Capitalism
and
Equality
in
America

Capitalism and Equality in America

Edited by

Peter L. Berger

**INSTITUTE FOR
EDUCATIONAL AFFAIRS**

Hamilton Press

LANHAM • NEW YORK • LONDON

Copyright © 1987 by

Hamilton Press

4720 Boston Way
Lanham, MD 20706

3 Henrietta Street
London WC2E 8LU England

Printed in the United States of America

British Cataloging in Publication Information Available

Library of Congress Cataloging in Publication Data

Capitalism and equality in America.

Bibliography: p.
1. Capitalism—United States.   2. Equality—
United States.   3. Income distribution—United
States.   I. Berger, Peter L.   II. Institute for
Educational Affairs (New York, N.Y.)
HB501.C2423   1987   330.12'2   86-24739
ISBN 0-8191-5572-1 (v. 1 : alk. paper)
ISBN 0-8191-5573-X (pbk. : vol. 1 : alk. paper)

Co-published by arrangement with the
Institute for Educational Affairs

All Hamilton Press books are produced on acid-free
paper which exceeds the minimum standards set by the National
Historical Publication and Records Commission.

Hamilton Press

CONTENTS

(VOL. I)

Preface

CAPITALISM IS AN ACCEPTED DESCRIPTION of the modern world. At its core a particular mode of organizing economic activity, with a flexibility equally amazing to its friends and discouraging to its critics, capitalism has the widest social, political, and cultural ramifications. Capitalism created the new secular order dreamed of by men like Francis Bacon. It began the revolution proclaimed by Karl Marx as needful of violent completion.

Yet it is only the critics of capitalism who have produced for contemporary intellectuals a persuasive, comprehensive critical study that integrates the manifold elements of capitalism. That critique now has the status of an ideology—Marxism—itself divided into numerous schools of thought and political factions. One measure of Marxism's hold on the modern mind is that while we adopt its name for the phenomena of a commercial republic, we forget that to Adam Smith and its other champions this social system was said to have a "low but solid" foundation in human nature.

If Marxism, or a variety of its Neo-Marxist offspring, provides satisfactory interpretation of this modern phenomenon, there is no problem—except for the continuing, healthy persistence of capitalism in its homelands, its growth in the Third World, and its resurrection in socialist countries. The problem is, capitalism is not understood.

The widespread and long-lasting attraction of Marxism, to be sure, is not primarily due to its theoretical force (and certainly not due to the decency of its politics). Marxism, by its own definition, is not just a theory, scientific or otherwise, but also a militant creed intended to inspire people to revolutionary action to destroy existing, that is, capitalistic society. Marxism is a myth, in George Sorel's meaning of the term. One cannot successfully counter a myth with a scientific theorizing. Yet, at least for intellectuals, the attraction of Marxism surely *also* lies in its capacity as an ideology to provide a comprehensive intellectual framework for the integration of initially disparate realms of experience.

It follows that the absence of a comprehensive alternative to the Marxist framework has political and philosophic implications. While Marxism has a near monopoly on the categories of social analysis, the disinterested scholar, who may also possess moral preferences for the basis of capitalism, has a serious problem in devising alternative categories of explanation.

Modern democratic industrial society is not the capitalism perjoratively labeled by its most compelling critic. The intellectual twins to Marx, Adam Smith and James Madison, called it a system of "natural liberty," but just as that system has grown into what we now know, that antique term has been lost.

On these premises, the construction of a comprehensive theory of modern capitalism's social and political working is a very important, even urgent, task. It must be evident, however, that no single individual is likely to be capable of undertaking this task, given the massiveness of the phenomenon and the awesome amount of relevant data. Inevitably, then, one is led to think of interdisciplinary collaboration over long periods of time, of teams, seminars, and the like. Such a procedure has obvious risks and shortcomings. Yet there is no realistic alternative.

The moral, political, cultural, and even literary dimensions of capitalism all require separate analysis. Capitalism is too important to be left to the economists, who by their own estimates now avoid the questions of capitalism's moral worth in preference for judging its efficiency and calculating its benefits and costs. What is missing today for the friends of capitalism is a careful, clear look at that society.

The present volume of essays is a first step toward assessing the practical benefits of capitalism against the egalitarian standard of its critics. This modest start is offered to our readers in the hope that once again serious thought, and perhaps some small measure of encouragement, will be brought to the examination of modern society.

This volume combines empirical and normative assessments of American capitalism. The essays combine the best of what has been learned and thought about modern capitalism. It is a project conceived and executed by the Institute for Educational Affairs in the hope that it might prompt renewed analysis of capitalism in

America. These essays were prepared during a year's seminar on Modern Capitalism, held in Boston, 1981–82. The essays proceed in a logical manner from the agreed to the arguable, describing what capitalism is and what it means.

The Seminar was funded by an educational grant from the SmithKline Beckman Corporation, which owing to the courage and farsightedness of its Chairman of the Board Robert F. Dee and his colleagues, saw the need for a reassessment of the intellectual roots of modern society. The participants of the Seminar are, of course, solely responsible for their own chapters and views. In light of our extensive discussions, one hopes there was a cross-fertilization of ideas among the participants that makes the volume more than the sum of its parts.

Philip N. Marcus, then president of the Institute for Educational Affairs, administered this grant and contributed much more, including his own considerable talents as a political and social analyst. Without his involvement, his careful attention to the details of running meetings and publishing books, and his own appreciation of what this project aimed to accomplish, this Seminar would have been a much less fruitful undertaking.

The initiators of this project, including the editor of this volume, openly prefer a capitalist society to any of the practical alternatives. This means that their interest in understanding modern capitalism is normative as well as cognitive. For this very reason it should be stressed as emphatically as possible that the project is an educational exercise. In the study of society, values become both inspirations and specific hypotheses. Openly stated hypotheses can be used as foils for analysis both for those who share the belief and for those who do not. The results of disinterested inquiry, empirical as well as theoretical, are open to use by both advocates and critics of American capitalism. In this instance, one may say that the master hypothesis has been that America is a highly egalitarian and equitable society. For the purposes of the inquiry, one could easily reverse the hypothesis and proclaim that America is a highly inegalitarian society—and reach the same conclusions. In any event, every participant was free to follow his own lights, and indeed some of the participants were vocal in their dissent from the beliefs of the editors.

Irving Kristol, Leslie Lenkowsky, and Michael Novak, among others, gave invaluable advice during various stages of the project. Ann Wortham served with enthusiasm and competence as administrative assistant of the Seminar. Naomi Munson, Miranda Reid and Thomas Skladony served as copy-editors for both volumes.

Washington, D.C.

If one is to address this question empirically, the concept of "equality" must be clarified. All but the most starry-eyed egalitarians will admit that perfect equality, in the sense that all members of a society will have fully equal shares of the available resources and services, is impossible in the real world. The question then, inevitably, becomes one of *relative* equality. To answer it, one must compare. Two comparisons are relevant, with the past and with other societies in the present. Thus one may ask: if one looks at the history of capitalist societies, have they become more or less equal? And if one compares them with existing non-capitalist societies, how do they stand up in terms of equality? It goes without saying that no conclusive normative statement can be made on the basis of such comparisons. One observer will regard the glass as being half full, the other as half empty, and it is exceedingly difficult to pin anyone down on just how much inequality is morally tolerable in a society. In view of all this, it might be more prudent to speak of "equity" rather than "equality", but this would not resolve the normative issue either. Nevertheless, the empirical examination of the inequalities to be found in capitalist and non-capitalist societies, past as well as present, is an essential element in any intelligent discussion of the merits of capitalism, even if many advocates of the latter will regard such an examination as morally penultimate.

The case of America is pivotal for this discussion, and by no means only for Americans. From its beginnings, America has been a symbol of equality for vast numbers of people, both admired and despised for this by both Americans and outside observers. Today, for many (again, both inside and outside its borders), America has become a precisely opposite symbol—supposedly a society with crass inequalities, oppressive and exploitative, a bastion of privilege and hierarchy. And for most of those who see America in this light, American capitalism is at the very least one of the important factors that have made for inequality. This is obviously so with critics of America from the left, but it is interesting that even those who criticize America from other ideological vantage points, such as racial or sexual liberation, commonly cite capitalism as one of the features that have made America oppressive: capitalism, supposedly, fosters the inequalities of "racism" and "sexism." These perceptions, of course, have made for a considerable affinity between the left and the various movements of socio-cultural liberation of recent decades. For people sharing these perceptions, there is by now a considerable cognitive investment in the proposition that American capitalism is, essentially and irrevocably, a structure of inequalities.

Once again, an empirical inquiry into this proposition is very important, even if it cannot finally resolve the normative issue of whether American society is "just" or "unjust" in its distribution of resources and services. To put it graphically, it is finally a normative issue whether a man is entitled to beat his wife, but if one is to make a responsible judgment about a particular man, it is of more than marginal interest to inquire whether he is in fact beating his wife or not.

Every human society (and indeed every human individual) has unique features. Americans have long been conscious of the highly distinctive character of their society. If one is then intent on exploring the relation of capitalism and equality in America, how can one be sure that it is the factor of capitalism that one is dealing with, as against many other distinctive features of the American case? Put differently, if one concludes that America either is or is not, comparatively speaking, an egalitarian society, is it capitalism that should be either praised or blamed for this fact? Clearly, there is no certain way of knowing. There are many other factors to be taken into account—industrialism as such (regardless of its organization in capitalist or non-capitalist forms), political democracy, and a miscellany of geographical, demographic, social and cultural factors—such as the continental size of American society, the waves of mass immigration, the frontier tradition or the Puritan heritage. Minimally, what one may conclude about the egalitarian or non-egalitarian effects of American capitalism cannot be transposed, *tout court*, to capitalist cases elsewhere. Nevertheless, the American case, because of its sheer magnitude and importance in the world economy, must be given high priority in any larger investigation of the issue. To return to an earlier illustration, if one is interested in the phenomenon of wife-beating, one will want to know whether the biggest guy on the block (or the one with the biggest stick) is or is not beating his wife.

The first and larger part of this volume deals with equality (or, if one prefers, equity) as a social reality in America. It deals, in other words, with the question of how much equality there *is* in America, as distinct from the question of how much equality there *should be*. The second part of the volume then discusses equality as a normative idea.

When equality is discussed today, two quite different approaches can be found. One explores the gaps between different groups in terms of income and wealth (a favorite comparison is between the highest and the lowest fifth, or quintile, in the income pyramid); the other looks at the standard of living of everyone in the society (with special attention given to the lower-income groups), regardless of what gaps may or may not remain in terms of the distribution of income and wealth. Choosing between the two approaches already implies a certain preference for either the equality or the equity standard. Those to whom equality is a very important norm in and of itself, no matter how much the standard of living of the poorer groups may have improved, the society is deemed unjust because the standard of living of the more affluent groups is still higher or may have improved even more. Those less egalitarian in their norms will not care that much about the latter eventuality, provided that all or most people, including those at the bottom of the pyramid, have a better life. In terms of American society, very few analysts question the remarkable improvement in the standard of living of all or nearly all strata over time, while the issues of income and wealth distribution are more controverted. Still, whatever one's norms about the relative importance of equality as against (even putatively unequal) improvement in the standard of living, it is relevant to look at the empirical data with regard to the latter.

Samuel McCracken provides eloquent testimony of the dramatic changes in American living standards since the beginning of the 19th century. In discussing the general availability of cheap and efficient energy, increasingly available to Americans of all strata, he speaks of "the liberating transformation of man from a beast of burden into a master of machines"; the phrase is equally applicable to other aspects of what nowadays is called "the quality of life". Whether one looks at sheer life expectancy (surely the most basic aspect of any standard of living), the incidence of diseases, nutrition, the prices of basic commodities and the resultant accessibility of inexpensive consumer goods, housing, clothing, leisure, transportation or communications—even the American poor today enjoy a standard of living which, for most of human history, would have been beyond the dreams of all but royalty, and in some respects (beginning with life expectancy) even beyond the dreams of the latter. To be sure, this cornucopia of industrial capitalism is not necessarily linked to equality, although in many of the above-listed items the gaps between poor and rich have been narrowing significantly (again, very notably so in the area of life expectancy, in which the relative gains of blacks and women have been particularly remarkable too), it is obviously true that the rich enjoy yet more of most of these benefits. Take one of the items to be brought up by McCracken, travel for enjoyment. Working-class Americans from the Northeast may travel by bus to Florida, middle-class Americans by charter to Hawaii, while their rich fellow-citizens fly first-class to Bali. These differences, to be sure, constitute evidence of continuing inequality. The fact remains that the working-class American enjoys access to the good things of life in a measure unparalleled in human history, anywhere or anytime, and this fact in itself has egalitarian implications. Put simply, industrial capitalism in America (and in other advanced societies of the capitalist type) has vastly raised the standard of living of virtually everyone in the society. For many, this fact in itself is tantamount to saying that American society is one of high equality and that it is the incredibly productive economy of American capitalism to which this achievement must be credited.

Even so, one may ask about the persisting inequalities of wealth and income. Jeffrey Williamson discusses the historical record in this regard. The picture emerging from this discussion is quite clear: America is no exception to what economists now call the "Kuznets curve", following the thesis of Simon Kuznets to the effect that modern economic growth first increases, later decreases inequality. According to Williamson, the curve leveled after 1929. In comparison with its own past, then, American society has become *more* egalitarian in the distribution of wealth and income. And compared to other societies of the capitalist type, America once again comes out as *more* egalitarian, even beating Sweden with its long-standing redistributionist policies. (Williamson gives credence to statistics that would indicate greater equality in industrialized societies of the socialist type. There are good reasons to be skeptical of these statistics, but this point cannot be pursued here.) While these results are persuasive, any reader of Williamson's paper will get a healthy sense of how difficult it is to interpret them. Williamson argues that the basic process "driving" the Kuznets curve is not any specifically American phenomenon (such as immigration), nor capitalism as such, but rather the underlying dynamics of industrialization. In other words, the persisting inequalities, and their changes over time, are endemic to modern economic growth, capitalist or non-capitalist. Certainly this can be said of the Kuznets curve, which can be found in socialist societies as well. (The seeming exceptions, in some of the capitalist societies of Northeast Asia, posit fascinating problems of interpretation, but these too cannot be followed up here).

If Williamson is correct (he very probably is), his findings have an important relation to the picture presented by McCracken: Capitalism as such does not make for equality in terms of the distribution of wealth and income; what makes for *greater* equality is progress in economic growth caused by industrialization in its more mature phases; but capitalism, far beyond any competing system, has the productive capacity for sustained economic growth of vast scope; to *that* extent, at any rate, capitalism brings about egalitarian effects. To see the human meanings of this, one may look ahead to the story told by McCracken.

The critics of capitalism, even if they concede all these points, will frequently argue that these achievements have been at the expense of other societies. In other words, some societies are rich *because* others have remained poor. This view, of course, is the core of the Marxist theory of imperialism, as first formulated by Rudolf Hilferding, Rosa Luxemburg, and V. I. Lenin, and it has now become a central component of what, broadly speaking, may be called Third World ideology. The next volume in the present series of studies on modern capitalism will take up this question; it is only mentioned here to point to the fact that, if capitalism is to be defended, this criticism too will have to be answered; that is, to defend capitalism it is not enough to describe the great cornucopia for some societies unless one is prepared to argue that other societies are *not* the ones at whose expense it pours out its benefits. However, leaving this question aside here, there is yet another point that the critics make: granted that modern economic growth produces certain inequalities, these are not beyond deliberate interference. Put differently, one need not necessarily "sit out" the Kuznets curve; rather, one may decide to intervene in order to hasten its "leveling" phase. Thus Williamson raises the question as to whether government actions of a redistributionist sort could not have made for more equality earlier; his answer is "perhaps."

This is the question to which Edgar Browning addresses himself. His paper deals with the existing inequalities in American society and with the effect on these of redistributionist policies by government. For a number of reasons, he believes that existing inequalities are *less* than the usually cited statistics indicate. Be this as it may, he has no doubt about the effects of government action since World War II (especially, of course, since the anti-poverty policies of the 1960's): "There would be nearly twice as many poor persons were it not for government transfer programs."

It is at this point that the adjective in the phrase "democratic capitalism" becomes significant. Capitalism in America, of course, is not an economic machine churning away without political interventions. The state has intervened all along, massively so since the enactment of the progressive income tax (and thus the establishment in America of that new political animal baptized "the tax State," or *Steuerstaat,* by Joseph Schumpeter), and even more massively with the establishment of the modern welfare state (in America coming in two great spurts, first in the 1930's, then in the 1960's). If Browning is correct (he probably is), the impact of these political interventions on the distribution of wealth and income has been very substantial. It is evident from his paper that he has doubts about the beneficence of these redistributionist interventions, especially in their effects on economic incentives and thus eventually on the average standard of living. At the very least, redistributionist policies will have economic as well as political costs. Whether one regards these costs as worth paying or not, one conclusion may be drawn: *democratic* capitalism generates political processes that reduce inequality. These political processes modify the "natural" development of the Kuznets curve, hastening and intensifying the onset of its "leveling" phase. The costs and benefits of these political processes are key subjects of the contention between right-of-center and left-of-center parties within the societies of democratic capitalism; the social reality of these processes is all that must be registered here.

Even in a society in which income and wealth are distributed in fairly stationary ways, in the sense that the gaps between the strata are more or less fixed, this state of affairs does not necessarily mean that individuals cannot move from one stratum to another. Most individuals, indeed, are likely to be much more interested in their own chances of moving into a more privileged stratum, or at least of *not* moving down into a less privileged one, than in the overall picture as to the distribution of privilege. Thus *distribution* is a quite different matter from *social mobility*. The two phenomena vary independently, in principle. Thus one may have a society with very unequal distribution of income and wealth in which there is, nevertheless, a high degree of social mobility; conversely, a society with an egalitarian distribution may have little social mobility. Yet the question of social mobility is very relevant to the issue of equality, precisely because equality is likely to be perceived by the individual in terms of his own chances of improving his lot or the lot of his children.

This question is addressed by Walter Connor. As in the area of distribution, data on social mobility in America are complex, incomplete and subject to different interpretations. Yet the overall picture given by Connor is, once again, fairly clear: either when compared with its own past or with other societies, America has a substantial amount of intergenerational mobility. Since much (indeed surprisingly much) mobility is downward rather than upward, it is also a society in which there is a high "circulation of elites" (to use Vilfredo Pareto's phrase). Put simply: the son of the

truck driver has a reasonable chance of making it into the world
of professional or business privilege; but individuals in the latter
world have a high chance of failing to prevent *their* sons from
ending up as truck drivers. From the point of view of the individuals concerned, of course, the first proposition is good news, the
second bad news. *Both* propositions, though, offer empirical validation of the egalitarian dynamics of the society. Thus, for example, a small majority of sons of the upper white-collar stratum
replicate their fathers' status, but almost half descend to the ranks
of manual labor. Close to one third of sons from the upper
manual stratum and close to one fourth from the lower manual
stratum reach elite status (that is, move into the upper white-collar
stratum). Even more interestingly, the majority of persons in the
elite originated below the manual/non-manual divide, and that
majority is increasing over time (51.6% in 1962, 54.1% in 1973).
This increase in mobility chances is also reflected in the data
showing that either the advantage or the handicap of the individual's starting position has been lessening; that is, it is *less* of an
advantage to start out at the top, *less* of a handicap to start out at
the bottom. Or, if one prefers: it is becoming less important to
make a careful selection of one's parents. Very significantly, since
1973 this lessening importance of starting position also applies to
blacks; the inroads of women into the labor force are sufficiently
new so that intergenerational data are as yet sparse, but it seems
plausible to hypothetize that what holds for the mobility of blacks
would hold *a fortiori* for women. One final comparative finding
reported on by Connor is particularly striking: the mobility rates
from manual to white-collar occupations are *higher* in America
than in other industrialized societies, capitalist or socialist; on the
other hand, the reverse rates of downward mobility are *lower* in
America than in several other comparable societies. Put simply: it
is still true that the individual has a better chance in America of
improving his lot; he also has a pretty good chance of holding on
to his gains for the benefit of his children.

The "Horatio Alger myth" has been a favorite target for the
debunking activities of social critics. To be sure, the idea that every
newspaper delivery boy, if he only works hard enough, will end
up as chairman of the board is now and always was illusionary.
What is surprising, though, is the degree to which this myth does
indeed correspond to reality. America continues to be a land of
opportunity. Indeed, it is *increasingly* this, and for an increasing
proportion of the population, as old barriers of prejudice and
discrimination are dismantled. A new question is beginning to

suggest itself: what are the sources of the "*anti*-Horatio-Alger myth?" This question will be taken up presently.

The market has often been depicted as a perfectly democratic, even egalitarian system, with prices recording the "votes" of all the participants. Insofar as capitalism is market economics, capitalism can then be defended on democratic or even egalitarian grounds. Many critics of capitalism (especially the non-Marxist ones) are quite willing to go along with this idea of the market (indeed, in the ideological bestiary of the times there is now a strange animal called "market socialism"). The same critics, however, point out that the American economic system today is not exactly an ideal market model; rather, it is "corporate capitalism" or "monopoly capitalism." The villain here is not so much capitalism as such, but the modern corporation as a new institution, supposedly both non-democratic or non-egalitarian in both character and effects. The degree to which contemporary capitalism incorporates both market and non-market features, and the role of the corporation in this, is beyond our present scope (the two questions, incidentally, are not identical; after all, it is not only the corporation, but the state, labor unions and other interest groupings that have modified the market dynamics of capitalism).

It is appropriate to ask, though, whether the American corporation is indeed a villain in its effects on equality or equity in the society. The chapter by Laura Nash and Alan Kantrow deals with this question. Again, the data are complex and inconclusive. Minimally, though, Nash and Kantrow make a good case for saying that it is simplistic to cast the corporation in the role of villain. Within itself, the contemporary corporation serves as an important vehicle of social mobility. And, by way of corporate philanthropy, the corporation has been an instrument of what Nash and Kantrow call the "beneficent re-distribution of profits." Their chapter leaves open the question as to whether the corporation is indeed becoming increasingly "open," reaching out to recruits from the lower strata of society (though they do discuss this matter briefly in terms of women and blacks); that assertion is often heard in business circles, though it is usually backed up by rather impressionistic evidence.

This last phrase also describes Richard Neuhaus' chapter on equality in everyday life in America, inevitably so, since it would be very difficult to marshall "hard" data on this phenomenon. It is very much part of social reality nonetheless. Indeed, the rough-and-ready egalitarianism of American life and manners is what has always been prominent in the minds of both Americans and outside observers when thinking about the issue of equality. The prototypical proposition, Neuhaus suggests, is "I'm as good as you are"—an assertion of individual dignity originally made against the pretensions of European aristocracy and continuing to permeate American life in distinction to other western societies with a feudal past. Neuhaus, probably correctly, argues that this proposition expresses an "ontological equality," with deep roots in the Christian heritage of America. The egalitarianism of American life may be taken as demonstrated; it is debatable to what extent it is linked to capitalism. Here the most interesting portion of Neuhaus' chapter is the one that deals with the sense of "arbitrariness, contingency, luck, choice," all notions that run counter to *ressentiment* and class struggle. It is very likely that capitalism is not the only factor that has engendered these American sentiments; there are also such factors as the frontier, the wide open spaces of this country, the ethos of immigration, and others. But it is also likely that capitalism has been *one* of the factors behind this constellation. If so, very interestingly, it is capitalism in its *non*-rational aspects, the risk-taking and gambling aspects, which George Gilder has recently (and perhaps exaggeratedly) characterized as an expression of "faith." Neuhaus remarks on the "game-like nature of economic activity" (*capitalist* economic activity, one must add). He who looks on economic activity as a big gamble is likely to accept the "approximate justice of capitalism" (Neuhaus might have cited another prototypical American expression: "You win some; you lose some"). It is because of this, one might also add, that Las Vegas could become a powerful symbol of the economic aspirations of Americans—surely an example of "false consciousness," *unless* one concedes that much of economic life is indeed a wild gamble rather than an exercise in rationality. Perhaps a theoretical task ahead is a careful analysis of both the similarities and the differences between Las Vegas and Wall Street; if the common sense of ordinary Americans is to be trusted, the similarities will be greater than the differences. In this connection it is also interesting to recall (as Neuhaus does) the empirical findings on the role of "luck" or "chance" in the mobility of individuals—findings that so deeply troubled Christopher Jencks and other advocates of "equality of result." In sum: it has always been the American ideal that all comers should be given a roughly equal opportunity to play the game; it continues to be the case that most Americans resist the idea that everyone should be made to win equal (or even roughly equal) shares in the stake.

It would obviously be foolish in the extreme to pretend that the chapters which follow in this volume present conclusive evidence on the question of the degree of equality in American society. Yet the evidence which they do present is not all that esoteric or new. The basic facts have been generally known to anyone taking the trouble of investigating them. And the overall picture that emerges is fairly clear: by any reasonable standard, and by comparison both with the past and with other societies in the present, America has not done badly at all by the standard of equality. Indeed, it is not at all a *tour de force* to say that America is a highly egalitarian society and that, as time passes, it is becoming increasingly that. But equality as a social reality, as an aggregate of empirical data, is not what the debate is finally all about, it seems. There is equality as an idea, utopian perhaps, but powerful all the same. In the name of this idea, *all* existing inequalities appear intolerable, and so does the society that generally tolerates them. There is also the myth of *in*equality, in which the empirical equalities of the society are denied *so that* this society can be condemned. This latter mental exercise is not so much utopian as grounded in hatred. In this instance, America is hated for other reasons, and a way is found to *also* hate it for its alleged inequality; under no circumstances must the object of hatred be allowed any virtues at all. There now ensues a curious inversion of symbols: America, which has been both praised and despised as a symbol of equality, is now condemned as the prime symbol of inequality in the world.

It is fair to assume that the man-in-the-street notions of equality and justice, as described by Neuhaus, have been dominant since the beginnings of American capitalism. These common-sense notions corresponded roughly with the ideas that served to legitimate American society on a theoretical level—ideas concerning the rights of property, ideas on equality as legal and political rather than economic, and because of this an acceptance of most existing economic inequalities as just. These ideas, of course, became enshrined in law. They served as an overall ideology for American capitalism which, until recently, was only challenged at the margins of the society.

Yet, as Stephen Miller shows in his chapter on equality as reflected in American literature, American intellectuals have long been ambivalent about capitalism and about the commercial civilization it engendered. Some, in the Puritan tradition, decried it for its greediness. Others, nostalgic for a (real or imagined) past of agrarian simplicity, despised capitalism for its ugliness and vulgarity. A third strain in American literature, the one Miller calls individualist, did indeed celebrate the rough world of capitalist enterprise. The very curious fact is that, of those three strains, the individualist is, it seems, the most egalitarian. In other words, those who admired American capitalism at least in part did so because of the egalitarianism they perceived in it, with each man, on his own, seeking to make his way in the world and perhaps toward fortune. Conversely, those who most despised American society and its grubby commercial economy were closest to the sentiments of European aristocrats; they despised America *because* it was egalitarian, in their perception.

This leads to certain, one may say, quasi-Freudian suspicions, which both Marc Plattner and Delba Winthrop touch upon in their explorations in the idea of equality. It is possible that many of those who uphold the banner of equality are not really concerned with equality at all; rather, they may be concerned with their own status, as intellectuals, in a society that has not allowed intellectuals much power or prestige compared with other societies. It is even possible that many of those who, contrary to the empirical evidence (some of it daily before their eyes, if they live in this country), maintain that America is a bastion of inequality are, on the contrary, bothered precisely by the *equalities* rampant in this society—most important, the political and (thanks to the market) cultural equality between themselves and all those *hoi polloi* who make up the majority of the population. H. L. Mencken and his contempt for the American populace (the "booboisie") may be seen as a prototype of this group of cultured despisers of America. What distinguished Mencken from many intellectuals today was his (one may say) healthier and more universalistic cynicism: he may have cynically misperceived America, but at least he did not fall for this or that foreign utopia, as so many intellectuals have done in the last two decades.

These considerations take one into a murky zone of ideological pathology that cannot be entered here. Let it be stipulated that only a minority of those who criticize America for its inequalities are denizens of this zone (though, unfortunately, they have been a very vocal minority). Most of the critics do not hate America and most of them are not entranced by the alleged egalitarian wonders of this or that socialist experiment abroad. Rather, they are genuinely outraged by whatever inequalities they continue to perceive in America, and their outrage is grounded in a vision of egalitarianism to which even one who does not share it must concede some nobility. It is, *au fond,* the same vision as that of socialism at its best—a vision of a world in which all men will be brothers and in which all the barriers between them will have been broken down in an all-embracing solidarity. Needless to say, the social reality of any empirical society (and, one may add, any realistically conceivable one) will fall short and thus merit condemnation.

It is these utopian themes in contemporary egalitarianism that make it so very difficult to deal with. Empirical falsification of egalitarian propositions can only go so far. Thus one can show that America or other capitalist societies cannot be adequately described as bastions of inequality or oppression. Conversely, one can show that the socialist societies in existence today are very far indeed from the equality they espouse as an ideal. For many, though, such empirical exercises do not touch on the core of their concerns. The mythopoetic appeal of equality remains untouched. No amount of empirical equality in America will, for them, justify the remaining inequalities. Comparison with either the past or with other societies will then be dismissed as irrelevant, the only relevant comparison being with the *ideal* of equality. And for those whose egalitarianism has taken a socialist form (still a minority in America) no empirical exposé of this or that socialist society and of its glaring inequalities will quench the hope that sometime, somewhere, the truly egalitarian socialist society will appear.

In different ways, the authors of the final chapters in this volume confront the built-in difficulty of those who would defend capitalism. It is essentially the difficulty of one who would defend a (necessarily imperfect) reality against a dream of perfection. Capitalism, by its very nature, is a sober, practical, prosaic affair. It fails to inspire, even when it works efficiently and humanely. The aforementioned authors are students of political theory; understandably, they think that political or philosophical theory will meet the needs of legitimation. Those in other fields may be skeptical about this. To be sure, there is a great need for a more comprehensive theory of capitalism, including a political theory; indeed, the present volume is understood as part of such a theory-building enterprise. But theories avail little against myths. And capitalism, by its very nature, is not a mythogenic entity: entrepreneurs and managers are very different human types from poets and prophets.

A more convincing procedure is always to stay close to the empirical evidence. It may not provide what students of political theory would call a "truly philosophical analysis"; that would not matter so much, except to philosophers. But, by its very "calculating" procedure, the political culture of capitalism too cannot inspire, and thus cannot *by itself* counter the mythopoetic inspiration of the egalitarian and socialist visions. Because our authors, however, understand this, they emphasize the "cultural" system, which has been historically linked with the economic and political development of America and of western civilization in general. This "culture," on closer inspection, turns out to be the sedimentation of that Judaeo-Christian religious tradition without which there would have been no western civilization and no America. It is this tradition which continues to inspire and which continues to evoke a mythic vision of its own, one of enduring power. It is all the more important to stress that this cannot possibly be an ultimate legitimation of capitalism. This religious vision necessarily relativizes and transcends capitalism, or any other socio-economic system. At the same time, it makes it possible to tolerate the imperfections and to acknowledge the merits of any existing socio-economic reality, precisely because the latter is perceived in relative terms.

The purpose of this volume is more modest than a comprehensive defense of capitalism, let alone the generation of new myths. It is an inquiry into the question of how American capitalism stands up when confronted with the ideal of equality. This inquiry leads to certain specific results. The logic of the project of which this volume is a part will inevitably lead to other societies. America is the biggest and perhaps, still, the most important capitalist society. It is not the only one. Anyone who follows the present inquiry to the end of this book will inevitably ask to what extent the findings concerning capitalism and equality in America are, or are not, applicable to other societies. Put differently, if America constitutes a socio-economic model, a key question is that of its "exportability." Volume II of the Modern Capitalism Seminar will address that question.

Democratic Capitalism and the Standard of Living 1800–1980

Samuel McCracken

I

THE FIRST PROBLEM we must face in such a study as this is the relationship between capitalism and industrialism. This distinction can be cited for capitalism and against it: one can absolve capitalism from the sins of modern society by arguing that they are after all merely the fruit of industrialism; and one can deprive capitalism of credit for its virtues by urging that *they* are after all merely the fruit of industrialism. This latter position is often allied to the view that industrialized non-capitalist states control industrialism better than capitalist ones do.

For the purposes of this study I shall treat industrialism as no more or less than capitalism's child: one that takes after its parent. It is so clearly derived from capitalism that its benefits no less than its defects are distinctively capitalist and both should be entered to capitalism's account.

This is not to treat the problem of the relationship as a Gordian knot, for the evidence for the practical identity of capitalism and industrialism is massive and detailed. It begins with the plain fact that industrialism arose in capitalist states, a fact acknowledged by

15

capitalism's critics and its supporters alike. The relationship is nowhere more evident than in the works of Marx and Engels.

What is less widely understood but no less obvious is that industrialism flourishes only in capitalist society. Although the socialist world (by which I mean the eastern bloc nations) is now heavily industrialized, its industrialism is marked by two qualities: its extreme ineffectiveness and its extreme derivativeness. This fact is beginning to be appreciated more clearly in the light of the collapse of the Polish economy. Here is a country which in theory has been free of the blighting effect of capitalism for more than a generation; and yet it cannot feed itself. Poles queue up for hours in hopes of buying the selfsame hams that are available in any American supermarket at a lower real cost. The Soviet camera industry produces largely shoddy copies of obsolete Japanese cameras, and one of its most prestigious cameras is a copy of a German one designed before World War II and marketed just after it. It should not be surprising that a heavily bureaucratized industry should lack imagination. What is surprising is the widespread failure to see that this should be so.

Nor are these failures limited to consumer goods. When, a few years ago, Western military analysts came into possession of an MIG-25 flown to Japan by a Soviet defector, they were astounded to discover that its electronic equipment ran on vacuum tubes rather than on transistors. Soviet failure to provide this aircraft with an ejection seat may be regarded as a cold-blooded calculation of cost benefit by people who hold life cheap; but the decision to give it only the most primitive electronic gear represents a crucial failure at being an industrial nation. Industrialism under socialism is for the most part rather like this, and the exceptions are almost entirely in countries with a tradition of capitalism before World War II, such as East Germany and Czechoslovakia.

But it is only when allied to capitalism—and, it should be said, political democracy—that industrialism retains its creative power. There have of course been claims to the contrary, and much innocent amusement can be had by reading the Reverend Dr. Hewlett Johnson's great work *The Socialist Sixth of the World,* which among other oddities contains extended praise of the industrial creativity of socialism. The problem is that every example cited originated under capitalism and had been merely applied—or rather misapplied—by Stalin. To read the Red Dean's remarkable paean to electricity, one would think that it had been invented in Semipalatinsk ca. 1921.

Such claims are belied—if by nothing else—by trade patterns between the Soviet Union and the capitalist world. Judged from this viewpoint, the arsenal of socialism looks more like a developing nation than a developed one, exporting largely raw materials and importing, besides food, the machinery it cannot make.

One cannot, in fact, find a single basic discovery on the order of the steam engine or the transistor made in the socialist world. Indeed, as regards the fundamentals of knowledge, Tsarist Russia produced a number of landmark workers in basic science: the Struves in astronomy, Mendeleev in chemistry, Tsiolkovsky in mathematics. Since the revolution, the Soviet position in basic science is indicated by fact that Soviet scientists have won a total of eight Nobel prizes, a figure easily eclipsed by the scientists of the Netherlands.

So, with the proviso that in a limited way some of the end products of capitalism can be transferred to socialist societies, I shall be treating the industrial society of the past two centuries as functionally and more or less exclusively defining capitalist society.

When to date the beginning of capitalism? Like most historical evolutions, the more understanding one gains of capitalism the easier it is to see its precursors at increasingly remote distances. I am going to begin this study with 1800, partially because that is a very rough equivalent of the start of the industrial revolution, but more important, 1800 is the earliest date for which we have reasonably reliable and comparable statistics for a variety of important variables, e.g., the start of the Department of Labor's Consumer Price Index.

II

"Standard of living" is an extremely complex concept. Some of its components are unambiguous in concept and easily quantifiable. Life-span is the most obvious of these. The universality of human desires for self-preservation suggests that a longer life, of whatever quality, is generally thought better than a shorter life, of whatever quality. Generally speaking, at least in western culture as we have known it for the past few centuries, to prefer a shorter but happier life to a longer but less happy one, and to act on the preference through suicide, is to offer up evidence of insanity.

Although it is also fashionable to bewail various "epidemics," as of cancer and heart-disease, calling them the result of industrialism or of capitalism, the lengthening lifespan is incontrovertible evidence that by the most important single measure the national health continues to improve. In 1900, the life expectancy at birth of the average American was 47 years; in 1980, it was 73. This is an astonishing figure, and it needs to be understood precisely. It does not, of course, mean that the human species has begun to live longer. It seems clear that the maximum useful lifespan has not varied significantly in historical times. The evidence is clear from the case of Sophocles and his sons* that in 5th century Athens 92 was thought a great age and yet it was an age at which an exceptional man might function exceptionally. These figures mean, rather, that a great many people who used to die in the first year of life, or in the second, or the eighteenth, now live more or less complete lives. The net addition to the sum of human existence made thereby is not easily quantifiable, but it is certainly immense.

Although the concept of life-span integrates a wide variety of health considerations into one convenient bottom line, an analysis of lifespan cannot serve as a replacement for a closer look at its components. For progress in health is a more complex matter than increased longevity.

For example, our reduction of appendicitis into a minor ailment has certainly increased the life-span. But it has also almost entirely removed from our human experience an extraordinarily painful way of dying before one's time. More than that, it has removed a threat that formerly hovered over everyone—once, a threat of painful death, later, a threat of dangerous surgery requiring long recovery, still later, of serious surgery requiring several weeks *hors-de-combat*.

Although before modern medicine kidney-, bladder- and gallstones did not usually prove fatal, their victims may well have been tempted to wish they were. There was no safe long-term analgesic for their excruciating pain, and surgery was risky. As late as 1870, Napoleon III preferred the agony of the stone to the risk of curing it, and was as a result hardly fit for command at the battle of Sedan.

Two more serious diseases have been essentially conquered: tuberculosis and syphilis. In 1865 in Massachusetts, the death rate per 100,000 of population for tuberculosis was 365; in 1900 nationwide it was 194, and by 1960, it had fallen to 6.1, by 1978, to 1.3. In 1900, the death rate for syphilis was 12; by 1960, it had

---

*The sons sued to gain their inheritance *vita patris suae* on the grounds that at 92 he was past it. He successfully countered by reading to the jury his latest play, the *Oedipus at Colonus*.

fallen to 1.6, and by 1978 the statistical column contains only a dash meaning "zero or rounds to zero." There hardly needs telling the former effect of these two scourges; the names of their more eminent victims suggest the years of achievement these two took from them and from us. These diseases, which killed Keats at 36 and at the height of his career deprived Lord Randolph Churchill first of his reason and then of his life, are no longer consequential.

There have been two principal areas in which mortality has increased: cardiovascular disease, from 345 per 100,000 in 1900 to 442 in 1978, and cancer, from 64 in 1900 to 182 in 1978. These increases should be considered against the backdrop of an overall decline from 1720 to 950. It is also inevitable that as increasing numbers of children survive infancy and childhood they will begin to die of adult diseases, which heart disease and cancer pre-eminently are. Part of the so-called cancer "epidemic" is simply the result of increasing numbers of people surviving long latency periods.

Syphilis and smallpox, like cancer and heart disease, are chronic diseases that work their harm over extended periods of time. They could, therefore, in a certain sense be accommodated to and prepared for. Once 19th century people received the diagnosis "consumption," they had a new sense of where their lives were leading. Epidemic diseases such as smallpox, yellow fever, and malaria presented a different problem: the dislocation of society by a sudden increase in deaths. The most famous example of these is certainly the great epidemic of the plague that swept Europe between 1348 and 1350, the so-called "Black Death." As but one example of the effect of such an epidemic, it can be noted that the plague was much more virulent in the crowded cities than in the countryside, and that in mid-14th century England English was predominantly a rural language and French predominantly urban. The plague noticeably shifted the demographic balance between the two languages and was thereby influential in the rapid rise of English to be once more the official language of the realm.

From such socially powerful effects of disease we have now been largely set free. The liberation has come comparatively recently, even in this country. As recently as 1919–20, it was visited by the last of the real pandemics, the so-called Spanish influenza. Persons born after 1930 who have talked with those who passed through this epidemic are sometimes surprised to learn how many thousands of deaths it caused. In the recollections of the survivors it does not seem particularly sensational, although in this time it would be so. The reason for the disparity of perception is probably that the survivors grew up in a world in which such things had been comparatively common.

Two of these diseases were conquered as byproducts of what many would call typically capitalist-imperialist adventures: the Spanish-American War brought an end to malaria, and the building of the Panama Canal eliminated yellow fever. To be sure, Carlos Finlay, the martyred Jesse Lazear, Walter Reed, and William Crawford Gorgas were the effective conquerors of the *anopheles* and *aedes Aegypti* mosquitoes. But it was the America of Mark Hanna and J. P. Morgan that gave them scope for action. This indirect medical benefit of capitalism must be added to the direct effects embodied in the medical institutions created by philanthropy. The Rockefeller Institute was preeminent among them, but hundreds more ranged down to small hospitals.

Yet another example of the profound influence of medicine on the standard of living can be seen in the decline in infant mortality. This to be sure, appears as part of the overall increase in lifespan. That is to look at infant mortality from the point of view of the infant. But it can also be looked at from the point of view of his parents and relations. Until comparatively recently, to have a family was to undergo a high risk of losing a child—or a sibling or a niece or nephew—to death. Between 1870 and 1874 in Massachusetts, the infant mortality rate stood at 170.3 per thousand births. That is to say, nearly one child in five. Although the extreme rarity of such loss in our time has made it a devastating blow for those to whom it occurs, familiarity with it does not seem to have bred indifference. Ben Jonson, writing in an era when the recurrent visitations of the plague had sharply multiplied already plentiful intimations of mortality, mourned the death of his firstborn in terms and tones that would be appropriate today, and through much literary and journal material it is clear that the loss of children was a lamentable and lamented occurrence. It is an occurrence now so rare that no one is prepared for it. The nearest thing to an immunizing experience we now have is experience, direct or vicarious, with miscarriage.

Thus some of the manifold ways in which medicine has increased the standard of living not only by allowing for more life, but allowing for life of a higher quality. But who has gotten the benefit? And has it been equally distributed? The answer to the first question is "everyone." That is, these health improvements have been so generally accessible that their transforming influence has been generally experienced. The answer to the second question is, "It has not." But the nature of the inequality may surprise one. Consider the following table:

Thus, whites as a group have improved much less than blacks as a group, but black women have done best of all, followed by black men. White men have done the worst, following black men distantly. The gap between the sexes in 1900 was 2, favoring women. The gap between the sexes in 1979 had widened to 7.9, favoring women. In 1920 the gap between the races was 14.6, favoring-whites. By 1979, it had narrowed to 4.5, still favoring whites.

It is not easy to explain these inequities of result. They do not spring from any social policy that intended them, for no such policy existed during the period, except for an increasing belief that all gaps between the races ought to be narrowed. The dramatic improvement in the female lifespan may be attributable to improvements in managing childbirth. As the next table shows, the improvement since 1915 for both races has been spectacular, but because the black starting place was so low, the black improvement has been numerically much greater.

The inferences from these figures are clear: we have not distributed good health—as mirrored in the lifespan—with exact equalness. But the system has strikingly improved the lifespan of both racial groups and sharply narrowed the gap between them. In terms of improvement, it has done much better by blacks than by whites. The "inequality" now stands at approximately 3% on either side of the average. It would be interesting to know how many societies manage, over various groupings, to be more even-handed.*

III

An essential element in the standard of living is ease of access to basic materials. This issue can be tracked from 1800 to 1970** through a series of wholesale prices for basic commodities. I have chosen six of these—coal, copper, cotton, flour, nails, and sugar—simply because they are the six for which continuous figures are available back to 1800. Charts 1–6 give costs for the six com-

---

*Similar improvements might, of course, be cited with regard to the Soviet Union. But on the typical measures this may appear to be no more than an inefficient transfer of the benefits of capitalism. Life expectancy in the Soviet Union is lower by two or three years than in every country in Europe except Spain, and the Soviet infant mortality rate was nearly three times that of the United States and still rising when last reported in 1975.

**I have not brought these figures current to 1980 because of a lack of fully comparable data. But rough analysis suggests that most of these commodities have remained at or gone below their 1970 real prices.

modities in current dollars, constant dollars, and in days needed
to earn a given amount.*

In 1970, each of the commodities was, in terms of prices unadjusted for inflation, selling below its 1800–1970 high point. These
high points were for the most part results of the War of 1812 and
the Civil War. With the exception of coal and flour—which was
below its historic high—each commodity was available at or below
its 1800 current-dollar price. In terms of constant dollars, every
commodity was well below its 1800 price and far below its historic
high. Finally, expressed in days of labor needed to earn a given
unit, each commodity was selling far below its 1860** price, and
after the Civil War the trend has been relentlessly downward.

The oscillation from year to year even in this last figure has
been sufficient that in a number of years the labor/cost of these
commodities has been higher than in the years just previous, and
many people might have thought themselves to be losing ground;
but as can be seen from the chart, periods of real increase have
never lasted more than a few years, and have always been followed by periods of decline. The overall evidence is unmistakable:
the average man's command over the basic commodities—although exercised at second- or third-hand—has improved immensely since the start of industrial capitalism. If one had to rely
on one statistic, it might be the one that sometimes leads to
revolutions: the price of bread. The wholesale cost of flour, over
the span 1860–1970, has fallen to a tenth of its starting price.

IV

Another method for comparing standards of living in consumer goods is through the historical prices of a short list of
common ones as offered in the Sears, Roebuck and Company
catalogue.

---

*This is a difficult concept to assign over a long period. I have found reasonably
consistent figures for average American salaries running back to 1860. The precise
amounts of labor needed to earn those salaries have at all times varied and have been
historically in decline, so that for some workers the 1982 figure would be little more than
half the 1860 one. I have arbitrarily chosen to call a "day" of labor 1/365 of a year's salary.
This allows for some comparability of figures that are themselves derivative and constructed, and builds in a bias against the accomplishments of democratic capitalism.

**The first year for which reliable salary figures are available.

Throughout this span, there can hardly be a more representative sample of the goods available to most Americans. To be sure, the selection and range of quality would always be better in the stores and shops of the great cities, but the catalogue was infinitely superior to the inventories of the small-town merchant—which can be studied to good effect in Carole Kennicott's appalled first shopping walk on Main Street—and remained so until after the Second World War, when Sears retail stores began to multiply and provide the provinces with immediate access to many of the goods that had been available only by mail.

My shopping list is brief, and I make no claim to its scientific inclusiveness. I have tried for some variety, and for items that have appeared as nearly the same as possible in the catalogue over the whole period.

Adjusting for variable quality in products and services represents a considerable problem. To use no more rarefied example, any serious consumer of beer, looking back on the history of hopped and malted beverages 1890–1982, would be quite sure that the beer was better in the good old days, and would probably be right in the assumption. There is no easy and reliable way to re- or de-value a modern product for the purpose of comparing it with its earlier analogue. Not, of course, that somewhere on the dark underbelly of social science someone may not have tried to produce a proper beer-enjoyability factor, and it may even have been published.

I propose to assume that the range of qualities available over time are comparable and to note the most obvious improvements and deteriorations.

The cheapest bicycle in 1897 cost $55.88 in 1967 dollars; in 1981, the cheapest bicycle cost $22.61 in 1967 dollars. The most expensive bicycle in 1897 cost $140 in 1967 dollars, and the most expensive bicycle in 1981 cost $49.12 in 1967 dollars. The cheapest bicycle in 1897 would have cost about 12 days work; the most expensive, 28 days. In 1981, the comparable figures are a little over a day and just under three days.*

Although the cheapest 1981 camera is approximately twice as expensive in constant dollars, it is half as expensive in terms of labor. The most expensive camera required three days labor to earn in 1981, but seventy days in 1897. As with the bicycles, the capabilities of the more modern devices are so much greater as to render comparison almost pointless.

---

*It must be remembered that the definition of *day's work* used here biases the later figures upward.

One of the most dramatic examples of steep decline is the expensive watch: in 1897 it required a month to earn, in 1981, less than a day. Another striking case is the phonograph. In 1897 a cheap one cost over eight days in labor; in 1981, the cheap one cost a third of a day. Some items, however, have made real advances in price. The 1897 expensive sewing machine was a little over half the cost of the 1981 one in constant dollars; however, when salaries are taken into consideration, it is seen to have cost twice as much. These figures are based on comparing what was quite a primitive sewing machine to a modern electronic marvel. The fairer comparison would be the 1981 cheap machine against the 1897 expensive one. This would yield an advantage of approximately thirteen times to the later device, and would ignore such improvements as electrification and portability.

An equally important contrast with the 1897 Sears catalog would be with its non-existent issue for 1800. It would be possible to make a stab at composing an 1800 Sears catalog by striking out of an 1897 issue all the devices that had not been invented yet or which would have been far beyond the means of the farmers of 1800. Even making the probably dubious assumption that the variety of types and styles of what remained was equal to that of 1897, the 1800 catalog would certainly have been very thin by comparison—almost certainly much too thin to have served the secondary function it acquired at the end of the century.

V

Energy consumption is an extremely illuminating measure of the standard of living, especially if we except food. (It is not that diet is not an important component of standard of living, but the evaluation of adequacy in this area is comparatively simple.) Non-food consumption of energy is largely an index of the liberating transformation of man from a beast of burden into a master of machines. In 1850, the United States had a population of approximately 24 million. The horsepower of all the non-human prime movers—all the steam engines, sailing ships, windmills, water wheels and work animals—in the country amounted to about 8.5 million. There was, consequently, about a third of a horsepower per person. The rest of the work of the country was done by human exertion. By 1970, the population had reached 203 million, and the horsepower of all the prime movers, 20.4 billion.

There were now approximately 100 horse power available for each person.

About 95% of this additional horsepower resides under the hoods of automobiles, where it is responsible for a transformation in mobility that would have astounded anyone born before this century. The total increase, however, is so great that the non-automotive horsepower has increased since 1850 from a third of one horsepower to 5.3 hp per person. Which is to say, nearly twenty times.

It is common to hear this development decried on the basis of some of its more trivial artifacts, such as electric toothbrushes and can-openers. But the horsepower used up by these devices is also trivial. The real appreciation of the liberation brought by the horsepower revolution is to watch a man loading wallboard into a building under renovation. He drives up in a flatbed truck stacked high with hundreds of sheets of board bound together in pallets; at the front of the truck bed reposes a large electric crane worked by a controller which the man holds in his hands. At his command the crane slews around and places lifting fingers under the top pallet, lifts it up and swings it over the sidewalk, through a second-story window and gently lowers it onto the floor inside. And then the process is repeated. The man might be wearing evening dress for all the physical exertion he is put to. Doubtless the truck was loaded by a similar device, also controlled by a single man, perhaps the same one. Looking at this extremely ingenious machine, one might well reflect on the labor that would be required of an entire crew of men to unload the wallboard as quickly and carefully. Such agonizing and relatively unproductive labor still exists in this society, but it is increasingly rare.

This is one way that capitalism has transformed the nature of work for the better, but not the only one. The relation of capitalism to domestic service is more complex than might be imagined. Post-revolutionary America was pre-eminently a nation of farmers and hence of people who do for themselves. In 1800, there were barely 40,000 domestics out of a population of 5.3 million. By 1850, there were 350 thousand domestics in a population of 23 million—approximately 1.5%; in 1870 there were a million domestics out of 40 million—2.5%; in 1900, 1.8 million domestics out of 76 million—2.3%; in 1920—down to 1.5; and by 1960 the proportion had receded to 1.3 million out of 176 million—.7%.

Although hard statistics are lacking, it seems reasonable to believe that the nature of this domestic workforce has changed drastically over the period: at the start, largely in residential service, but latterly working in such institutional settings as hotels and college dormitories. Hotels, to cite only the foreshortened baseline available, went in number from about 30,000 to about 90,000 between 1933 and 1967; most of the millions of beds in college dormitories are comparatively recent in origin, the fruit of the great expansion that came to higher education after 1950. Just as the relative size of the domestic force shrank, its clientele and its relationship with it shifted from one that closely resembled pre-capitalist norms to one that converted domestics from servants to workers and the clientele from masters to customers.

This transfer of domestics out of the home and into the hotels was made possible by the development of a wide range of what forty-years ago were still invariably known as "labor-saving devices."

The transfer of labor from servants to machines was already well under way ca. 1910 when a Maytag advertisement spoke of how a marvellous new appliance would lighten the work of "washday," and the beneficiary was clearly seen not as the scullion but the mistress. The phrase "washday" was probably for most housewives an exaggeration, but certainly far more applicable then than now. The ad cheerily advises prospective customers that their washday labors will be converted from serious drudgery to healthful exercise! In later years the process was to be transformed out of recognition, and doing the washing became, like many another household task, a collaboration between the housewife and the unseen factory worker in which most of the drudgery of both was taken over by machines. That is, the sensational future forecast by the more extravagant and technologically-oriented leftists was quietly achieved by capitalism.

VI

Statistics make it abundantly clear that in the approximately two centuries since capitalism began to operate it has enriched mankind almost beyond belief by liberating and thereby vastly increasing its productive capacities. Moreover, even the most casual march through the Sears catalog shows that by the turn of the century the production of capitalism was increasingly made available to an extremely wide range of people at a decreasing price in terms of their labor: that is, that increases in productivity were and have been shared with the producer. But all these effects might be consistent with the notion that capitalism is a rising tide on which all boats float but which nevertheless maintains at the flood the inequalities that existed at the ebb.

Capitalism is almost never thought of as increasing equality, an increase in which is generally taken as a desideratum, one for which most people look elsewhere than capitalism. The received view among American intellectuals of the relationship obtaining among capitalism, socialism, economics and politics is the one crystallized by Barry Commoner at the end of his 1976 book *The Poverty of Power:* ". . . no existing example of a socialist society— whether the U.S.S.R., China, or Cuba—is consistent with both the economic democracy of socialism and the political democracy inherent in the U.S. tradition . . ."

This opposition between political democracy and economic democracy is not original with Commoner, for it goes back at least to Henry Wallace's 1948 presidential campaign. The implication of the dichotomy is as clear as it is misleading: freedom may suffer under communism, but equality can flourish better there. Even before one can conduct empirical research into this formulation, theoretical problems arise. For example, the equality of the prison is a very marked phenomenon: at the top, an autocrat; just beneath him, a comparatively few Praetorians; and at the bottom, constituting the overwhelming majority of the population, everyone else, arranged in an equality so absolute that everyone has the same living space, the same clothes, the same food, and the same lack of freedom. The model is as apt an account of the Soviet Union as of Sing Sing.

Commoner states the common theory: when we turn to the practice the reality is astonishingly different from what everyone knows. Consider housing. We still have with us the artifacts of the heavily class-bound housing system that antedated capitalism and indeed continued barely changed through its early stages. At the top, palaces. Splendid palaces in Europe, typified by Blenheim, Versailles and the Schoenbrunn; palaces at first much more modest in the United States, but eventually palaces on the grand, if often tasteless, scale, as at Newport. These the democratic tradition required to be called cottages.

That American palace-building flowered on the grand scale so late is perhaps attributable to a democratic society's pioneer impatience with gross distinctions of class as embodied in living arrangements. It is noteworthy that James Hoban took for the model of the White House not a stately home on the scale of Castle Howard or Chambord, but the Duke of Leinster's relatively modest Dublin house. When Robert Lucas came to Iowa City to be governor of the Territory of Iowa, he built Plum Grove, a vest-pocket country house of some elegance, but in size and exterior no grander than the solider farmhouses of the surrounding county.

But such as they are, we still have our ancient palaces. And we have our ancient dower houses and our ancient homes of the bourgeoisie, greater and lesser. And we have our ancient tenements, home of the proletariat. We have in great abundance the homes of our yeoman farmers. What we do not have in any quantity are the homes of our peasants and our lumpen-proletariat. The hovels of the past have not come down to us.

This is an interesting fact, but even more interesting is the question of what parts of the pre- and early-capitalist housing stock is still residential. When palaces survive, they are almost always museums, as often as not museums of themselves, as at Newport. Part of the spice of the Von Bulow murder trial of 1981–82 lay in the fact that the principals actually *lived* in the sort of Newport "cottage" that is mostly now a museum. Many such palaces have been demolished, and those that survive more often than not provide housing for eleemosynary institutions. Our society seems unable to produce individuals rich enough to live in them. More often than not, the rich live in apartments, like everyone else in the cities where they cluster, and when they live in houses these are likely to be houses rather than estates.

The estates themselves, when they do not house colleges educating the daughters of the affluent proleteriat, are more often than not converted into condominiums, the Big House broken into flats and its lawns accroached by what are curiously called town-houses. Meanwhile, back in the cities, the rich and the aspiring huddle near to each other in apartment buildings distinguished largely by total area and by the elaboration of security measures. The poor live in what would have been thought of in the pre-capitalist period as ill-maintained castles.

Most of the housing stock of the country dating from before 1837 consists of farmhouses. These are, for the most part, still occupied by something approximating the yeoman class, even though it sometimes now tills computers rather than fields.

My own house was built as a farm cottage about 1835, almost certainly on the foundations of an earlier one. In its original form it had four smallish rooms and a loft above. About 1870 the owners sold off the land around the house and a large number of houses considerably more grand were built. These are now occupied by a vigorous mixture of artisans and college students.

Only my house appears to be occupied by the middle-class sort who built it.

My people—as I like to think of them—appear to have used their gains from the land sale to erect a bewildering array of small extensions for which "wing" would be a pretentious term. A series of chances—two successive ownerships each lasting a half-century and acquisition by ambitious and hard-working immigrants as income property—explain why it has not passed into the hands of people who would have lived less substantially a century ago.

The effect of a century and a half of capitalism has been to level living accommodation to a degree that would have been thought impossible by all but a few Utopians. The gulf between Raskolnikov's lodging and the palaces of St. Petersburg was a gulf between worlds; the gulf between a college dormitory and the apartments of the Upper East Side is that between tutelage and achievement.

VII

Another striking levelling tendency is in clothes. While there remains a formidable gap in the prices the rich and the less-rich pay for their clothes, Americans—especially when dressing up— tend increasingly toward a common sartorial habit. If one looks at the photographs of the Lincoln conspirators, it is fairly easy to place them in their proper socio-economic niche by the *kinds* of clothes they are wearing. It is clear that as late as the turn of the century, there was considerable truth in the sardonic account of the capitalist "uniform" given in *1984*. Walking down Fifth Avenue in 1900, one could have estimated the income of a man walking toward one from a considerable distance. Now, you must get near enough to see the quality of his stitching and his fabric. Once, a laboring man would have been denied the chance to regale himself with an occasional meal in a good restaurant simply because he would not have owned the clothes necessary to get in. Today, the three-piece suit—a capitalist uniform of sorts until quite recently—is found everywhere and vests are regularly supplied with the cheapest suits.

The copying of expensive women's dresses for sale in bargain stores is of course a tradition of considerable antiquity; even the extremely expensive and elegant little black dress of the sort that

the Duchess of Windsor made famous gets copied and ceases to be
a badge of affluence at more than a few paces.

Thus much for comparatively formal clothes. Recreational
wear seems even more levelled. Such feeble attempts to put a little
class back into the uniform of the '60's as designer jeans seem
fated to cheap copying and consequent demystification. Recent
press reports indicate that the LaCoste company has decided to
throw in the towel and license its alligator more widely in the
interests of selling it *tois pollois,* and gaining revenue now being
lost on less worthy imitators. Perhaps the most remarkable sartorial development of the age is the resurrection of the medieval
custom of livery; there is not a shop or bar in Boston's Quincy
Market that does not have its distinctive T-shirt, often as not worn
by customers as well as employees. When, in *You Can't Fool an
Honest Man,* W. C. Fields entered a fancy party wearing an opera
cape emblazoned with an ad for "Larsen E. Whipsnade's Circus
and Raree-Show," he outraged his hostess and tickled his audience; if some one tried to do that today, he would probably start
a fad.

Levelling of costume is especially important because highly
stratified organizations have often separated the strata with sartorial labels; the uniforms of military organizations and of European civil services are a case in point. A society in which people
have began to dress more alike is almost by definition, one in
which they have come to be more equal.

VIII

Capitalism has thrown up a number of systems of transportation; each has been an equalizer and resisted by the opponents of
equality.* When it was eight days between London and Edin-
burgh, the style of one's accommodation on the way made a
considerable difference to the pleasure of the trip, e.g., whether

---

*This phenomenon is as marked today as ever. Aristocratic opposition to the railways in
England was very strong; the Fellows of Eton College were successful in preventing the
Great Western Railway from having a station nearby, and it was not until the more
bourgeois residents at Windsor took up the railway that the College got service. In the
1930s, the surviving baronial class of Long Island did everything they could to prevent
Robert Moses' parkways from spilling the Manhattan hordes into their forest primeval.
Aristocratic liberalism in Massachusetts counts one of its proudest victories in having
prevented the completion of Interstate 93 through Boston. For much enlightenment on
the modern alliance between privilege and anti-capitalism, see William Tucker's work.

one rode inside or on top, slept in a room or in the stable. But when with the coming of the railway, the time was reduced to eight hours, such distinctions became irrelevant. This is probably one reason why the railways were at some pains in England to introduce class systems of conveyance as a moderator of their new device's levelling tendencies, and why class accommodations were by and large resisted on American railroads.*

In creating the railroad system of the United States, capitalism established a remarkable public utility that by being open to all could not help but induce greater equality among all. Railroad statistics are not always gripping, but there is something dramatic in the fact that in each of several years after 1911, the American railroads carried a billion passengers. With a population hovering around 100 million, this was the equivalent of ten or more rides a year for each man, woman and child in the country.

It is typical of the prodigal genius of capitalism that having created a mass transportation system of this magnitude, it should in a comparatively short time replace it with two more. One of these, the airline system, now logs five times as many passenger miles annually as the railroads did at their height. The breadth of its use may be judged from the fact that in 1980 this system served 300 million passengers. It may also be judged from the exiguous and ill-patronized remnants of first-class service; aircraft are now fitted to carry a small fraction of their passengers in first-class— when they carry any of them—and the first-class cabin is rarely full.

The airplane is one of the most transforming creations of capitalism. For business and pleasure alike, the passenger airplane makes possible a multiplicity of journeys that simply could not have happened before the Second World War. Not the least of these has been the provision of foreign travel, long a preserve mainly of the rich and the bohemian, to an increasingly large cross-section of the country. So long as a trip to Europe began and ended with a week on the sea, Europe was not a place for a secretary's vacation. Getting there might have been half the fun, but getting there and back would have taken all the time. The invention of the jet airliner, marketed by the entrepreneurial device of the charter, has changed all that, and Americans, once for the most part untravelled by European standards, become more and more aware of the worlds that lie across the seas.

The second system of mass transportation is the automobile.

---

*There is a certain irony in the fact that the class distinctions on the Trans-Siberian Railway are such as are no longer maintained in Europe or the United States.

This nearly universal possession, in conjunction with a universal system of public highways, allows anyone to traverse great distances at a mile a minute. The gap between the rich man in a new Mercedes and a poor man with a 1973 Oldsmobile is much less than that between either of them and a man on foot or a man reduced to using inadequate public transportation.

The utilization of this system beggars the imagination: American automobiles now log over a *trillion* vehicle miles a year. Access to this capability for motion increases apace. As recently as 1965, each American possessed a little more than a third of a car; by 1980, he or she had nearly half a car. Since we may reasonably assume that in 1965 the rich owned as many cars as they could use, it appears that the increase has been to the benefit of everyone else and in the interest of narrowing distinctions.

The mere ownership of a car, to be sure, confers no mobility in the absence of gas in the tank. And probably no useful commodity is more widely assumed to be skyrocketing in price under the manipulations of monopoly capital than gasoline. In this light it is instructive, even amusing, to consider the price of gasoline since 1919. Gasoline prices since 1919 are given in charts 7a, 7b, and 7c. Because the combined state and federal gasoline taxes have been a substantial part of the price at the pump, these charts give data for the price of gasoline, the tax, and the combined figure which most motorists think of as the price of gasoline.

These charts make several revelations. The first of these is that from the time the Motor Age began in full swing until the arrival of OPEC, the price in real terms of gasoline at the pump declined sharply. And even the exactions of OPEC had not, by 1981, succeeded in bringing the real price of gasoline to a new historical high. Moreover, if we consider the price of the gasoline itself, setting the tax on it aside, the long decline before the boycott is even more striking. The historical low point for the real price of gasoline came in 1973, when the price of gasoline at the pump was roughly one-third tax. Since then, OPEC has been substantially more greedy than the government and the tax has receded to a rate of approximately 10% of the total.

It is probably unfair to call the government greedy at all, for the tax in question builds the roads the cars run on. But it is necessary to understand that a considerable proportion of the historical movement of "gasoline" prices has nothing to do with gasoline or with the wicked oil companies. It has to do, rather, with our decision to build a massive highway network and to pay for it largely through a user fee rather than a general tax.

Finally, it should be noted that since 1973 even in current

dollars OPEC prices for crude oil have risen about fifteenfold, and that the price of gasoline itself has risen about fourfold.

Given the historical ability of the oil companies to supply all the gasoline we want at declining real prices, and their comparative success in moderating the impact of OPEC, the only explanation for their present massive unpopularity must be that there is some truth in the saying that no good deed goes unpunished.

The effect of these gasoline prices upon standard of living is moderated by alterations in the cars we use it in. The most obvious of these is in gasoline mileage. We do not have reliable and comparable historical figures on automobile mileage before it became a matter of legal interest to the EPA, but the long-term trend is obviously sharply up. Changes in mileage are, however, intimately linked to considerations of quality. Thus, the fleet mileage fell in response to a more widespread use of air-conditioning, just as it is now rising in response to the prevalence of lighter and smaller cars, themselves ambivalent creatures that are easier to park and harder to get into and possibly more dangerous in a crash.

All things considered, it is probably rash to try to adjust these gasoline prices for mileage. It can be observed that the nadir in mileage came in 1973–74, when very large cars that were more likely to be air-conditioned came up against EPA emissions standards that for the time being could be met only by radical detuning of the engine—that is, by making it radically inefficient. The more recent climb in mileage figures began when the arrival of the catalytic converter in the 1975 model year made lower emissions compatible with higher mileage. These have been dramatic: the Corporate Average Fuel Economy (CAFE) of all cars produced in 1974 was 12 mpg; in 1982 it is projected to be 24. This improvement outruns the real price increase of gasoline over the same period. That is, one who buys a new car is gaining on OPEC, and in a comparatively few years the entire fleet will have gained similarly over current OPEC prices.

IX

One could multiply examples of the levelling inventions of capitalism almost indefinitely. Before the industrial revolution, communication between two persons at a great distance was slow, uncertain, and generally expensive, especially to the extent that it was faster or more certain. The telegraph was to change that within a few years at mid-century, and the telephone was to build on the transformation wrought by the telegraph: for the first time in the history of man, there could be knowledge of action at a great distance that was essentially simultaneous with the action.

By 1978, 98% of the households in the United States had telephone service. The number of individual telephone instruments was approximately 77% of the population, and they threaten at present rates of increase to outnumber us at no very distant date. Few commodities have dropped in price quite so sensationally as long distance telephone calls. In 1915, the price of a call from New York to San Francisco was $20.70. This was, in 1967 dollars, $68.10. By 1982, the price in current dollars had dropped to $1.72, or $.61 cents in 1967 dollars. The earlier call would have cost nearly twelve days to earn; the later one, 1% of a day! The comparison ignores the fact that the call in 1915 would have needed to be booked through a central operator, whereas the 1982 call could be set up by the caller himself.

Without belaboring the details, I should note that even in its present deformed state the U.S. Postal service would have seemed an unlikely miracle at any time before this century, and that the cost of sending a first-class letter has, in 1967 dollars, gone down from 18 cents in 1847 to 8 cents in 1900 to 7 cents in 1982. In 1900, a day's wages bought 57 first-class stamps; in 1982, 250. The bad news is that the second of these price cuts has been accompanied by a considerable decline in the quality of service.

Finally, not to prolong endlessly this catalog of the universally distributed benefits of capitalism, let us consider the universal provision of safe drinking water. Many of the effects of this change have already been noticed in the discussion of lifespan; but as an extension of simple convenience it can hardly be matched. Capitalism did not of course invent the notion of a universal public water supply; but it did organize and implement it with a speed and thoroughness that the world had never seen before. That water "companies" were typically, but not invariably, municipal, should not confuse the issue, for the civil engineering works that were necessary for these companies' operations were capitalism's children.

X

Capitalism does not, it must be said, conduce to perfect equality. It is especially ill-adapted to produce equality of result, for its failure to achieve that is precisely what makes it work. It is not even especially well-adapted to guarantee instant equality of opportunity, for the freedom which is necessary for capitalism to work at all is a freedom in which people are free to hold deplorable ideas about civil rights and to act on them in ways harmful to such equality. Generations of such mistaken choices taken in freedom largely account for the economic differentials between blacks and whites. The existence of these differentials as an artifact of racial prejudice is distressing, and no one can doubt the desirability of their prompt disappearance. But nothing suggests that we can get rid of them by scrapping or mischievously altering capitalism. In the medium to long run capitalism appears to be the only system that maintains inequalities only when necessary to make it work. The workings of capitalism are such as to make its comparative failures more attractive than the other firm's successes.

The great mystery remains, when one has thought on these things, as to why capitalism should have such a bad name. Even its unacceptable Victorian face looks benign compared to the more acceptable faces of communism. During the two decades when the Trusts were presumed to be oppressing the poor most effectively, the prices of sugar and flour, in terms of the hours needed to earn them, dropped to a third of their starting values.*

And when we consider the extent to which even socialism's successes have been parasitic upon a capitalist base, the wonder grows that capitalism should be so widely abused by all the best people. Michael Novak, in his recent *The Spirit of Democratic Capitalism*, has made a start at diagnosing the sources of hostility to capitalism, but we are still wanting an explanation of why millions who regularly benefit from it should be routinely hostile to it. That is a question of intellectual and social pathology I shall not follow further. What is beyond serious doubt is the role of capitalism as a liberating and equalizing force.

---

*In this connection it is worth remembering that the effect of the organization of the Standard Oil Company was to lower the price of petroleum sharply. During the period of the Rockefeller monopoly, its greatest critics were not consumers but its erstwhile competitors—that is, John D.'s fellow capitalists.

TABLE 1
LIFE EXPECTANCY AT BIRTH, 1900 AND 1979

	Total			White			Black and Other		
	Total	Male	Female	Total	Male	Female	Total	Male	Female
1900	47.3	46.3	48.3	47.6	46.6	48.7	33.0	32.5	33.5
1979	73.8	69.9	77.8	74.4	70.6	78.3	69.9	65.5	74.5
+	26.5	23.6	29.5	26.8	24.0	29.6	36.9	33.0	41.0

TABLE 2
MATERNAL MORTALITY, 1915 AND 1970

	Total	White	Black and Other
1915	60.8	60.1	105.6
1970	2.2	1.4	5.6
−	58.6	58.7	100.0

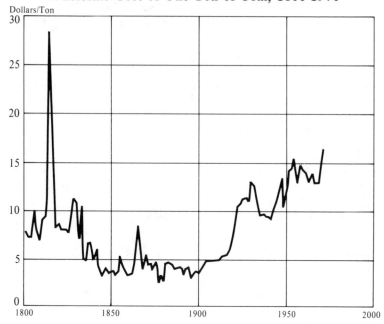

Figure 1a
Wholesale Cost of One Ton of Coal, 1800-1970

Dollars/Ton

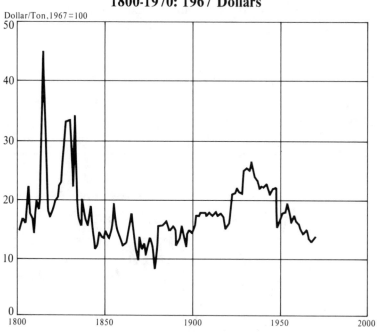

Figure 1b
Wholesale Cost of One Ton of Coal,
1800-1970: 1967 Dollars

Dollar/Ton,1967=100

Figure 1c
Wholesale Cost of One Ton of Coal, 1860-1970: Days to Earn

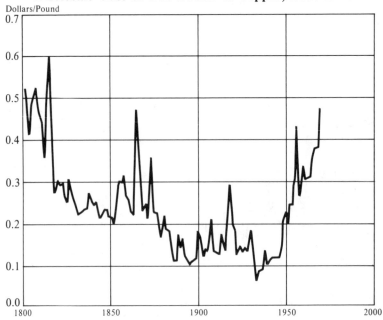

Figure 2a
Wholesale Cost of One Pound of Copper, 1800-1970

Figure 2b
Wholesale Cost of a Pound of Copper,
1800-1970: 1967 Dollars

Figure 2c
Wholesale Cost of One Pound of Copper,
1860-1970: Days to Earn

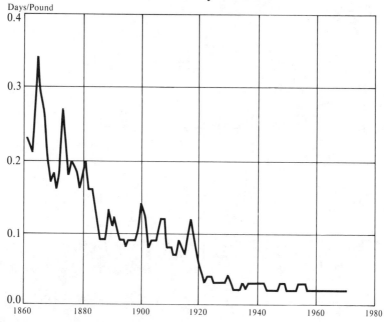

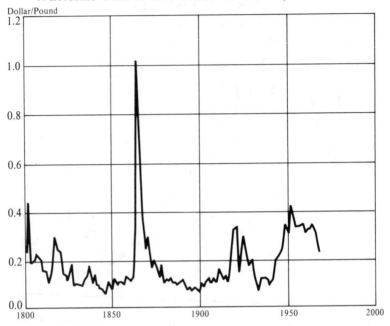

Figure 3a
Wholesale Cost of One Pound of Cotton, 1800-1970

Dollar/Pound

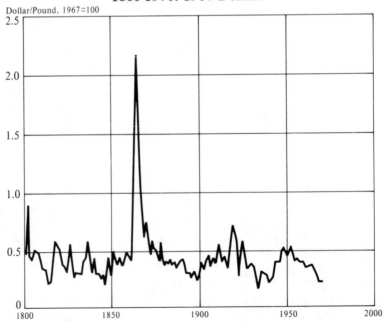

Figure 3b
Wholesale Cost of One Pound of Cotton, 1800-1970: 1967 Dollars

Dollar/Pound, 1967=100

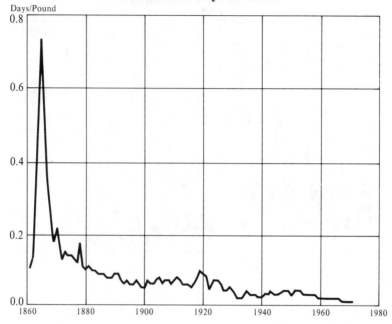

Figure 3c
**Wholesale Cost of One Pound of Cotton,
1860-1970: Days to Earn**

Days/Pound

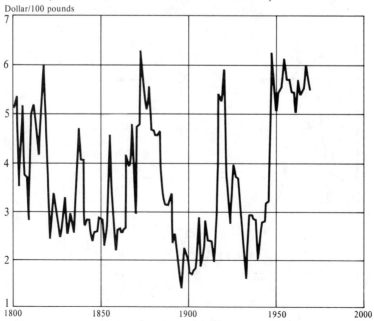

Figure 4a
Wholesale Cost of 100 Pounds of Flour, 1800-1970

Dollar/100 pounds

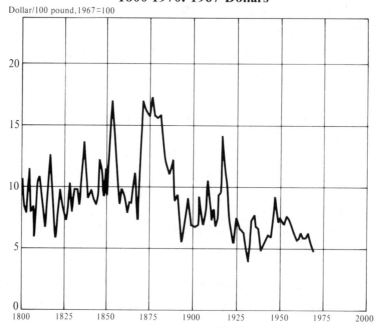

Figure 4b
Wholesale Cost of 100 Pounds of Flour,
1800-1970: 1967 Dollars

Dollar/100 pound, 1967=100

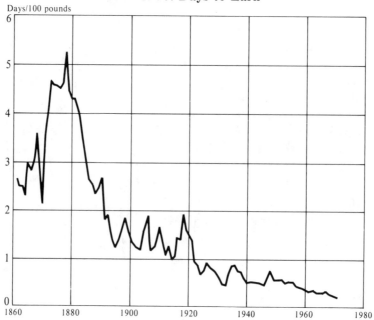

Figure 4c
Wholesale Cost of 100 Pounds of Flour,
1860-1970: Days to Earn

Days/100 pounds

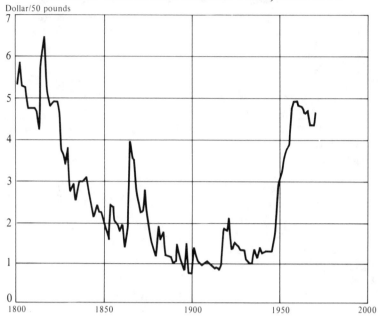

Figure 5a
Wholesale Cost of 50 Pounds of Nails, 1800-1970

Dollar/50 pounds

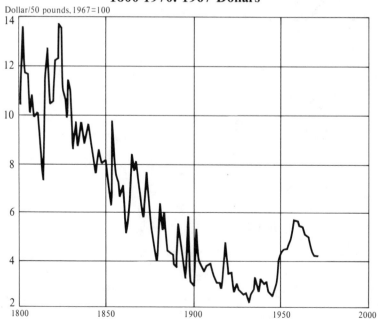

Figure 5b
Wholesale Cost of 50 Pounds of Nails,
1800-1970: 1967 Dollars

Dollar/50 pounds, 1967=100

Figure 5c
Wholesale Cost of 50 Pounds of Nails, 1860-1970: Days to Earn

Figure 6a
Wholesale Cost of One Pound of Sugar, 1800-1970

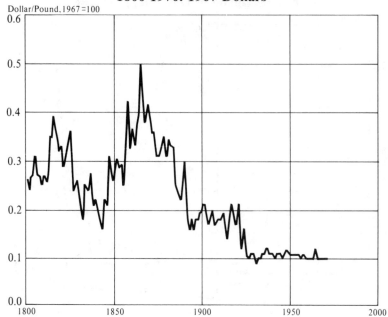

Figure 6b
Wholesale Cost of One Pound of Sugar, 1800-1970: 1967 Dollars

Dollar/Pound, 1967=100

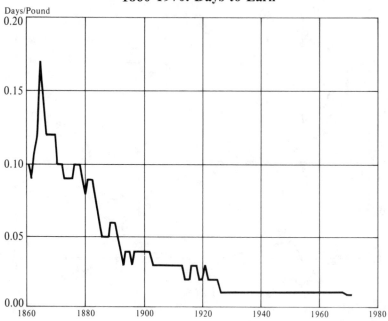

Figure 6c
Wholesale Cost of One Pound of Sugar, 1860-1970: Days to Earn

Days/Pound

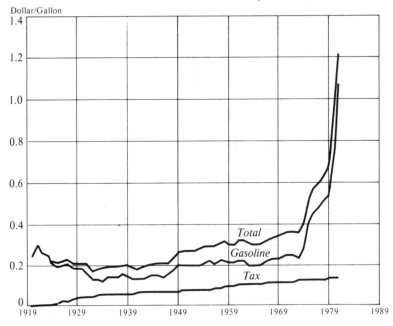

Figure 7a
Cost of One Gallon of Gasoline, 1919-1980

Dollar/Gallon

Total

Gasoline

Tax

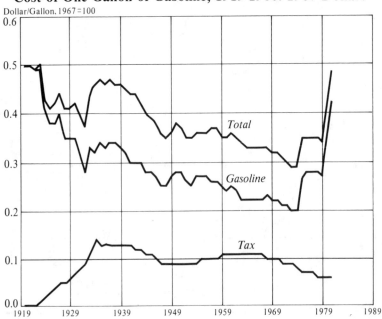

Figure 7b
Cost of One Gallon of Gasoline, 1919-1980: 1967 Dollars

Dollar/Gallon, 1967 = 100

Total

Gasoline

Tax

Figure 7c
Cost of 500 Gallons of Gasoline, 1919-1980: Days to Earn

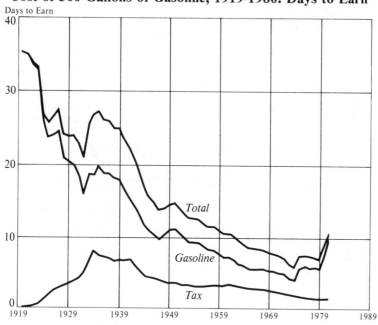

Is Inequality Inevitable Under Capitalism? The American Case

Jeffrey G. Williamson

I. The Critics of Capitalism: The Great Debate

DID WESTERN CAPITALISM breed inequality in its heyday? Would it continue to do so in Europe and America were it not for government intervention and the welfare state? Does it breed inequality in the developing Third World?

Opinion has always been divided on the inequality issue whether in American political campaigns of the 1980s, in 19th century British debate over social reforms or in debate over the World Bank's efforts to shift from passive "trickling down" policy in the developing Third World to active implementation of projects which target the bottom 40 percent. But for hot rhetoric, the critics of 19th century British capitalism are hard to beat. Indeed, Marx and Engels have been the source of inspiration for the critics ever since they fired their first volley at capitalism more than a century ago.

Writing in 1845, Friedrich Engels deplored *The Condition of the Working Class in England* and thought it had deteriorated under capitalism. Before the Industrial Revolution, the worker's

". . . standard of life was much better than that of the factory worker to-day. They were not forced to work excessive hours; they themselves fixed the length of their working day and still earned enough for their needs. . . . Most of them were strong, well-built people, whose physique was virtually equal to that of neighbouring agricultural workers. Children grew up in the open air of the countryside, and if they were old enough to help their parents work, this was only an occasional employment and there was no question of an eight- or twelve-hour day." (Engels, 1845, p. 10)

Three years later *The Communist Manifesto* added to the classic description of middle and lower class impoverishment in the midst of accelerating economy-wide growth (Marx and Engels, 1848, pp. 34, 35, 46):

"Owing to the ever more extended use of machinery and the division of labour, the work of these proletarians has completely lost its individual character and therewith forfeited all its charm for the workers. The worker has become a mere appendage to a machine. . . . Wages . . . decrease in proportion as the repulsiveness of the labor increases. . . .

"Those who have hitherto belonged to the lower middle class—small manufacturers, small traders, minor recipients of unearned income, handicraftsmen, and peasants—slip down, one and all, into the proletariat. . . .

". . . in extant society, private property has been abolished for nine-tenths of the population; it exists only because these nine-tenths have none of it."

In an otherwise theoretical work, Marx devoted much of the first volume of *Capital* to empirical issues, concluding that

"The greater the social wealth, the functioning capital, the extent and energy of its growth . . . the greater is the industrial reserve army . . . and the greater is official pauperism. *This is the absolute general law of capitalist accumulation.*" (1947 ed., pp. 659, 660, emphasis in original)

Like Engels, Marx asserted that the lot of the workers necessarily grew worse, though it can be argued that both had relative "immiseration" in mind rather than absolute impoverishment.

Engels and Marx were hardly alone in stating publicly that inequality was on the rise in 19th century England. Speaking to the House of Commons at the dawn of progressive income taxation, Philip Snowden made a statement that has now become part of our common lexicon:

"The working people are getting poorer. The rich are getting richer. . . . They are getting enormously rich. They are getting shamefully rich. They are getting dangerously rich." (As cited in Whittaker, 1914, p. 44).

Apologists for capitalism were equally vociferous. In Victorian Britain, Porter and Giffen countered the radical critique by using limited tax return data to suggest an egalitarian trend. Alfred Marshall (1910, p. 687) added his weighty influence to the optimistic camp:

"It is doubtful whether the aggregate of the riches of the very rich are as large a part of the total national wealth, . . . in the United States or in England, now as they have been in some earlier phases of civilisation. The diffusion of knowledge, the improvement of education, the growth of prudent habits among the masses of the people, and the opportunities which the new methods of business offer for the safe investment of small capitals: all these forces are telling on the side of the poorer classes as a whole relatively to the richer. The returns of the income tax and the house tax, the statistics of consumption of commodities, the records of salaries paid "to" the higher and the lower ranks of servants of Government and public companies, tend in the same direction, and indicate that middle-class incomes are increasing faster than those of the rich; that the earnings of artisans are increasing faster than those of the professional classes, and that the wages of healthy and vigorous unskilled labourers are increasing faster even than those of the average artisan."

Yet in both America and Britain, the debate raged with almost no hard data. We can sympathize, since until recently few were publicly available. In Britain, 19th century critics of and apologists for capitalism had only occasional Parliamentary income tax and estate tax returns. Around the turn of the century, Arthur Bowley and his colleagues added an impressive compilation of 19th century wages, thus improving the empirical content of the debate. Beyond these, the participants had only back-of-the-envelope guesses at national income distribution, fragmentary estimates of the distribution of earnings among "manual workers" in manufacturing, and street-level impressions of the sort that Engels used to heat up the debate in the 1840s. And there was no information on the distribution of wealth at all.

We have stressed the history of British inequality for one important reason. Britain underwent the first Industrial Revolution, she did so under capitalist institutions, and America followed her lead. Supply-side economics dominated, growth was the dominant social goal, and the apologists' belief in "trickling down" held sway. Furthermore, Britain's experience spawned critics like Marx whose views of 19th century capitalism help justify alternatives to capitalism in much of the world today.

Why didn't America produce a Marx or an Engels? Certainly there were critics of American capitalism. And certainly political activism had an impact on social reform around the turn of the present century, but the reforms came much later in America, they were far less important, and inequality was never the issue that it was in 19th century Britain. Why? Was it that America escaped the inequality which Marx and Engels saw in Britain?

Certainly the New World always held an image of egalitarianism and opportunity in the eyes of the Old World beholders. Visiting contemporary observers were unanimous in describing colonial America as a utopian middle-class democracy, where economic opportunities were abundant and egalitarian distributions the rule. Lord Adam Gordon said so after his 1764 visit to Boston, and Brissot de Warville was even more explicit, stating in 1788 that he "saw none of those livid, ragged wretches that one sees in Europe (Kulikoff, 1971, p. 383.)." Of colonial Philadelphia, visitors pronounced "This is the best poor man's country in the world (Nash, 1976, p. 545)." According to early America's most famous foreign observer, Alexis de Tocqueville (1839) thought things were pretty much the same by the 1830s. Modern social historians have done nothing to overturn these early impressionistic judgments, and they encouraged the dream that the New World would avoid the Old World conflict between growth and equality, a conflict so painfully obvious to Marx and Engels shortly before Tocqueville made his visit to America.

If America was the best poor man's country in the 1830s, something must have gone wrong in the decades following. If the colonial era was one of relative egalitarianism, it must have been followed by a very long episode of rising wealth concentration since by the early 20th century wealth was as concentrated in America as it was in France or Prussia, and almost as concentrated as it was in England. As we shall see below, this episodic rise in wealth concentration seems to have occurred primarily in the antebellum period, with the most dramatic shift towards inequality taking place in the second quarter of the nineteenth century. The timing offers support for Marx and Engels' thesis: Since American industrialization and capitalist growth also begins in the 1820s, the growth-inequality correlation appears to be confirmed, and the view that capitalism breeds inequality appears to be reinforced—even in the "land of opportunity."

If America underwent increasing inequality during her 19th century experience with modern economic growth, what about the 20th century? Evidence has now accumulated suggesting that

America underwent a "revolutionary" income leveling in the middle of the present century, falling from peak levels of inequality in the 1920s. When it first appeared, this evidence was not accepted by the critics without attack. Indeed, Perlo (1954) and Kolko (1962) denied that any leveling had taken place! Furthermore, the critics' views have become embedded in both the popular and the professional literature, the best example being Martin Bronfenbrenner's (1971) oft-cited book on income distribution.

Social scientists are now armed with far better and more abundant data than they were two decades ago, let alone a century ago.

What, then, are the lessons of history? Is inequality inevitable under capitalism?

II. How Does America Stack Up Today?

The Kuznets Curve

In his 1955 Presidential Address before the American Economic Association, Nobel-laureate Simon Kuznets formulated an hypothesis which has since come to be called the "Kuznets Curve." Kuznets argued that inequality followed an inverted U-shaped pattern with inequality first increasing then decreasing with development. Following Kuznets' lead, the hypothesis received considerable attention, especially the inequality phase which has such great relevance for the contemporary Third World (Kuznets, 1963; Adelman and Morris, 1973; Paukert, 1973; Cline, 1975). Given the scarcity of historical data on inequality at the time of writing, most of these authors appealed to cross-national comparisons in testing the Kuznets hypothesis. While even the cross-national data were limited in these early studies, they tended to support the thesis nevertheless. Since then, a vastly augmented data base has been exploited by a World Bank team (Chenery and Syrquin, 1975; Ahluwalia, 1976; Ahluwalia, Carter and Chenery, 1979; Chenery, 1979). These newer studies throw even stronger support behind the Kuznets hypothesis.

The Kuznets Curve is a statement about relative incomes: periods of rising inequality are characterized by the poor lagging behind so that the income gap between them and the rich widen. More recently an even stronger version of the thesis has been advanced, namely that the poor do not share at all in the income growth during phases of rising inequality, and may even suffer an absolute deterioration in their living standards (Adelman and Morris, 1973, pp. 179–183; Ahluwalia, Carter and Chenery, 1979; Chenery, 1979). This extreme view of absolute impoverishment certainly had its defenders among the "pessimists" in the old historical debate over Britain's standard of living during the Industrial Revolution, but based on accumulating evidence the "optimists" appear to have won the day (Lindert and Williamson, 1983). As a consequence, the remainder of this paper will focus on the weaker version of the thesis as it deals with relative income.

How Does America Stack Up?

Table 1 offers a summary of inequality levels across 60 nations in the 1960s and 1970s. The countries are arrayed by levels of development as measured by gross national product per capita. The inequality measures are based on household pre-tax income. Economists have developed far more sophisticated inequality indicators than those presented in Table 1, but the income shares reported there are sufficient to reveal evidence of the Kuznets Curve. The target group for World Bank analysts, for example, is the bottom 40 percent of the population, and it is clear that their share in national income first falls then rises with development. Among "capitalist" nations, the very poorest (GNP per capita at $300 or less) have their bottom 40 percent claiming only 13.66 percent of national income, the middle group (GNP per capita ranging from $300 to $700) have their bottom 40 percent claiming even a smaller share of 10.88 percent, and the richest of the developing countries (GNP per capita ranging from $700 to $1300) show an improvement in the bottom 40 percent share, 14.12 percent. The 13 developed countries have their bottom 40 percent claiming an even larger share of 16.12 percent. The opposite trend appears for the top 20 percent.

Figure 1 summarizes the evidence in Table 1 using regression analysis.[1] Not only is the Kuznets Curve confirmed in Figure 1, but it also tells us something about turning points: Inequality appears to reach its peak among "middle group" countries who have developed sufficiently to attain GNP per capita levels ranging between $300 to $700. And indeed, this range includes those successfully developing "capitalist" countries where inequality and social discontent appear to have been most pronounced over the past two decades: e.g., Colombia, Brazil, Jamaica, and Mexico. In contrast, the 13 advanced "capitalist" countries with far longer successful growth experience have much more equal distributions.

Table 1 and Figure 1 also suggest that America is more egalitarian—at least in the distribution of pre-tax incomes—than almost any of the other 53 "capitalist" countries. America even looks more egalitarian than the 12 other advanced "capitalist" countries with whom she is often compared. While the richest 20 percent claim on average 43.46 percent of the national income among the 13 developed countries (DCs) in Table 1, they claim only 38.8 percent in America. While the poorest 40 percent claim on average 16.12 percent of national income among the 13 DCs, they claim 19.7 percent in America. Of course, *post-tax* income distributions would offer a less egalitarian assessment of America compared with the 12 other advanced "capitalist" countries.

Table 1 also suggests that incomes are more equally distributed in socialist countries. No doubt the problems of comparability are enormous when assessing pre-tax "capitalist" and post-tax (but pre-transfer) "socialist" societies' distribution of economic welfare, but certainly no one would deny the egalitarian advantage of socialism revealed by these statistics. The focus of this section, however, is where America stands today relative to other countries which have a similar pattern of development.

In summary, the cross-national evidence offers two unassailable stylized facts: First, countries seem to pass through stages of inequality experience, early stages of development generating increasing inequality and late stages producing a leveling; second, America today appears to have a relatively egalitarian distribution of pre-tax income, even when compared with the more advanced countries of Western Europe and their offshoots.

III. Historical Dynamics: How Did America Get Here?

The Kuznets Curve Again

Did America always have this relatively egalitarian distribution? Or did she too pass through a Kuznets Curve from early industrialization to the present? Did America ever reveal inequality typical of countries like Brazil and Mexico in the middle stages of industrial development? If so, when? And when did America undergo the leveling of incomes and wealth to reach the relatively egalitarian conditions of today?

An impressive amount of historical evidence has accumulated over the past two decades which makes it possible to document the Kuznets Curve in American history. The evidence has been analyzed elsewhere at length (Lindert and Williamson, 1976; Williamson and Lindert, 1980a, 1980b), and this section will only summarize those findings. First, we shall review long-run wealth inequality trends, focusing attention on the rising concentration of wealth prior to the Civil War, the plateau of high and persistent inequality from the 1870s to the 1920s, and the "revolutionary" leveling of wealth holdings from the 1920s to the early post-World War II years. Second, we shall review the evidence on the distribution of income, earnings and the structure of pay. The evidence here also confirms the Kuznets Curve.

Trends in Wealth Inequality Since 1774

Table 2 reports wealth distribution at three benchmark dates: 1774, based on the impressive research on colonial probate records by Alice Hanson Jones (1978); 1860 and 1870, based on Lee Soltow's (1975) recent analysis of the unique manuscript census data for that period; and 1962, based on a Federal Reserve Board survey (Projector and Weiss, 1966). The measures of wealth inequality are based on net worth and total assets, and the degree of concentration is summarized by the percent of wealth held by the richest 1 percent, the richest 10 percent, and the Gini Coefficient,[2] a statistic which summarizes inequality across households at all levels of wealth.

In 1774, the top 1 percent of free wealth holders held 12.6 percent of total assets, while the richest 10 percent held a little less than half of total assets. While such measures of wealth concentration hardly suggest complete equality in colonial America, they are very low by the standards of 19th century America. That is, the richest percentile held 29 percent of total assets in 1860, and the richest decile held 73 percent. Thus, the top-percentile share more than doubled and the top decile increased its share by half again of its previous level. Among free adult males, the Gini coefficient on total assets rose from .632 to .832. The rise in wealth inequality took place within the North, within the South, as well as for America as a whole. It is also evident whether one includes slaves as part of the population or as assets only.

The figures in Table 2 reveal an epochal surge in wealth concentration between 1774 and the Civil War. Tocqueville (1839) anticipated this trend, pointing to the rise of an industrial elite which he feared would destroy the economic foundation of American egalitarianism:

"I am of the opinion . . . that the manufacturing aristocracy which is growing up under our eyes is one the harshest that ever existed . . . The friends of democracy should keep their eyes anxiously fixed in this direction; for if a permanent inequality . . . penetrates into [America], it may be predicted that this is the gate by which they will enter (1963 ed., p. 161)."

Jackson T. Main (1971) suspected that Tocqueville's fear was borne out by subsequent events, at least based on his early rough estimate of wealth inequality on the eve of the Revolution. Gallman (1969) also suspected a rise in wealth inequality after 1810. Edward Pessen (1973) took a similar position, debunking "the era of the common man" with evidence of rising wealth inequality and social stratification in northern cities. The evidence in Table 2 now confirms this view. Furthermore, additional evidence reported elsewhere (Williamson and Lindert, 1980b, pp. 43–46) strongly suggests that almost all of this drift towards inequality took place in the relatively short period of early industrialization, from the early 1820s to the Civil War.

Following this inequality surge, America appears to have bumped along a high plateau of inequality. There was a leveling across the 1860s, in part due to the freeing of the slaves, but Table 2 suggests that it was modest and/or short-lived. There was also a leveling across the World War I decade (1912–1922) which was reversed largely or entirely by 1929. This suggests that American wealth reached its greatest inequality around 1860, 1914 or 1929. That each of these pinnacles was followed by a major upheaval— civil war and emancipation, world war, or unparalleled depression—may suggest interesting hypotheses regarding the effects of these episodic events on wealth inequality, but the important point is that a *permanent* leveling in the distribution of wealth did not take place until after 1929.

Inequality at the Peak: International Comparisons

The quality of the available data around the turn of the century makes comparisons between American and European wealth inequality hazardous. Yet a rough assessment can at least be attempted by appealing to probated wealth. Taking Table 3 at a face value, it certainly appears that America had reached Old World inequality levels by World War I. Whatever egalitarian influence our frontier, our alleged upward mobility and "opportunity," and our more rural orientation may have imparted, this influence was not a significant leveling force in mature America. Tocqueville was right: less than a century after his visit, the egalitarian "dream" had been lost.

Is the comparison with Europe biased against America? Immigrants and young people tend to be poor, and America had more than her share of both prior to World War I. Could it be that America would look far more egalitarian if we could somehow adjust for the departure of emigrants from the bottom of Europe's size distribution and their arrival at the bottom of America's size distribution? No doubt America's inequality in 1912 would look less concentrated than Europe if such immigrant adjustments were made, but no one has yet offered such an adjustment. What about the relatively young American population produced by decades of more rapid population growth both due to immigration and higher native fertility? If Robert Gallman's (1974) mid-19th century comparisons can be used as a guide, international differences in age distributions may matter a great deal. Yet these age and immigration influences deal with international comparisons *at one point in time*. What about wealth inequality *trends*? Since it is well established that American wealth was far more equally distributed than English wealth in the 18th century (Kulikoff, 1971), it follows that America underwent far more pronounced inequality trends across the 19th century. And elsewhere it has been shown that neither of these forces can directly account for our wealth inequality trends, especially for the ante bellum surge (Williamson and Lindert, 1980a). The inequality surge is no mirage induced by age and nativity forces.

The 20th Century "Revolutionary" Wealth Leveling

Our understanding of levels and trends in wealth inequality since World War I rests on two kinds of data. The first relies on estimates of shares of top wealth holders using estate tax returns. The second relies on the Federal Reserve Board's survey taken in December of 1962. We have already used the latter in Table 2 to document the long-run secular decline in wealth inequality in the century following the Civil War. The former can now be used to identify precisely when that long-run leveling took place.

Table 4 reveals unambiguous trends. Top wealth holders increased their share markedly between 1922 and 1929, apparently recovering their pre-World War I position. Their share then dropped over the next twenty years, hitting a trough around 1949. This leveling in wealth distribution also parallels a "revolutionary" income leveling over the same period, about which more will be said below. The leveling had three striking attributes: First, it was not solely a wartime phenomenon, since an equally dramatic leveling took place early in the Great Depression. Second, while America had undergone leveling over short time periods before, for the first time the leveling stuck. That is, it was not followed by a "return to normalcy" as, for example, was true of the 1920s. Third, the leveling was not simply an artifact of changes in the age distribution and what economists call "life-cycle effects." This latter point requires elaboration.

Between 1930 and 1960 the American population aged. Since young adults tend to be poor, wouldn't the "aging" produce an egalitarian leveling by itself? While young adults declined in relative numbers from the 1920s to the 1960s, the percentage of adults above age 55 also increased. Since the young *and* and old tend to have less wealth, these demographic trends have ambiguous impact on inequality. Did the "net life-cycle impact" serve to contribute to the leveling? This issue has now been resolved (Williamson and Lindert, 1980a), and in sharp contrast to the implications of the so-called "Paglin debate" over post-World War II trends (Paglin, 1975 and the subsequent exchange), age/life-cycle effects appear to have *increased* apparent wealth concentration between 1930 and 1960. Thus, the post-1929 leveling in wealth distribution is understated, and proper adjustment for life-cycle effects would serve to make the trend towards greater wealth equality even more pronounced.

Wages and Earnings Inequality Up to 1880

Shortly before World War I, the premium on skilled labor was extraordinarily high in America. Skills were expensive even by

West European standards. For example, the ratio of skilled to unskilled wages in the U.S. building trades was 2.17 in 1909, while just two years earlier the ratio was as low as 1.54 in the United Kingdom.[3] In contrast, English visitors a century earlier characterized America as a nation endowed with abundant and cheap skills. That is, the pay advantage which skilled workers had over common labor was slightly *lower* in America than Britain in the 1820s. In short, compared to England and the Continent, skilled labor in America may have been relatively cheap at the start of modern industialization, but a century later conditions had reversed.

Do these pay ratios correlate with overall distribution trends? Apparently so: We have already seen that an extraordinary rise in wealth concentration was compressed within four antebellum decades. The same inequality surge reappears when we look at trends in the structure of pay.

Figure 2 presents five time series documenting movements in the pay structure. Massachusetts pay ratios in the building trades surge after 1820, peaking in the 1850s. Pay ratios in northern cities as a whole also rise steeply over the antebellum period, from a low in 1816 to a high in 1856. The ratio of public school teachers' salaries to pay for unskilled common labor also rises prior to the Civil War, as does the ratio of engineers' to common labor wages. All of these series document a brief but sharp decline in the skill premium during the Civil War itself, a finding which is repeated in both 20th century World Wars. But from the mid-1870s onwards, these pay ratios appear to be relatively stable, much like the wealth distributions discussed above. What is most striking, however, is the surge in the relative price of skills and the abrupt widening in the pay structure from around 1816 to around 1856. The movements after 1856 pale by comparison. In four short decades, the American Northeast was transformed from the "Jeffersonian ideal" to a society more typical of developing countries with very wide pay differentials and marked inequality in the distribution of wage income.

Income and Earnings Inequality: Civil War to Great Depression

While the data hardly match the quality and coverage of today's size distributions produced by the Census Bureau's Current Population Surveys, the time series in Figure 3 are at least adequate to mark out the entire period between 1860 and 1929 as one of far greater inequality than that which surrounds us in the 1980s.

The federal government experimented with income taxes on the very rich first around the Civil War, again briefly in the 1890s, and then permanently just before World War I. While these early tax returns tell us little about the distribution of income among the majority of Americans escaping the tax, they do tell us about the share received by the top as well as the distribution in income among those at the top. Both measures show peak inequality on the eve of World War I and again in the late 1920s (Figure 3, "Tucker-Soltow" and "Kuznets"). The income tax data also suggest a plateau of high income inequality from the Civil War to 1929.

While space limits us to a summary, the ratio of wages of skilled to unskilled closely correlate with the income and wealth distribution trends uncovered thus far (see Williamson and Lindert, 1980, pp. 80–82). Pay gaps narrowed a bit during the Civil War, returned to something like their prewar levels by about 1873, drifted towards a very gentle convergence up to 1896, and then widened from 1896 to 1916. During World War I, however, unskilled labor became very scarce and its wages jumped. The wages of skilled and professional groups, by contrast, were bid up much less, the net result being an unprecedented contraction in pay ratios between 1916 and 1920. This leveling was undone in the 1920s, with higher-paid groups increasing their pay advantage over both the urban unskilled and farm labor. By 1929, the gaps between traditionally high-paid and low-paid jobs were almost as wide as in 1916, when the widest gaps in American history seem to have prevailed. This is exactly the same chronology suggested by the income inequality trends in Figure 3. The shares of income going to the top 1 percent dropped between 1916 and 1920 and rebounded strongly across the 1920s. The return to inequality in the 1920s was so great that the bottom 93 percent of the population may have enjoyed no real income gains whatsoever.

The Income "Revolution", 1929–1951

With the appearance of the federal income tax returns around World War I and with the 1940 census, more and more data have become available on the overall size distribution of income. Based on this evidence, Simon Kuznets and others (Kuznets, 1953; Goldsmith, 1969) began to supply estimates which clearly showed that income inequality had diminished sharply between the late 1920s and the late 1940s. Indeed, Arthur Burns (1954, p. 137) viewed this leveling as "one of the great social revolutions of history." Does the evidence accumulated over the past quarter-century confirm or deny Burns' early judgment?

Figure 3 does indeed confirm the earlier findings: there was a dramatic and pervasive shift toward more equal incomes between 1929 and the Korean War. While some gained more than others, the entire income spectrum seems to have converged. But the greatest changes over the two decades as a whole were the rise in the poorest fifth's share and the decline in the top fifth's share (especially the top 5 percent). In 1929, the average income of the richest fifth was 15.5 times that of the poorest fifth. The figure had dropped to 9 by 1951.

The leveling is remarkable in many respects, but one should be emphasized. The series in Figure 3 measure the leveling *before* the effects of government are included. Indeed, this decrease in "pre-fisc" inequality appears to have been as great as the entire equalization achieved by postwar government tax-transfer programs. That is, the leveling in pre-fisc incomes between 1929 and 1951 was as great as the difference between the distribution of pre-fisc and post-fisc incomes in 1950, the latter including *all* state, local, and federal tax-transfer expenditure policies (Reynolds and Smolensky, 1975).

Could the leveling be a mirage? If so, it can't lie with the exclusion of capital gains, since including the latter *magnifies* the egalitarian trend.. Adjustment for changes in the age composition also appears to reinforce the egalitarian trend. Although such demographic influences were never very large, the equalization of life-cycle incomes was even more dramatic than of measured incomes reported in Figure 3. Could it all be due to tax-avoidance and lying? Perlo (1954) and Kolko (1962) thought so, but even when assumptions most favorable to their position are applied, the leveling still remains.[4] Furthermore, tax-avoidance is not a serious problem in household surveys or in pay data, and these series document the same leveling. For example, between 1929 and 1951 the urban unskilled reaped far greater percentage pay gains than workers above them on the income scale. Unskilled workers gained ground on skilled blue-collar workers, lawyers, dentists, engineers, army officers, teachers, professors, and even physicians. And what is true of urban unskilled is also true of farm labor. Furthermore, trends in the civilian economy are mirrored in the military as well.

IV. What Drove the Inequality Trends?

How Should We View Inequality Trends?

It is one thing to document historical trends in inequality. It's quite another to explain them. What drove the Kuznets Curve across American history?

Since Adam Smith's *Wealth of Nations*, economists have found it useful to simplify the income distribution problem by aggregating households by "class". Those households with limited wealth were lumped together in the "working class"; those whose incomes were dominated by land rents were lumped together as "landlords"; and those whose incomes were dominated by profits and returns to other investments were lumped together as "capitalists". No doubt these sharp distinctions get blurred in real world applications, but this class trilogy survived for more than a century as an analytical device for apologists (Ricardo, Mill, Malthus) and critics (Marx, Engels) alike. Both thought that most inequality issues could be handled quite adequately by the simplification. The trick was to understand the determinants of factor shares—the share of wages, rents and profits in national income, and factor costs—wages, land rents and profit rates. Once distribution of factor income between these three "classes" was understood, then the more complex "size" distributions across households would readily follow, or so the classical economists thought.

Only over the past two decades or so has the modern economist come to realize that the class trilogy simply won't do. While the critical reader might wonder why the classical model survived for so long in the face of contrary evidence, recall that truly comprehensive evidence documenting the distribution of income has appeared only fairly recently. Without such evidence, we never would have known that changes in the distribution of *earnings* are a central force behind changes in the distribution of income. Nor would it have been clear that the distribution of *human* capital is at least as important as the distribution of conventional wealth in determining inequality patterns. So it is that the very same historical evidence recently accumulated and summarized above in this paper also motivated the so-called "human capital revolution" led by Nobel prize winner Theodore Schultz (1963) and his Chicago colleague Gary Becker (1964). Yet, these modern advances in distribution theory hardly imply that the 19th century classical economists' focus on factor income distribution is irrelevant or that "class" is a useless concept. Rather, they simply suggest that the trilogy needs to be expanded to include *four* factors of production, not just three: land, labor, capital, *and* skills.

The American evidence reviewed above suggests that trends in earnings inequality have played a crucial role in driving trends in income inequality. The evidence also suggests that occupational pay ratios and income gaps by skill may account for most of the historic changes in the distribution of earnings, a finding documented for 19th century Britain as well (Williamson, 1980). Indeed, the historical evidence on British and American inequality suggests that the explanation for the relative surplus and scarcity of low-skilled labor lies at the heart of any theory of the Kuznets Curve. Such explanations will serve to account for the initial fall and subsequent rise in the relative economic position of "common" labor, for the initial fall and subsequent rise in the bottom 40 percent's share in national income, for the initial rise and subsequent fall in earnings inequality, and thus for the Kuznets Curve more generally. Certainly this wasn't the only force at work, but it is the most pervasive and systematic force common to capitalist development everywhere, past and present.

But what about the distribution of wealth? What follows is motivated by the belief that wealth and its distribution is the tail wagged by the current-income dog. We shall find it more helpful to take the existing distribution of human and conventional wealth as given, then to explore the impact of various economy-wide events on the return to that wealth, and finally to infer inequality trends as a result. This does *not* mean that we ignore the influence of changing wealth distributions and social mobility on changing income distributions. Rather, we believe that wealth distributions respond to, or are determined simultaneously with, rates of pay and returns to assets.

Disequilibrium and Price Signals?

While rising inequality can be, is, and was viewed as an unsightly blemish on early capitalist growth, it can also be viewed as a set of price signals which eventually triggered a health supply response. In a nutshell, herein lies the core of the Great Inequality Debate. Does rising inequality reflect demand-side disequilibrium forces unleashed by rapid industrialization? In the American case were these disequilibrium forces made worse by the flood of immigrants fleeing European harvest failure, political repression and other events over which America had no control? According to this view, capitalist inequality comes out smelling like a rose. Indeed, this has been the position of apologists for capitalism since it all began two centuries ago: Capitalist inequality was a necessary condition if industrialization and growth were to continue, for how could the shortage of skills and capital be alleviated if the incentives to accumulate both human and conventional capital weren't there? Rising inequality simply reflected price signals necessary to induce the accumulation of capital and skills which eventually would eliminate those scarcities and bottlenecks. So said apologists in the past. And so say contemporary apologists who advise Third World governments beset by inequality today.

In reply, the critics have raised an embarassing question: Why, then, does capitalist inequality persist for so long? The critics have supplied their own answer: Capitalism's supply response to these disequilibrium forces was and is slow, sluggish and inelastic. Rising pay ratios, occupational income gaps, and earnings inequality did little to foster skill accumulation and class mobility since the poor were least able to make the necessary investment, and the skilled and middle class did everything they could to discourage upward mobility into their ranks. Furthermore, capitalists—so say the critics—didn't respond to high profit rates with sharply rising savings and accumulation. Thus, profit rates remained high, wealth inequality persisted, and the "robber baron" era lasted for decades from Civil War to Great Depression.

Defenders of capitalism could reply that inequality persisted because America was continually subjected to disequilibrating shocks induced by the success of previous industrialization. Inequality finally declined from its peak in 1929 because the immigrant flood finally ceased and industrialization slowed down to a creep, not because of social reforms legislated in the wake of the Great Depression.

Since this debate between the critics and apologists for capitalism has been ongoing since the First Industrial Revolution in Britain, we are unlikely to resolve it in these pages. But we can examine the sources of the disequilibrating demand and supply shocks which appear to be associated with America's Kuznets

Curve. Perhaps we shall then be better equipped to evaluate the ability of capitalist institutions to deal with the social impact of modern economic growth. The answers may be helpful in anticipating the future shock of fuel and resource scarcities as well.

The Hard Knocks of Industrialization: Factor Demand Problems

If modern economic growth tends to economize on some factors of production and to favor the use of others, then income distribution may be significantly influenced as a consequence. Labor-saving technological change can widen income gaps by worsening job prospects and relative earnings for "common" labor. Capital and skills-using technological change may have the opposite effect, bidding up the return to skills and machines, thus generating inequality. These complex technological forces are commonly abbreviated by the label "labor-saving technological change."

Labor-saving has long been part of the lexicon of growth theorists, economic historians and development economists. It can be broken down into three parts.

First, economy-wide labor-saving may be due to the discovery and application of new technologies in all firms, farms, and industries in the wake of rapid productivity advance associated with the Industrial Revolution. This is certainly the labor-saving that Marx was talking about, and it is also the labor-saving of which so much has been made in the contemporary development literature (Morawetz, 1974). Furthermore, the past two decades have seen case after case confirming the labor-saving bias in American history, although fewer studies are available for the 19th century in spite of Habakkuk's (1962) brilliant attempt to goad the historian into empirical research on the problem.

Second, economy-wide labor-saving may be induced by unbalanced rates of productivity advance across sectors, regardless of its bias within firms and sectors. To the extent that modern sectors exhibit the highest rates of productivity advance during the Industrial Revolution, and given that modern sectors tend to use skills and machines intensively, then the demand for skills and machines is driven upwards, contributing to inequality. Labor-intensive sectors, like agriculture and traditional services, tend to lag behind. Unskilled labor suffers as a result. Unbalanced productivity advance of this sort has been at the heart of conventional histories of the Industrial Revolution ever since the "wave of gadgets" swept England in the late 18th century. In spite of the Green Revolution in the contemporary Third World, it is also at the heart of 20th century Industrial Revolutions taking place in Africa, Asia, and Latin America.

Third, economy-wide labor-saving may be induced by shifts in aggregate demand also favoring modern sectors. But here it's not technology doing the work, but rather domestic demand and government policy. The most famous of these are so-called Engel Effects, which simply describe how household expenditures shift out of food and into manufactures as income per capita increases. As domestic demand shifts to the products of modern industry, skills and machines receive a further boost in demand, augmenting their scarcity. A government tariff policy which protects young industry simply makes matters worse.

These "labor-saving" forces are not simply a once-and-for-all shock to the system either. The quantitative work of Simon Kuznets (1966) and others has established that modern economic growth tends to exhibit trend acceleration, per capita income growth rising from low to high rates over periods stretching over decades. Furthermore, economists have come to realize that most of this trend acceleration is accounted for by a quickening in the pace of technological progress. It is but a short step from this to conclude that the rate of labor-saving must also have quickened across the 19th century. In short, not only did the disequilibrating forces persist, but they appear to have increased in magnitude from the 1820s onwards.

The inherent Industrialization Bias has other attributes too. It also seems to be true that the rate of productivity advance was most rapid in the capital goods sector, especially in the producer durables sector. Indeed, one of the attributes of modern economic growth is the shift of investment out of plant and into equipment. A classic example is offered by the shift out of farm-formed land improvements—a very unskilled labor-intensive investment activity, into steam engines used in modern transport, coal extraction, and textile manufacturing—a very skill-intensive investment activity. Urban social overhead and sophisticated urban services should be added to the Industrialization Bias. To the extent that urbanization associated with the Industrial Revolution requires skill and/or machine intensive inputs, the labor-saving bias of industrialization is reinforced.

The inequality bias is completed by the addition of capital

formation forces. Modern economists now believe that machines and skills are what they call "relative complements." By this they mean that an investment boom tends to augment the demand for skills. Earnings inequality results. The influence is likely to be important, both for the surge in 19th century inequality, when capital accumulation rates were very high, as well as for the 20th century leveling, when capital accumulation rates fell to very low levels.

Absorbing the Immigrant Host: Factor Supply Problems

There is a long tradition in American historiography which argues that the mass migrations of the 19th century introduced inequality where little had previously prevailed. The same tradition reappears when labor historians attempt to account for the behavior of pay ratios after the 1920s when these mass migrations ceased. These and other strands of thought imply the operation of what might be called an "immigrant-inequality trade-off" in American history (Williamson, 1981). The time series in Table 5 certainly encourages the view; not only is the overall correlation between labor force growth and inequality quite close, but the historical correlation is closely related to immigration itself.

Most countries in the contemporary Third World undergoing high and rising inequality are doing so in the absence of mass immigrations. And the same is true of much of Western Europe, which, indeed, underwent emigration during their Industrial Revolutions. True, the contemporary Third World has undergone unusually rapid rates of population growth, but it seems unlikely that demographic/migration forces are the common force driving the Kuznets curve in so many capitalist societies, past and present. In the American case, however, it surely must have been a major contributing factor.

If immigration experience is to help explain the American Kuznets Curve, we certainly know where to look for its most pronounced impact: the first great flood during the "hungry 'forties", led by the Irish fleeing the potato famine; the rising mass migrations of increasingly unskilled laborers from the late 19th century to World War I; and the cessation of the mass migrations following the imposition of quotas in the 1920s.

The Evidence: Sources of the Kuznets Curve

Converting these plausible hypotheses into explicit models, esti-
mating the models, and then using them to unravel history is a
complex process. We have no intention of leading the reader over
that rough ground. But we certainly can summarize the findings
that have accumulated thus far.[5]

The surge in earnings inequality and the rise in pay gaps before
the Civil War appears to have been due to two forces, rapid capital
accumulation and labor-saving technological change. The very
high rates of capital accumulation favored skilled and high-wage
workers in two ways. First, machines served to displace unskilled
labor far more rapidly than skilled labor, thus creating skills
scarcity and earnings inequality. To get some idea of the rate of
accumulation which appears to have created the earnings inequality, capital per worker grew at 3.2 percent per annum between
1839 and 1859 while it grew at only 1.5 percent per annum
between 1929 and 1966. Second, the rapid accumulation contributed to high rates of GNP growth which, through Engel's Law,
speeded the relative demise of agriculture and manufacturing
dominance. Since technological change was centered on manufacturing, it reinforced these effects and hastened the shift of industrial output towards the modern sectors. Indeed, the rate of
industrialization was at no time in our history more rapid than
between 1839 and 1859, the growth rate in manufacturing
reached 7.8 percent per annum while agriculture lagged behind
at 3.3 percent. This shift in output favored those sectors which
used high-paid urban skills intensively, and earnings inequality
was generated as a consequence. Immigration seems to have made
no net contribution to rising inequality in the pre-Civil War episode. Of course, the inequality surge would been quite a bit less in
the absence of the immigrant influx, perhaps diminished by half.
But the upswing of the Kuznets Curve would have remained,
driven by the Industrialization Bias.

Why, then, did inequality remain at this high plateau from Civil
War to Great Depression? Why didn't inequality rise still further?
It turns out that the disequilibrating forces associated with modern economic growth quieted down as the American economy
entered her mature phase of capitalist development, and the
intensity of the Industrialization Bias diminished as a consequence. But the disequilibrating forces were still present with
sufficient force to keep inequality high. The Industrialization Bias
quickens again around the turn of the century—this time associated with dramatic growth in the modern service sectors, all of

which were highly skilled and capital intensive. After the inter-
ruption of World War I, the Industrialization Bias resumes
through the 1920s, although here the leading sectors were automobiles, consumer appliances, petrochemicals and electric util-
ities. Indeed, so pronounced was the labor-saving Industrialization Bias in the first third of the 20th century, that in its absence
an income leveling would have been set in motion long before
1929. Perhaps that's why Britain began her downswing of the
Kuznets Curve in the late 19th century, decades before America
underwent the same leveling. While Britain underwent a productivity slowdown in the late 19th century and lost her technological
leadership, she did find it easier to cope with inequality, undergoing a leveling almost a half-century before America (Williamson,
1985).

What about the post-1929 leveling, the downswing of the
Kuznets Curve, and the "income revolution?" The second third of
the 20th century, from 1929 to 1951, ushered in a pattern of
technological change and factor supply growth that America had
not seen since the Industrial Revolution began in the 1820s. No
longer was technological advance biased in favor of the more skill
and capital intensive sectors. About half of the shift to post-1929
leveling can be explained by this change in the pattern of productivity advance. The labor-saving embedded in the Industrialization Bias had disappeared from the American scene, and America
joined Britain sliding down the Kuznets Curve.

Demographic changes accounted for another third of the shift
to leveling between 1909–29 and 1929–48. The leveling was dramatic because the fertility rate declined, because the quotas ar-
rested the immigrant tide, and because America shifted its mode
of accumulation from physical capital to human capital and skills.
The finding is important and deserves stress. If immigration had
remained at its pre-World War I peak rates, the post-1929 leveling
in incomes would *still* have occurred. But the leveling would have
been far less dramatic. If immigration had stayed at the 1920's
rates, the leveling would have been reduced by about a third.
Immigrant-induced and fertility-induced demographic changes
mattered, but the demand-side forces would still have produced
the Kuznets Curve in their absence.

V. Was This Trip Necessary?

Nowhere in this account have we mentioned inflation, unions,
the rise of government, monopoly power, and other favorite

themes which color the pages of our traditional histories. This does not imply that "institutional forces" played no role at all, but rather that there are more systematic forces associated with modern economic growth that drove the Kuznets Curve. If this interpretation is correct, it also implies that *all* countries, capitalist and non-capitalist, must face the same disequilibrating influences associated with changes in economic and demographic structure during modern economic growth. One manifestation of the structural adjustment is inequality. Stagnant economies undisturbed by demographic shocks are unlikely to be faced with the social problems which accompany the Kuznets Curve.

It is also hard to imagine a bigger shock to an economic system than the rapid growth and structural change associated with the Industrial Revolution, especially when complicated by population explosions—as in the contemporary Third World, or by the absorption problems produced by an immigrant host—as in pre-1929 America. But the future *does* contain elements of structural adjustment not unlike those through which America suffered over the past century and a half. Current inequality problems are clearly exacerbated by the presence of the post-World War II babies who now glut the labor market. But if Richard Easterlin (1978) is right, these inequality-inducing effects will disappear as we move into the late 1980s, unless, of course, immigration over our southern borders swells to much higher rates. There is yet another structural adjustment which shall continue to beset the American economy in the late 20th century— learning to live with increasing fuel scarcities. Economists now believe that energy, capital and skills tend to cluster together, and that any effort to diminish our reliance on energy will bring with it an economy which is more labor-using. Certainly the Industrial Revolution over the past century and a half was extremely fuel-intensive: any switch from that dependence is likely to take the bite out of the Industrialization Bias.

Modern economic growth breeds inequality, whether capitalist or non-capitalist. But could America have done it better under some other system? Perhaps. If inequality patterns over the Kuznets Curve are simply price signals offering an incentive to accumulate skills and capital, couldn't the public sector have assumed a bigger role as a "saver" sooner, especially in fostering human capital accumulation among the bottom 40 percent? This is certainly the direction which much of the Third World has taken, and most of the advanced countries in eastern and western Europe do a far better job in delivering "basic needs" to low income groups than was the case under old-style capitalism. But as Reagan has pointed out, a large public sector has its costs.

Is inequality inevitable under capitalism? Apparently so. Is it unique to capitalism? Certainly not. Is it necessary? This paper takes us no further in resolving this classic question on growth versus equity, but it should help clarify what the trade-off was like in our past.

TABLE 1
INCOME DISTRIBUTION AT DIFFERENT LEVELS OF
DEVELOPMENT:
CROSS-NATIONAL COMPARISONS

Country (Year)	Per Capita GNP in US$ (1970 prices)	Income shares of		
		Bottom 20%	Bottom 40%	Top 20%
Developing Countries				
Chad (1958)	79.5	7.5	18.0	43.0
Malawi (1969)	80.0	5.8	14.9	53.2
Dahomey (1959)	91.3	5.0	15.5	50.0
Pakistan (1963/64)	93.7	6.5	17.5	45.5
Tanzania (1967)	103.8	5.0	14.0	57.0
Sri Lanka (1969/70)	108.6	6.0	17.0	46.0
India (1963/64)	110.3	5.0	16.0	52.0
Malagasy (1960)	138.7	5.5	13.5	61.0
Thailand (1962)	142.8	5.7	12.9	57.7
Uganda (1970)	144.3	6.2	17.1	47.1
Kenya (1969)	153.2	3.8	10.0	68.0
Botswana (1971/72)	216.6	1.0	6.9	58.9
Philippines (1965)	224.4	3.9	11.8	55.4
Egypt (1964/65)	232.8	4.2	14.0	47.0
Iraq (1956)	235.5	2.0	6.8	68.0
El Salvador (1961)	267.4	5.5	12.0	61.4
Korea (1970)	269.2	7.0	18.0	45.0
Senegal (1960)	281.8	3.0	10.0	64.0
Average	300 or less	4.92	13.66	54.46
Honduras (1967/68)	301.0	2.0	6.4	65.0
Tunisia (1970)	306.1	4.1	11.4	55.0
Zambia (1959)	308.2	5.6	14.6	57.0
Ecuador (1970)	313.6	2.5	6.4	73.5
Turkey (1968)	322.2	3.0	9.5	60.6
Ivory Coast (1970)	328.7	3.9	10.1	57.2
Guyana (1955/56)	350.8	4.0	14.0	45.7
Taiwan (1968)	366.1	7.8	20.0	41.4

TABLE 1 (continued)
INCOME DISTRIBUTION AT DIFFERENT LEVELS OF DEVELOPMENT: CROSS-NATIONAL COMPARISONS

Country (Year)	Per Capita GNP in US$ (1970 prices)	Income shares of		
		Bottom 20%	Bottom 40%	Top 20%
Colombia (1970)	388.2	3.5	9.4	59.4
Malaysia (1970)	401.4	3.4	11.4	55.9
Brazil (1970)	456.5	3.1	10.0	62.2
Jamaica (1958)	515.6	2.2	8.2	61.5
Peru (1970)	546.1	1.5	6.5	60.0
Lebanon (1955/56)	588.3	5.0	13.0	61.0
Gabon (1968)	608.1	3.3	8.8	67.5
Costa Rica (1971)	617.1	5.4	14.7	50.6
Mexico (1969)	696.9	4.0	10.5	64.0
Average	300 to 700	3.80	10.88	58.68
Uruguay (1967)	720.8	4.3	14.3	47.4
Panama (1969)	773.4	2.9	9.4	59.3
Spain (1964/65)	852.1	6.0	17.0	45.2
Chile (1968)	903.5	4.5	13.0	56.8
Argentina (1961)	1004.6	7.0	17.3	52.0
Puerto Rico (1963)	1217.4	4.5	13.7	50.6
Average	700 to 1300	4.87	14.12	51.88
Developed Countries				
Japan (1968)	1712.8	4.6	15.9	43.8
Finland (1962)	1839.8	2.4	11.1	49.3
Netherlands (1967)	2297.0	3.1	12.6	48.5
France (1962)	2303.1	1.9	9.5	53.7
Norway (1963)	2361.9	4.5	16.6	40.5
United Kingdom (1968)	2414.3	6.0	18.8	39.2
New Zealand (1970/71)	2501.5	4.4	16.9	41.0
Denmark (1963)	2563.9	5.0	15.8	43.2
Australia (1967/68)	2632.4	6.6	20.1	38.7
West Germany (1970)	3208.6	5.9	16.3	45.6
Canada (1965)	3509.6	6.4	20.0	40.2
Sweden (1970)	4452.2	5.4	15.3	42.5
United States (1970)	5244.1	6.7	19.7	38.8
Average	Above 1300	4.84	16.12	43.46

TABLE 1 (continued)
INCOME DISTRIBUTION AT DIFFERENT LEVELS OF
DEVELOPMENT:
CROSS-NATIONAL COMPARISONS

Country (Year)	Per Capita GNP in US$ (1970 prices)	Income shares of		
		Bottom 20%	Bottom 40%	Top 20%
Socialist Countries				
Bulgaria (n.d.)	406.9	9.8	25.0	35.0
Yugoslavia (1968)	602.3	6.5	18.5	41.5
Poland (1964)	660.8	9.8	23.4	36.0
Hungary (1967)	872.7	8.5	24.0	33.5
Czechoslovakia (1964)	887.7	12.0	27.6	31.0
East Germany (1970)	2046.3	10.4	26.2	30.7
Average	All	9.5	24.12	34.62

Source: Ahluwalia (1976), Table 8, pp. 340–341, which is based on data collected by the World Bank's Development Research Center.

TABLE 2
SELECTED MEASURES OF WEALTH INEQUALITY IN THE UNITED STATES,
1774, 1860, 1870, and 1962

	Net Worth			Total Assets		
	Percent Share Held by Top 1%	Percent Share Held by Top 10%	Gini Coefficient	Percent Share Held by Top 1%	Percent Share Held by Top 10%	Gini Coefficient
1774 (13 colonies)						
Free households	14.3%	53.2%	.694	12.6%	49.6%	.642
Free and slave households	16.5	59.0	n.a.	14.8	55.1	n.a.
Free adult males	14.2	52.5	.688	12.4	48.7	.632
All adult males	16.5	58.4	n.a.	13.2	54.3	n.a.
Southern free households	10.7	47.3	.664	9.9	46.3	.649
Non-South free households	17.1	49.5	.678	14.1	43.8	.594
1860						
Free adult males				29.0	73.0	.832
Adult males				30.3–35.0	74.6–79.0	n.a.
Southern free adult males				27.0	75.0	.845
Non-South free adult males				27.0	68.0	.813
1870						
Adult males				27.0	70.0	.833
Southern adult males				33.0	77.0	.866
Southern adult white males				29.0	73.0	.818
Non-South adult males				24.0	67.0	.816
1962						
All consumer units ranked by total assets, adjusted	20.6	38.5–46.1	n.a.	15.1	35.7	n.a.

Source: Williamson and Lindert, (1980b), Table 3.1, based on A. H. Jones (1978), Vol. 3, Table 8.1; L. Soltow (1975), pp. 99, 103), and D.S. Projector and G.A. Weiss (1962), Tables 8, A2, A8, A14, and A36.

TABLE 3
WEALTH SHARES HELD BY THE TOP 1% AND 10% OF
DECEDENTS AND THE LIVING: FOUR NATIONS, 1907–1913

| Country | Wealth Share of | |
	Top 1%	Top 10%
Among Decedents		
United States 1912	56.4%	90.0%
United Kingdom 1907–11	57.8–64.3	91.9
France 1909	50.4	81.0
Among the Living		
England and Wales 1911–13	70.0	n.a.
Prussia 1908	49.1	82.3

Source: Williamson and Lindert, (1980b), Tables 3.6 and 3.7.

TABLE 4
SHARE OF U.S. PERSONAL WEALTH HELD BY TOP
WEALTH HOLDERS, 1922–1972

| Year | Top 1% of Adults (Lampman) | Top 0.5% of Population | | Top 1% of Population (Smith and Franklin) |
		(Lampman)	(Smith and Franklin)	
1922	31.6%	29.8%		
1929	36.3	32.4		
1933	28.3	25.2		
1939	30.6	28.0		
1945	23.3	20.9		
1949	20.8	19.3		
1953	24.3	22.7	22.0%	27.5%
1954	24.0	22.5		
1956	26.0	25.0		
1958			21.7	26.9
1962			21.6	27.4
1965			23.7	29.2
1969			20.4	25.6
1972			20.9	26.6

Source: Lampman (1962), pp. 202, 204 and Smith and Franklin (1974), unpublished estimates, all reported in Williamson and Lindert, (1980b), Table 3.8.

TABLE 5
WAGE-STRETCHING, LABOR FORCE GROWTH AND IMMIGRATION,
1820–1948

Period	(1) Gross Annual Immigration per 1000 U.S. Population	(2) Rate of Labor Force Growth (% per annum)	(3) Rate of change in the Skilled-Wage Premium (% per annum)
1820–1840	2.67	2.95	4.49
1840–1860	8.61	3.38	1.48
1860–1880	6.15	2.24	0.47
1879–1899	7.00	2.80	0.59
1899–1909	9.37	2.35	1.06
1909–1929	5.11	1.62	− .09
1929–1948	0.62	0.32	− 1.99

Sources: Col. (1): Average annual gross immigration over period divided by mid-period resident population, in Williamson, (1981), Table 1.

Cols. (2) and (3): Williamson and Lindert, (1980b), Table 9.1.

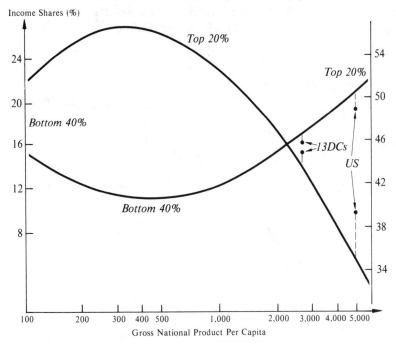

Figure 1
The Kuznets Curve: Cross-National Comparisons

Income Shares (%)

Gross National Product Per Capita

Figure 2
American Pay Ratios Across the 19th Century, Various Skilled Occupations Relative to Unskilled Common Labor

Ratio of Wages by Occupation

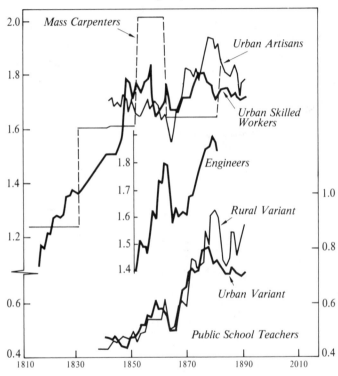

Source: Williamson and Lindert, 1980b, Figure 4.1.

Figure 3
A Century of Income Inequality in America

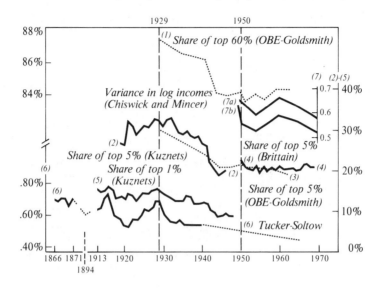

Source: Williamson and Lindert. 1980b. Figure 4.3.

79

NOTES

*This paper draws heavily on almost a decade of past research on inequality in history. Much of this work has been in collaboration with Peter H. Lindert, at the University of California at Davis, to whom I owe a great deal. Section I leans heavily on an unpublished paper which I presented at the Conference on *Economic Growth and Social Change in the Early Republic, 1775–1860* at the University of Illinois in the Spring of 1980 (Williamson, 1980, section I). Section III summarizes the inequality evidence which Professor Lindert and I analyzed at great length in our recent book *American Inequality: A Macroeconomic History* (Williamson and Lindert, 1980b), although this material was also reported in two earlier papers (Lindert and Williamson, 1976; Williamson and Lindert, 1980a). Much of the "theorizing" in Section IV is taken directly from Chapter 5 of my book on British 19th century inequality entitled *Did British Capitalism Breed Inequality?* (Williamson, 1985). The similarities between British and American experience are striking, as the text above suggests. The pages dealing so briefly with the "sources of the Kuznets Curve" are based on Part III of *American Inequality* with Professor Lindert, although it was preceded by some earlier work which both of us pursued independently (Lindert, 1978; Williamson, 1976, 1979). It also draws heavily on a subsequent study of mine which focuses on immigration (Williamson, 1981). The interested reader is encouraged to explore these items upon which this paper draws. It will be quickly apparent to those who do so that this paper makes no effort to "survey the literature" but rather presents my own view of a problem which is still actively debated in the literature.

1. Figure 1 is derived from the regression equations reported in Ahluwalia (1976, Table 1, equations A.1 and A.4). The regressions are based on the full sample of 60 countries in Table 1, where the income share of interest is regressed on log per capita GNP, the square of log per capita GNP, and a socialist dummy variable.

2. The Gini Coefficient is commonly used in the literature. A value of unity indicates greatest inequality and a value of zero indicates a completely egalitarian distribution. This is hardly the only statistic used by economists to summarize complex size distributions, but it's the most popular. In recent years, we have learned that it is *least* sensitive to changes in distribution, and thus may well understate inequality trends in history.

3. Phelps-Brown (1968, p. 47). This was the dominant view of contemporary analysts, too, including such notable economists of the time as Frank Taussig.

4. Williamson and Lindert (1980b, pp. 86–88). There is reason to believe that the introduction of progressive income taxes—even if partially avoided by lying and loop-holes—would tend to make pre-fisc incomes more unequal. In order to secure a supply of high-skill workers, white collar professionals, and able managers, firms may be obliged to pay even higher pre-tax incomes so that post-tax incomes coax out the supply. Since the data in Figure 3 are "pre-tax", the "revolutionary" leveling is likely to be suppressed, not exaggerated.

5. My collaborative work on America with Peter Lindert has been reported most recently in *American Inequality: A Macroeconomic History* (1980b). Analysis of 19th century Britain has produced similar results (Williamson, 1985, Chapters 8–11).

REFERENCES

Adelman, I., and Morris, C. T. 1973. *Economic Growth and Social Equity in Developing Countries*. Stanford: Stanford University Press.

Ahluwalia, M. S. 1976. "Inequality, Poverty and Development." *Journal of Development Economics, 3*, 307–342.

Ahluwalia, M. S., Carter, N. G., and Chenery, H. B. 1979. "Growth and Poverty in Developing Countries." World Bank Staff Working Papers, No. 309 (May). Washington, D.C.: World Bank.

Becker, G. 1964. *Human Capital*. New York: Columbia University Press.

Bronfenbrenner, M. 1971. *Income Distribution Theory*. Chicago: Aldine.

Burns, A. F. 1954. *The Frontiers of Economic Knowledge*. Princeton, N.J.: Princeton University Press.

Chenery, H. 1979. *Structural Change and Development Policy*. New York: Oxford University Press.

Chenery, H. and Syrquin, M. 1975. *Patterns of Development, 1950–1975*. Oxford: Oxford University Press.

Cline, W. R. 1975. "Distribution and Development: A Survey of Literature." *Journal of Development Economics, 1*, 359–400.

Easterlin, R. A. 1978. "What Will 1984 Be Like?" *Demography*, 15, 4 (November), 397–432.

Engels, F. 1845. *The Condition of the Working Class in England*. Translated and edited by W. O. Henderson and W. H. Chaloner. Oxford: Basil Blackwell, 1958 ed.

Gallman, R. E. 1969. "Trends in the Size Distribution of Wealth in the Nineteenth Century: Some Speculations." In L. Soltow (ed.), *Six Papers on the Size Distribution of Wealth and Income*. New York: National Bureau of Economic Research.

Gallman, R. E. 1974. "Equality in America at the Time of Tocqueville." Unpublished. Department of Economics, University of North Carolina, Chapel Hill.

Goldsmith, S. F. 1967. "Changes in the Size Distribution of Income." In E. C. Budd (ed.), *Inequality and Poverty*. New York: Harper and Row.

Habakkuk, H. J. 1962. *American and British Technology in the Nineteenth Century*.Cambridge: Cambridge University Press.

Jones, A. H. 1978. *American Colonial Wealth: Documents and Methods*. New York: Arno Press.

Kolko, G. 1962. *Wealth and Power in America*. New York: Praeger.

Kulikoff, A. 1971. "The Progress of Inequality in Revolutionary Boston." *William and Mary Quarterly, 28*, 375–412.

Kuznets, S. 1953. *Shares of Upper Income Groups in Income and Savings*. New York: National Bureau of Economic Research.

Kuznets, S. 1955. "Economic Growth and Income Inequality" (Presidential Address.) *American Economic Review, 45*, 1–28.

Kuznets, S. 1963. "Quantitative Aspects of the Economic Growth of Nations, VIII. Distribution of Income by Size." *Economic Development and Cultural Change, 11*, 2 (January), Part II, 1–80.

Kuznets, S. 1966. *Modern Economic Growth*. New Haven, Conn.: Yale University Press.

Lampman, R. J. 1962. *The Share of Top Wealth-Holders in National Wealth, 1922–1956*. Princeton, N.J.: Princeton University Press.

Lindert, P. H. 1978. *Fertility and Scarcity in America*. Princeton, N.J.: Princeton University Press.

Lindert, P. H. and Williamson, J. G. 1983. "English Workers' Living Standards during the Industrial Revolution: A New Look." *Economic History Review,* Second Series, 36 (February), 1–25.

Main, J. T. 1971. "Trends in Wealth Concentration Before 1860." *Journal of Economic History,* 31, 445–447.

Marshall, A. 1910. *Principles of Economics,* 6th ed. London: Macmillan.

Marx, K. *Capital,* Vol. I. New York: International Publishers, 1947 ed.

Marx, K. and Engels, F. 1848. *The Communist Manifesto*. New York: International Publishers, 1930 ed.

Morawetz, D. 1974. "Employment Implications of Industrialization in Developing Countries: A Survey." *Economic Journal, 84,* 491–542.

Nash, G. B. 1976a. "Urban Wealth and Poverty in Pre-Revolutionary America." *Journal of Interdisciplinary History, 6,* 545–584.

Paglin, M. 1975. "The Measurement and Trend of Inequality: A Basic Revision." *American Economic Review, 65,* 598–609.

Paukert, F. 1973. "Income Distribution at Different Levels of Development: A Survey of Evidence." *International Labour Review, 108,* 97–125.

Perlo, V. 1954. *The Income "Revolution."* New York: International Publishers.

Pessen, E. 1973. *Riches, Class, and Power Before the Civil War*. Lexington, Mass.: D. C. Heath.

Phelps-Brown, E. H. 1968. *A Century of Pay*. London: Macmillan.

Projector, D. S., and Weiss, G. A. 1966. *Survey of Financial Characteristics of Consumers*. Washington, D.C.: Federal Reserve Board.

Reynolds, M., and Smolensky, E., 1975. "Post-fisc Distribution of Income: 1950, 1961, and 1970." Institute for Research and Poverty Discussion Paper 270–75. University of Wisconsin, Madison.

Schultz, T. W. 1963. *The Economic Value of Education*. New York: Columbia University Press.

Smith, J. D., and Franklin, S. D. 1974. "The Concentration of Personal Wealth, 1922–1969." *American Economic Review, 64,* 162–167.

Soltow, L. 1971b. *Men and Wealth in the United States, 1850–1870*. New Haven, Conn.: Yale University Press.

Tocqueville, A. de. 1839. *Democracy in America*. Reprint. New York: A. A. Knopf, 1963.

Whittaker, T. P. 1914. *The Ownership, Tenure and Taxation of Land*. London: Macmillan.

Williamson, J. G. 1976. "The Sources of American Inequality, 1896–1948." *The Review of Economics and Statistics, 58,* 387–397.

Williamson, J. G. 1979. "Inequality, Accumulation, and Technological Imbalance: A Growth-Equity Conflict in American History?" *Economic Development and Cultural Change, 27,* 231–254.

Williamson, J. G. 1980. "Earnings Inequality in Nineteenth-Century Britain." *Journal of Economic History* 40 (September), 457–476.

Williamson, J. G. 1981. "Immigrant-Inequality Trade-Offs in the Promised Land: American Growth, Distribution and Immigration Prior to the Quotas." In. B. Chiswick (ed.), *The Gateway: U.S. Immigration Issues and Policies*. Washington, D.C.: American Enterprise Institute.

Williamson, J. G. 1985. *Did British Capitalism Breed Inequality?* London: Allen and Unwin.

Williamson, J. G. and Lindert, P. H. 1980a "Long-Term Trends in American Wealth Inequality." In J. Smith (ed.), *Modeling the Distribution and Intergenerational Transmission of Wealth.* Chicago: University of Chicago Press, NBER Studies in Income and Wealth, Vol. 46.

Williamson, J. G. and Lindert, P. H. 1980b. *American Inequality: A Macroeconomic History.* New York: Academic Press.

Income Distribution and Redistribution

Edgar K. Browning

NO SOCIETY HAS EVER had an equal distribution of income, and the United States is no exception. Yet the idea of equality has increasingly come to influence social values and government policies. As *Business Week* noted a few years ago, "the greatest single force changing and expanding the role of the federal government in the United States today is the push for equality."[1] While the balance of forces may have shifted somewhat in the last few years, there is no doubt that the appeal of egalitarianism continues to be a powerful force in our society, especially in intellectual circles.

Economists have never been comfortable discussing whether, or how far, government is justified in redistributing income to achieve greater equality. This reflects a reluctance to exceed the bounds of their professional competence: As a scientific discipline, economics deals with *what is* or *what can be*, rather than with *what should be*. As an economist, I share this general orientation, and most of the present paper deals with income distribution and redistribution from an economic perspective. The first three sections cover primarily data interpretation problems like determining how equal (or unequal) the distribution of income really is. Sections four, five, and six consider how government efforts to redistribute income affect productive incentives, and the significance of this for evaluating redistributive policies. Section seven contains some concluding observations.

I. Income Distribution and Poverty

Two propositions are frequently held to characterize the distribution of income in the United States: First, income is distributed very unequally among households; and second, the degree of inequality has not changed perceptibly since World War II. As we will see later, there is reason to be skeptical of both these widely held views. For now, however, let's consider the basis for these beliefs.

Much of our knowledge about the distribution of income is based on the annual Current Population Survey conducted by the Bureau of the Census. The result of this extensive survey is, among other things, detailed estimates of the distribution of money income among families and unrelated individuals. Table 1 represents a convenient way of presenting some of these data. It gives the share of total money income received by families and unrelated individuals whose incomes place them in the lowest 20 percent (lowest quintile) of household units ranked by income, the second lowest quintile, and so on. Thus, in 1978, the most recent year the data was available, the lowest quintile received 3.8 percent of the total money income of the entire population.

Looking first at the figures for 1978, it is clear that there is substantial inequality among money incomes. Average money income of households in the lowest quintile was only 19 percent of the national average (3.8/20, since the share would be 20 percent if income were equal to the average), while members of the top quintile enjoyed incomes exceeding twice the national average. Perhaps the best indication of the degree of inequality is that the income of the top quintile was nearly 12 times as great (45.2/3.8) as the income of the bottom quintile. The absolute dollar magnitudes may be of interest. Average household income of each quintile, from lowest to highest, was $3183, $8127, $13,740, $20,778, and $37,870. Some people find it quite surprising how low the averages at various positions in the income distribution really are. In fact, any income above $25,222 in 1978 would place a household in the top quintile while an income in excess of $40,811 would place it in the wealthiest five percent of the population.

Table 1 also shows the income shares for selected earlier years. A comparison indicates that there has been almost no change in the distribution over the entire 30 year period covered. While the average real income of households has doubled over this period, the relative shares of income going to the various quintiles are virtually unchanged. Given the major changes that have occurred in work habits, living arrangements, demographic characteristics, government policies, and the like, this constancy in the relative distribution of income is truly surprising.

These estimates are the basis for the belief that the distribution of income is very unequal and has not changed in recent years. There are, however, many problems in interpreting these figures as measures of relative standards of living. At this point, let me mention that the income definition upon which these estimates are based is far from ideal. In the Census Bureau data, cash transfers are included but transfers in-kind (like Medicare and food stamps) are excluded, and personal taxes are not deducted. We will consider the significance of these and other problems in Section III.

One other indicator of inequality is the government's count of the number of persons living in poverty. To make this determination, the federal government establishes a set of poverty-level incomes that vary with the demographic characteristics of families. For example, the poverty level for a nonfarm family of four, headed by a male, and with two related children under 18 years old, was $6610 in 1978. Families with incomes below their respective poverty lines are officially designated as poor. The poverty lines are adjusted upward each year to reflect increases in the cost of living.

Table 2 provides the official estimates of the size and composition of the poverty population in recent years. The total number of poor persons declined from 39.5 million in 1959 to 24.5 million in 1978. Most of this decline, however, occurred during the earlier years. In fact,the number of poor persons today is no lower than it was in 1969. Looking more closely at the demographic groups, we see that the sharpest decline in the incidence of poverty occurred for nonaged, male-headed families. This reduction is attributable largely to economic growth and the higher real wages that accompanied it.

The figures in Table 2 give the number of persons who remain poor even after receipt of government cash transfers. It should be mentioned, however, that there would be a much larger number of persons counted as poor in the absence of government welfare programs. According to one recent estimate, 21 percent of the population had incomes below their respective poverty lines prior to receipt of governmental transfers in 1976, but only 11.8 percent remained officially poor after receiving transfers. Put differently, there would be nearly twice as many poor persons were it not for government transfer programs.

II. Government Redistributive Policies

Many government policies affect the distribution of income, and it would be impossible to describe them all. Some indication of the effort made by government to alter the distribution of income, however, can be obtained by considering "social welfare expenditures," which include all government spending on programs that provide cash or goods and services to persons and families. In fiscal 1979, total social welfare expenditures of federal, state, and local governments amounted to $428.3 billion, with the federal share equal to 62 percent of the total. This comes to an expenditure of almost $2000 per person in the United States, or just under $8000 per family of four.

Table 3 provides a breakdown of social welfare expenditures in 1979 by major functional categories. Actually, more than a hundred separate programs are included in the six categories identified in the table. For example, of the $193.6 billion spent on social insurance, $102.6 billion was spent on social security (OASDI), $29.1 billion on Medicare, $11.3 billion on unemployment insurance, and $33.8 billion on public-employee retirement programs with the remainder allocated to several smaller programs.

As will be clear from Table 3, not all social welfare programs are "welfare" programs for the poor, nor are they all intended to redistribute income. Nonetheless, it is important to consider all social welfare expenditures in an analysis of the way government affects the distribution of income. Although social security, unemployment insurance, and public schools are not intended exclusively for low income families, they do provide important benefits to some poor families. For many low income families, the provison of public schools is quantitatively more important than food stamp transfers.

Table 4 traces the growth of social welfare expenditures in recent years. In the 32 year period from 1947 to 1979, social welfare expenditures grew from $17.3 billion to $428.3 billion. Inflation is responsible for a large part of this growth since prices approximately tripled over this period. Nonetheless, in real terms, social welfare expenditures increased by a factor of more than eight. Relative to net national product, expenditures increased from 8.3 percent in 1947 to 20.8 percent in 1979.

Note in particular the rapid growth in social welfare spending since 1966, especially by the federal government. The mid-1960's saw President Johnson declare his War on Poverty, and the following years saw the enactment of several new programs and enlargement of existing programs. Medicare, Medicaid, and food stamps emerged from this period, and they were accompanied by substantial increases in social security. It seems fair to say that in this period a massive transformation occurred in the content of public budgets with a greatly increased emphasis on the use of government funds to help low income citizens.

Now let us consider somewhat further how these government programs, and the taxes that finance them, have affected the distribution of income. According to the official Census Bureau estimates discussed in the last section, this massive commitment of public funds has had little or no effect on income distribution or poverty. A more careful consideration, however, shows this conclusion to be wrong, due in part to the defects in the way in which income is defined and measured by the Census Bureau.

III. How Much Inequality Is There Really?

Despite widespread reliance on the Census Bureau's data regarding income distribution, it has become clear in recent years that these figures are inaccurate measures of relative living standards: they exaggerate the degree of inequality. Part of the problem lies in the definition of income used by the Census Bureau: it is basically a measure of before-tax money income. Personal taxes, principally income and social security taxes, should be deducted before household incomes are compared. In addition, since the Census Bureau figures include only money income, all types of income in-kind are excluded. Thus, government transfers in the form of Medicare, Medicaid, housing subsidies, food stamps, and the like are not counted as income. This omission has become very serious given the growth of in-kind transfers in recent years and helps to explain why the growth in social welfare expenditures has had no measured effect on the distribution of income—fully half of these outlays are in the form of goods and services provided to households and so are not counted as income by the Census Bureau.

To see how this treatment of taxes and in-kind transfers affects the measured distribution of income, consider Table 5. This table gives detailed information on the quintile distribution of income among households in 1976, and is based on a more comprehensive definition of income than employed by the Census Bureau. Unfortunately, data limitations prevented including all in-kind benefits provided by government, but Medicare, Medicaid, housing subsidies, food stamps, and child nutrition subsidies are included. (However, education benefits are a large item that is omitted.) Since government in-kind programs tend to concentrate benefits on lower income households, their inclusion tends to make the final distribution more equal. So does the subtraction of taxes, due to the fact that the tax system is progressive.

Two points should be noted in Table 5. First, the final distribution of income after taxes and transfers is more equal than the unadjusted Census Bureau figures in Table 1. According to the Census Bureau figures, the highest and lowest quintile shares are 44.7 and 3.8 percent, a ratio of 12 to 1. Using the more comprehensive measure of income in Table 5, the highest and lowest shares are 42.0 and 6.2 percent, a ratio of 7 to 1. Second, apparently government tax and transfer policies have a substantial equalizing effect on the distribution.[2] The percentage distribution of earnings (income before taxes are paid or transfers received) has the highest quintile receiving 50.1 percent and the lowest 2.6 percent, a ratio of 19 to 1, and this ratio falls to 7 to 1 after taxes and transfers are accounted for.

The omission of in-kind transfers and taxes also biases the government's estimates of the poverty population. Because low income families pay very little in taxes, this factor is relatively unimportant. However, the omission of in-kind transfers makes a significant difference in determining the size of the poverty population. Several studies have attempted to estimate the number of poor persons after counting the benefits of in-kind transfers.[3] They conclude that the number of poor persons, as of the mid-1970's, falls by 40 to 70 percent when in-kind transfers are included. The War on Poverty was far more effective in reducing poverty than has been generally acknowledged. The problem has been that official accounting procedures fail to record this achievement.

We may conclude that the distribution of income is more equal than government statistics indicate, but several other problems in interpreting this income data still remain. Basically, they involve questioning whether annual income differences among households are the proper index for measuring the degree of inequality. If households were identical in all respects except income, this might be a reasonable procedure, but it turns out, not surprisingly, that households differ enormously in other respects that most people would consider relevant.

To take just one factor that will illustrate the general problem, consider the influence of age on income. Most people's incomes vary over their lifetimes. Typically, income is relatively low early and late in life, but relatively high during middle-age. For example, in 1978, the average incomes of families where the head of household was under 24 years of age was $12,570, while average income was more than twice as great at $25,383 where the head of household was 45 to 54 years old, and then dipped to $13,754 when the head was over 65. To see how the age factor can affect income data, suppose that every person has the same income at any given age, but that people differ by age. In statistical summaries like Table 1 or Table 6, this would show up as the top quintile having more than twice the income of the bottom quintile because middle-aged persons, populating the top quintile, would have high incomes in the given year while younger and older persons would have low incomes. The statistics would display considerable inequality in annual income despite the fact that all people would have identical lifetime income profiles. In this case, most observers would probably agree that our hypothetical society was characterized by equality, but the income data would indicate otherwise.

This example is of more than theoretical interest since it turns out that half the households in the lowest quintile have heads of household under 24 and over 65, while fewer than eight percent of households in the top quintile do. Middle-aged households are found primarily at the top of the income distribution while young and old households predominate at the bottom. There are also other systematic differences in households in the various quintiles that should be taken into account. For instance, although there are the same number of households in each quintile, there are twice as many persons in the top quintile as in the bottom: Average family size rises with income. In addition, the total number of hours of work supplied by persons in the top quintile is five times as great as for the lowest quintile. Thus, income per person and income per hour of work—other plausible ways to measure inquality—are more equally distributed than household income.

For these and other reasons, it is unlikely that data like that presented in Table 1 or Table 5 convey a very accurate impression of the degree of economic inequality. It is, however, far easier to point these problems out than to overcome them. What I suggest is that a better (but certainly not perfect) index of the degree of inequality can be constructed by looking at an appropriate subset of families that are identical in terms of family size and age. Table 6 does this by considering the distribution of income among three person families with the family head aged 35 to 44.[4] In comparison to Table 5, this distribution displays less inequality in both the distribution of market earnings and the distribution of income after taxes and transfers. The ratio of net income for the top quintile to the bottom quintile is 4 to 1, a far cry from the 12 to 1 ratio in the unadjusted Census figures of Table 1.

Actually, the degree of economic inequality is probably even less than suggested in Table 6 because public education subsidies are not included and no adjustment is made for differences in hours of work. Net income per hour of work is, in fact, about the same for the bottom four quintiles ($5.78, $5.77, $5.68, and $6.66) and only rises to $9.82 for the top quintile. Per hour of work, families in the top quintile received less than twice as much as families in the lowest quintile.

It should be repeated that this exercise is not intended just to show that inequality is less among middle-aged families. Instead, it is intended as a clue to the degree of inequality in society at large when we remove the independent influence of age and family size on incomes. While this procedure can certainly be criticized, it seems to me far better than looking at the total population and thereby jumbling together families of different size and age.

We should also consider briefly whether there has been any trend in the degree of inequality over the postwar years. This is actually a more difficult problem because detailed data of the type that underlie Tables 5 and 6 do not exist for earlier years. However, the current consensus among people who have tried to grapple with this problem is that there has been a trend toward greater equality—once again the official data are misleading. Differences of opinion exist regarding whether the trend has been modest or substantial. It does appear, however, that whatever changes have occurred are due to the growth of government activity in this area. The distribution of market earnings has not become more equal and may have become slightly less equal over this period. There is, however, the possibility that growth in government tax and transfer policies have produced a more unequal distribution of market earnings than would have existed in the absence of that growth.

IV. How Redistribution Affects Productive Incentives

Many discussions of redistributive policies proceed on the implicit assumption that the income is just "there," and the only problem is to see that it is distributed in an equitable or just fashion. Perhaps the most important contribution economics can make is to emphasize that income must be produced before it can be redistributed, and that redistributive programs tend to undermine the incentives to produce income in the first place. Much of the remainder of this paper is devoted to emphasizing the significance of the incentive issue.

Most government efforts to redistribute income involve the use of tax and transfer policies, and I will concentrate on these. The most common way tax and transfer programs affect incentives is through the application of high *marginal* tax rates to income. It is essential to understand that it is the marginal tax rate, not the average tax rate, that adversely affects productive incentives. An example will make this important point clear.

Suppose the government sets out to collect $7500 in taxes from a person earning $30,000. It can attempt to do this with an income tax that exempts the first $20,000 of income and applies a flat rate tax of 75 percent to income in excess of $20,000. If the person continues to earn $30,000, he will pay $7500 in taxes. Thus, his average tax rate is 25 percent. His marginal tax rate, however, is 75 percent: earning a dollar more or less is associated with a change in tax liability of $0.75. The fact that this person pays "only" 25 percent of his income in taxes is not instrumental in affecting incentives to earn income. Instead, it is the 75 percent marginal tax rate, and its implication that his net income falls by only $0.25 when a dollar less is earned, that diminishes productive incentives. The higher the marginal tax rate, the less the taxpayer gets to keep out of each additional dollar in earnings, and it is this that diminishes the incentive to earn income. The average rate of tax may also have some independent effect, but it is high marginal tax rates that are most likely to undermine incentives. As we shall see, redistributive programs generally involve high marginal tax rates, even though average tax rates may be relatively low.

Most people are familiar with the way tax policies impose marginal tax rates on taxpayers, but less well known is the fact that many government transfer policies also involve high marginal tax rates on earnings. If the transfer a family receives is reduced when family earnings increase, this reduction in benefits has exactly the same effect as a marginal tax rate applied to income. Most welfare programs operate in this way, and for good reason: To insure that families with the lowest incomes receive the largest transfers, transfers must be gradually reduced as earnings increase. As an example, suppose that the transfer is reduced by $1 for every $2 earned. Then when earnings increase by $2, disposable income goes up by only $1—exactly the same as a 50 percent marginal tax rate is applied to earnings.

How high are marginal tax rates in the United States now? As a result of the many tax and transfer programs in existence, the effective marginal tax rates are already quite high for most people, but especially for those with high and low incomes. It should be emphasized that the marginal tax rate relevant for incentives is the combined, or effective, rate which results from all the separate tax and transfer programs taken together. For example, a family in a 20 percent federal income tax bracket and a 5 percent state income tax bracket, and subject to no other taxes or transfers, is subject to an effective marginal tax rate of 25 percent. This is the effective marginal rate, and it would be instrumental in affecting economic behavior.

Upper income families confront high effective marginal tax rates primarily for two reasons. First is the progressivity of federal and state income taxes, which apply the highest marginal rates on those with the highest incomes. Second is the fact that investment income is taxed more heavily than labor income, and upper income households receive a larger share of their income in this form.

Perhaps surprisingly, low income families typically confront even higher marginal tax rates than do high income families. The reason is the implicit marginal tax rates found in most transfer programs. Not only are the separate rates of different programs substantial, but when a family receives more than one transfer, the effect is cumulative. For example, when a low income family earns an additional dollar, it may lose $0.25 in food stamp benefits, another $0.25 in housing subsidies, and pay an additional $0.10 in social security taxes: Its effective marginal tax rate is 60 percent.

Table 7 presents estimates of the effective marginal tax rates on households (by income deciles) that result from the combined impact of the tax and transfer system. For reasons just mentioned, the highest marginal tax rates fall on low income households, with the bottom 40 percent of households facing rates in excess of 50 percent. Both tax and transfer programs interact in determining a household's marginal tax rate, and for low income households, the impact of transfer programs is especially important. At higher income levels, transfers become relatively unimportant, and the effective marginal tax rate is due primarily to the tax system. As a point of interest, it might be mentioned that taxes were about 32 percent of net national product in 1976, which is a measure of the national average tax rate. As Table 7 makes clear, all households confront marginal tax rates well in excess of the overall average rate for the nation.

Marginal tax rates are already quite high, in large part due to the redistributive activities of government. Now let's consider in more detail the relationship between the level of marginal tax rates and the amount of income redistributed by tax and transfer policies.

V. Financing Redistribution

It is obvious that redistributing income through tax and transfer policies results in marginal tax rates for both taxpayers and transfer recipients. What is far from obvious, however, is how sensitive the level of marginal tax rates is to the volume of redistribution. As it turns out, redistributive programs result in greater increases in marginal tax rates than do other expenditure programs. For example, by raising everyone's marginal tax rate by one percentage point, it would be possible to spend one percent more of national income on, for example, defense. By contrast, to redistribute one percent more of national income to low income families would require marginal tax rates of all households to be increased by an average of four to five percentage points.

The relationship between redistribution and marginal tax rates can best be illustrated through the use of an example. Assume that transfers take the form of equal grants to all members of society, and that they are financed by a flat rate tax on all income. In Table 8, it is assumed that society is composed of five households, A through E, with earnings of $5000 through $25,000 in increments of $5000. Now suppose that a tax of 20 percent is applied to income, and that there is no effect on incentives to work; earnings remain unchanged. This tax yields $15,000, 20 percent of total income of $75,000, which permits a transfer of $3000 to each of the five households. The results of the tax-plus-transfer on each household are shown in rows two through five in the table. Note that the net effect is a redistribution of $3000 from households D and E to A and B. Only four percent of total income ($3000 out of $75,000) is redistributed by this policy, yet the marginal tax rate for all households is 20 percent.

Although this example is based on a particular type of redistributive policy, the implication that marginal tax rates must rise by a multiple (here, five) of the percentage of national income that is redistributed, is generally true for virtually all actual, and potential, programs. Note that it would make no difference if the government only collected or dispersed the net change in each household's income. For example, if the first $15,000 in income is exempted from taxation and a 20 percent tax applied to income above $15,000, household D would still pay $1000 and E, $2000, and they would still be subject to a 20 percent marginal tax rate. Granting transfers of $2000 to A and $1000 to B implies that transfers are reduced twenty cents per dollar of income—the implicit 20 percent marginal tax rate of the transfer program. Thus, all households would still be subject to a marginal tax rate of 20 percent in this case, although the government would only be collecting and spending $3000.

There is simply no feasible way to avoid sharply increased marginal tax rates when redistributing moderate additional portions of national income. While it is possible to redistribute $3000 in our example in such a way that some households will have lower marginal tax rates than 20 percent, the result is always higher marginal tax rates for other households. For example, suppose only the first $10,000 is exempted from taxation. Then $3000 can be collected from households C, D, and E (who have a combined income in excess of $10,000 of $30,000) with a marginal tax rate of only ten percent. Transferring the $3000 to household A, however, implies marginal tax rates on income below $10,000 of 60 percent! (Since the transfer must be reduced to zero when income reaches $10,000, it must fall by 60 cents for each additional dollar of earnings from $5000 to $10,000.) There is just no way to avoid the fact that someone's marginal tax rates will go up sharply. For convenience, it is simplest to describe the situation by the increment in rates that result when everyone is subject to the same rate—here, marginal tax rates go up by five points for each additional percent of national income redistributed.

While the numbers in Table 8 are intended for illustrative purposes, the actual relationship between the share of national income redistributed and the necessary marginal tax rates is similar to this example. My research suggests that in the United States, a redistribution of one percent of national income requires marginal tax rates to rise by about four percentage points if it is accomplished using a flat rate tax and equal transfers. This means that increasing the percentage share of the lowest quintile of households by just one percent—a seemingly small increase— would require marginal tax rates to rise sharply for all households from their already high levels shown in Table 7. In fact, the required increase would be greater than four percentage points because when one percent of income is redistributed, only part of this can feasibly be transferred to the lowest quintile. (Recall that household B in our example received a third of the sum redistributed.) It would probably be necessary to redistribute at least two percent of national income to the lowest three quintiles to raise the share of the lowest quintile by one percent, and that means everyone's marginal tax rates would have to rise by about eight percentage points.

The arithmetic underlying redistribution demonstrates how difficult it would be to effect a significant increase in the share of income going to the lowest quintile. Many people think it must be simple to augment the small percentage share of the lowest quintile (in the Census Bureau tabulations) by two or three points. The harsh reality, however, is that the policies required to accomplish this would increase marginal tax rates by 15–20 points or more. This would push rates above 60 percent for most households (as is clear from Table 7). To the extent that these higher rates reduce incentives to earn—a matter we will consider further in the next section—the actual gain for low income households would be even smaller.

We can arrive at the same general conclusion by approaching the problem from a different direction. Let's focus on the marginal tax rates necessary to establish a given effective income guarantee, or floor, for all people. Using the example involving equal transfers for all households, the size of that transfer effectively becomes a guaranteed income since it will be the total income of a household with no earnings of its own. Suppose we wish to have an income guarantee equal to one-half the average household income: what marginal tax rate is required? Since total outlays on transfers must then equal half of total income, the required tax rate is 50 percent. In general, the necessary tax rate is the income guarantee divided by average income—to have an income floor of 50 percent of average income requires a marginal tax rate of 50 percent for all households. (Note that the guarantee of $3000 in Table 8 is 20 percent of average income, $15,000, and requires a tax rate of 20 percent.)

Once we recognize that the government requires tax revenues for nonredistributive purposes, the marginal tax rate necessary to establish an income floor at half the average can be seen to be even higher. Suppose, not unrealistically, that 20 percent of national income is required to finance defense, schools, police, interest on the national debt, and so on. These outlays necessitate a tax rate of 20 percent. To have an income floor of 50 percent of the average would require an additional 50 percent marginal tax rate, and therefore an effective marginal tax rate on all households of 70 percent.

These arithmetical relationships, simple as they are, are extremely important in understanding how limited our ability is to achieve a substantially more equal distribution of income through redistribution. Yet most people discussing these matters seem completely unaware of how difficult it would be for tax and transfer policy to materially alter the distribution of income further. For example, a common suggestion of scholars is that an income floor of half the average or median be established, or that the poverty line be set at half the median level and then poverty eliminated. Such things are always proposed as if they would be easy to accomplish, yet the discussion here shows that it would require marginal tax rates on all households to be increased by perhaps 20 percentage points, a 50 percent increase for the average household.

VI. The Trade-Off Between Equality and Efficiency

The higher marginal tax rates required to redistribute income would constitute no real problem except for the fact that economic incentives are affected by the level of these rates. When higher marginal tax rates operate to diminish the quantities of labor and capital supplied, redistributing income will reduce the total income of society. This does not imply that redistribution is necessarily undesirable, but it does imply that there is a cost associated with raising the incomes of the poor: the average level of income will fall.

Economists like to frame the issue of choosing the volume of redistribution as one involving a trade-off between equality and the average level of income, or more generally between equality and efficiency. To have a more equal distribution of income, it is necessary to accept a lower standard of living. Put somewhat differently, to raise the income of low income families requires us to reduce the incomes of upper income families by a larger amount because total earnings will fall in response to the higher marginal tax rates. Obviously, the magnitude of this trade-off should be an important consideration in determining the appropriate level of government redistribution. We do not know, however, the exact magnitude involved because we do not know precisely how powerful the disincentives associated with higher marginal tax rates are. Nonetheless, it is possible to get a general feeling for the likely order of magnitude involved, as well as a better understanding of the nature and significance of the trade-off, by considering a simple numerical example.

Consider a society with just two people, H who has (high) market earnings of $20,000 and L who has (low) earnings of $5000. We want to establish the trade-off involved when income is redistributed from H to L using the type of policy described in the last section—a flat rate tax financing equal per person transfers. Now, however, we assume that the level of each person's earnings declines as the marginal tax rate increases. The exact relationship is assumed to be that given in the first two columns of Table 9. For example, when the marginal tax rate is 20 percent, each person is assumed to earn 97 percent as much as when the rate is zero ($20,000 and $5,000, respectively), but when the rate is 40 percent, earnings fall to 90 percent of their initial value. This relationship is entirely hypothetical, and is intended only to show how the trade-off is related to earnings responses.

The earnings response relationship together with the prescribed tax-transfer policy allows us to calculate columns (5) and (6) that show the possible combinations of net income for H and L that can be achieved. To see how one row is filled in, suppose the tax rate is 30 percent. Then H's earnings are $18,800 and L's are $4700, or $23,500 together. The tax yields $7050 in revenue which permits a transfer of $3525 to each person. Thus, H's net income is equal to earnings of $18,800 minus his tax of $5640 plus the transfer of $3525, or $16,685. L's net income is calculated in a similar fashion.

Columns (5) and (6) thus show how all possible redistributive policies, with tax rates from zero to 100 percent, affect the incomes of both persons. The trade-off is shown by the fact that increasing L's income by a dollar results in a loss of more than a dollar to H since total earnings fall when the marginal tax rate is increased to finance the transfer. The size of the trade-off is given in the last column. For example, to raise L's income from $5000 to $5692 requires a ten percent tax rate that reduces H's income from $20,000 to $19,057, or by $943. A gain to L of $692 at a cost to H of $943 implies a cost of $1.40 to H per dollar of gain to L. which is entered in the last column as a loss/gain ratio of 1.4. The other figures are calculated in the same way. I think it is most useful to conceptualize the trade-off as in the last column of the table, which in effect shows the incremental, or marginal, cost (to H) of increasing L's income. Starting from any given position, this shows the additional cost we must impose on H in order to increase L's income by a dollar.

Table 9 illustrates two important general features of the trade-off implied by redistribution. First, the marginal cost of raising the income of low income households increases with the level of marginal tax rates. If the rate is currently zero, we can increase L's income by a dollar at a cost of only $1.40 to H. If the rate is currently 30 percent, however, the marginal cost follows from the fact that as marginal tax rates rise, each successive increment will reduce earnings by more than the last. This is why the fact that existing marginal tax rates in the U.S. are already quite high (as shown in Table 7) is important: it suggests that the marginal cost of moving closer to equality is also likely to be quite sizeable.

Second, complete equality in incomes is in general impossible except at a level of zero income. In fact, the highest level to which it is possible to raise the income of low income families will still imply substantial inequality in incomes. Note that in Table 9, the maximum income for L occurs at a tax rate of 50 percent, at which point H's income is still about double L's income. Any further attempt to redistribute income reduces earnings so much that net income of both H and L will fall. Consequently, no one would reasonably wish to go beyond this critical level, at a 50 percent tax rate in the example. In fact, John Rawls is almost unique among scholars in arguing that we should go even this far and try to maximize the position of the poorest household. If we attach any importance to the well-being of the nonpoor, we would not want to go this far.

Obviously, the important question is the size of the actual trade-off in the United States, given the current tax and transfer policies in place. The answer to this question depends on how responsive people are in their work and saving behavior to changes in marginal tax rates, and we do not know this with any great accuracy, so the exact size of the trade-off is not and perhaps cannot be known. Nonetheless, I believe the available evidence concerning the responsiveness of people to taxes and transfers suggests that the relevant trade-off is more severe than most people suspect. I cannot defend this judgment fully here since it relies on simulations of the effects of redistribution utilizing a range of plausible earnings responses, but it is possible to see from Table 9 why a sizeable trade-off is likely. Note that in the table it is assumed that a 40 percent tax rate—close to the existing level for most people—reduced earnings by only 10 percent, while an increase to 50 percent would reduce it by another five percent. These are not unrealistically large responses given available evidence on this matter, but they imply that raising the income of L by another dollar from the current level will cost H \$6.30. The key point is that what appear to be moderate, even modest, responses to marginal tax rates imply a surprisingly high marginal cost.

These remarks also suggest that the limits to redistribution—in the sense of how much it would be possible to raise the incomes of low income families—may be more restrictive than is commonly thought. In some research that is still in preliminary stages, I have estimated the maximum level of income possible for the lowest quintile of households using tax and transfer policies (analogously to the \$7437 that is the maximum for L in Table 9). These estimates suggest that the income of the lowest quintile can be increased *at most* by 15 to 25 percent (about \$10–\$17 billion in 1976), and that this would require policies that would reduce the incomes of the top four quintiles by about \$200 billion. These figures are intended only to be indicative of general orders of magnitude, but what they suggest is, I believe, correct: our ability to raise the incomes of low income households much beyond current levels using redistributive policies is rather limited, and the cost of moving in this direction is quite high.

VII. Is More Equality Worth the Cost?

In the introduction to this paper, I mentioned that economists don't like to discuss the question of how much government redistribution is desirable. The reason is that they recognize the type of trade-off identified in Table 9: it is possible to redistribute income so as to achieve greater equality, but the cost is having less of something else that is desirable, namely, a high average standard of living. Weighing one desirable goal (equality) against another (high average standard of living) requires the use of nonscientific value judgments, a matter on which reasonable people may disagree. Thus, there is no such thing as an objectively "best" distribution of income, or an "ideal" amount of redistribution.

Admitting that economics, or any other discipline for that matter, cannot conclusively resolve this important issue, however, is not the same as saying that it can make no contribution towards its resolution. In this paper, I have emphasized several facets of the problem which are routinely ignored or misunderstood, but which seem to me to be highly relevant. In particular, the evidence that differences in standards of living are much less pronounced than official income data imply and the likelihood that the trade-off implied by the incentive effects of taxes and transfers is more severe than generally recognized are both significant factors which deserve to be taken into account.

Notably absent from this discussion has been an evaluation of justice or fairness in the way income is distributed. Do considerations of fairness help in determining how far we should go in redistributing income? There is no doubt that this aspect of the issue is overwhelmingly important to many people, but justice is not an objective concept with a meaning people agree to. Some may believe each person is entitled to keep whatever he legally earns in a free society, while others believe the needs of the poor entitle them to share in the incomes of those better off.

Economics perhaps does have something to say about justice in that it provides an explanation of the principles that determine the prices of factors of production (like labor), and thereby strongly affect the distribution of income. In competitive markets, economics shows that the prices of productive factors tend to become equal to their marginal value productivity. As applied to labor, this means that workers tend to be paid the value of their contribution to output. When first discovered, this marginal productivity theory was widely hailed as proving that the market-determined distribution of income was fair.

If justice means that each person deserves an income equal to the contribution he and the resources he owns make to output, then insofar as markets are competitive the distribution of market earnings would be just. Most people, however, believe that justice involves more than this. Today, economists take pains to emphasize that payment according to productivity and justice are not the same thing. Some people do not have the mental or physical capacity to contribute much to output, and their earnings will be low, in some cases too low for survival. Justice in such cases certainly does not mean that these persons should be condemned to destitution or worse.

Economists, however, may have gone too far in coming close to denying that there is any connection between productive contribution and justice. There is much to be said for the justice of payment according to productivity since it means people are rewarded for effort, thrift, perseverance, honesty, foresight, and the like. I would suggest that market-determined incomes are, in fact, reasonably just for the bulk of the population. It is only when we consider the extreme cases involving people able to earn very little if anything that market-determined incomes violate our sense of fairness.

I think it is useful to make a distinction between those unable to support themselves and the remainder of the population, imprecise as any such distinction is bound to be. For those unable to support themselves, there is good reason to wish to supplement the market mechanism, and it is not surprising therefore that there is widespread agreement that helping the poor is a legitimate government responsibility. There is much less agreement, however, that the distribution of income among the remainder of the population is unfair, and for a very good reason: it isn't obviously unjust at all. Redistribution for the sake of equality among the bulk of the population has found little favor with the American people at the same time that they are quite generous in supporting welfare programs for the truly needy. As I understand it, there is no paradox in this: it just reflects an awareness of the distinction I am trying to make.

Many egalitarian-minded intellectuals do not accept the view that the market-determined distribution of income among the nonpoor is reasonably just. As an example, the late Arthur Okun explained that he would favor redistributing income from a family with $18,000 to a family with $10,000 (in 1974 when the average income was $14,000) even if it meant that the average income would fall due to incentive effects. My reaction is to question whether such a redistribution would be fair even in the absence of incentive problems. Without knowing anything about the age, composition, background, character, needs, occupation, etc., of the families in question, can we really be confident that justice is served by such a redistribution? In the absence of some compelling evidence to the contrary, I think the presumption should be that these families—both well above the poverty level—deserve to keep what they earn.

Whether or not the view that the distribution among the nonpoor is reasonably just is accepted, it should be emphasized that further expansion in redistributive policies will increasingly involve shifting income around among middle-income families. Thus, it is necessary to consider carefully the ethical basis and practical consequences of this type of redistribution. A case that we should help the needy and those unable to support themselves does not provide a justification for egalitarian policies of this sort.

TABLE 1

INCOME SHARES FOR HOUSEHOLDS, SELECTED YEARS

(Percentages)

Income Class	1978	1976	1967	1957	1947
Lowest Quintile	3.8	3.8	3.6	3.4	3.5
Second Quintile	9.7	9.9	10.6	10.9	10.6
Third Quintile	16.4	16.7	17.5	18.0	16.8
Fourth Quintile	24.8	24.9	24.8	24.7	23.6
Highest Quintile	45.2	44.7	43.9	45.5	45.5

Source: United States Bureau of the Census, "Money Income of Families and Persons in the United States: 1978," *Current Population Reports,* Series IP-60, No. 123, Table 13.

TABLE 2

SIZE AND COMPOSITION OF POVERTY POPULATION,

SELECTED YEARS

(In thousands)

	1978	1974	1969	1966	1959
Number of Poor Persons	24,497	24,260	24,147	28,510	39,450
65 years and over	3,233	3,299	4,787	5,111	5,679
Under 65 years					
Family with female head	10,989	9,891	7,930	7,841	8,115
Family with male head	10,275	11,070	11,430	15,558	25,696

Source: U.S. Bureau of the Census, "Characteristics of the Population Below the Poverty Level: 1978," Series P-60, *Current Population Reports,* No. 124 (1980), Table 1.

TABLE 3

SOCIAL WELFARE EXPENDITURES, FISCAL YEAR 1979

($ in billions)

Category	Total Expenditures	Expenditures from Federal Funds	Expenditures from State and Local Funds
Social Insurance	$193.6	$163.7	$29.8
Public Aid	64.6	43.6	21.0
Health and medical	24.5	12.2	12.3
Veterans' programs	20.5	20.3	0.2
Education	108.3	12.1	96.2
Housing and other social welfare	16.9	12.2	4.6
TOTAL	428.3	264.1	164.2

Source: Ann Kallman Bixby, "Social Welfare Expenditures, Fiscal Year 1979," *Social Security Bulletin,* Vol. 44, No. 11 (Washington, D.C.: U.S. Government Printing Office, November 1981), Table 1.

TABLE 4
SOCIAL WELFARE EXPENDITURES, SELECTED YEARS
($ in billions)

	1979	1971	1966	1959	1947
Total social welfare	$428.3	$171.9	$88.0	$49.8	$17.3
From federal funds	264.1	92.6	45.6	23.5	9.8
From state and local funds	164.2	79.3	42.4	26.3	7.5
Total social welfare as percentage of NNP (%)	20.8	18.5	13.5	11.3	8.3
Total government spending as percentage of NNP (%)	36.1	35.4	31.3	31.0	20.4

Sources: See Table 3; other government documents.

TABLE 5
DISTRIBUTION OF HOUSEHOLD INCOME, 1976
($ in billions)

Income Class	Market Earnings	Cash Transfers	In-kind transfers	Taxes	Net Income	% Shares, Net Income	% Shares, Market Earnings
Lowest Quintile	$ 35.7	31.8	10.2	10.1	67.7	6.2	2.6
Second Quintile	114.8	36.0	12.5	31.9	131.5	12.0	8.4
Third Quintile	210.2	27.9	7.9	60.6	185.3	16.9	15.5
Fourth Quintile	317.9	26.3	4.7	95.8	253.0	23.0	23.4
Highest Quintile	681.7	32.1	4.2	255.9	462.2	42.0	50.1

TABLE 6
DISTRIBUTION OF HOUSEHOLD INCOME AMONG THREE PERSON HOUSEHOLDS, AGED 35–44, 1976
($ in billions)

Income Class	Market Earnings	Cash Transfers	In-kind transfers	Taxes	Net Income	% Shares, Net Income	% Shares, Market Earnings
Lowest Quintile	$ 2.3	0.78	0.49	0.54	3.02	9.2	5.3
Second Quintile	5.4	0.46	0.11	1.43	4.56	13.8	12.6
Third Quintile	7.7	0.32	0.04	2.20	5.92	17.9	18.1
Fourth Quintile	9.9	0.57	0.04	2.95	7.56	22.9	23.0
Highest Quintile	17.6	0.43	0.02	6.06	11.99	36.3	41.0

TABLE 7
ESTIMATED MARGINAL TAX RATES, 1976
(percentages)

Income Decile	MTR of Transfer System	MTR of Tax System	Effective MTR
1 & 2	37.1	14.9	52.0
3	36.3	26.2	56.5
4	27.1	27.2	54.3
5	15.4	30.3	45.7
6	10.4	31.3	41.7
7	4.5	33.0	37.5
8	0.7	35.5	36.2
9	0.6	40.8	41.4
10	0.0	45.8	45.8

Source: Edgar K. Browning and William R. Johnson, "Taxation and the Cost of National Health Insurance," in Mark Pauly, editor, *National Health Insurance* (Washington, D.C.: American Enterprise Institue, 1980), Table 4.

TABLE 8
HYPOTHETICAL TAX-TRANSFER POLICY

Households	A	B	C	D	E
Earnings	5,000	10,000	15,000	20,000	25,000
20 percent tax	−1,000	−2,000	−3,000	−4,000	−5,000
Transfer	+3,000	+3,000	+3,000	+3,000	+3,000
Net Income	7,000	11,000	15,000	19,000	23,000
Change in income	+2,000	+1,000	0	−1,000	−2,000
	+3,000[a]			−3,000[b]	

[a] Sum of A and B.
[b] Sum of D and E.

TABLE 9
DERIVING THE EFFICIENCY-EQUALITY TRADE-OFF

Tax Rate	Earnings Response	H's Earnings	L's Earnings	H's Net Income	L's Net Income	H's Loss / L's Gain
0	100	20,000	5,000	20,000	5,000	
10	99	19,800	4.950	19,057	5,692	1.4
20	97	19,400	4,850	17,945	6,305	1.8
30	94	18,800	4,700	16,685	6,815	2.5
40	90	18,000	4,500	15,300	7,200	3.6
50	85	17,000	4,250	13,812	7,437	6.3
60	77	15,400	3,850	11,935	7,312	
70	65	13,000	3,250	9,587	6,662	
80	50	10,000	2,500	7,000	5,500	
90	30	6,000	1,500	3,975	3,525	
100	0	0	0	0	0	

NOTES

1. *Business Week*, "Egalitarianism: Threat to a Free Market," December 1, 1975, p. 62.

2. I say "apparently" because it is conceivable that the distribution of market earnings would be more equal than shown in the table in the absence of these policies. For instance, low income families may earn less because of the disincentive effects of welfare programs.

3. U.S. Congress, Congressional Budget Office, *Poverty Status of Families Under Alternative Definitions of Income*, Background Paper No. 17, January 1977; Timothy Smeeding, *Measuring the Economic Welfare of Low-Income Households and the Anti-poverty Effectiveness of Cash and Non-cash Transfer Programs*, unpublished Ph.D. dissertation, University of Wisconsin, Madison, 1975; Morton Paglin, *Poverty and Transfers In-Kind*, Hoover Institution Press, 1980.

4. The distributions of income for three other groups were also examined: three-person households with a 45–54 year-old head; and four-person households with 35–44 and 45–54 year-old heads. The results were similar in all cases.

SUGGESTED READING

1. Sheldon Danziger, Robert Haveman, and Robert Plotnick, "How Income Transfers Affect Work, Savings, and the Income Distribution," *Journal of Economic Literature*, Sept. 1981.

2. Alan Blinder, "The Level and Distribution of Economic Well-Being," in Martin Feldstein, editor, *The American Economy in Transition*, University of Chicago Press, 1980.

These two useful surveys deal with the empirical side of the issues.

3. Walter Blum and Harry Kalven, *The Uneasy Case for Progressive Taxation*, University of Chicago Press, 1953.

A classic analysis of many issues related to the role of government in redistributing income.

4. Arthur Okun, *Equality and Efficiency*, Brookings Institution, 1975. A liberal economist's view on the subject.

5. Colin Campbell, editor, *Income Redistribution*, American Enterprise Institute, 1977.

A collection of papers and commentaries, with interesting insights into the way people with differing ideologies and from various disciplines (but mainly economics) look at the subject.

Social Mobility and Democratic Capitalism in America

Walter D. Connor

THE VALUES AND BELIEFS surrounding social mobility in any society, in any political and economic order, tell us much about the society. In the case of the United States—democratic, capitalist—two values are central, and mutually in tension. A belief in *equality* has been part of the American ethos, as against older, traditionalist notions of natural order and hierarchy, of knowing and keeping one's "place." This has weighed heavily in American notions that people are entitled to an equal start in competition with others for scarce goods, and are vested with a legal and political equality which distinguishes no one as winner or loser before the race is run. The notion, however, that life is a race bespeaks the strong American acceptance of *achievement:* a readiness, up to some limits, to countenance unequal outcomes in money, in prestige, and in general "clout"—as long as these are prizes in the game as played by American rules.

As Seymour Martin Lipset has put it:

These values, though related, are not entirely compatible; each has given rise to reactions which threaten the other.

When I say that we value equality, I mean that we believe all persons must be given respect simply because they are human beings; we believe that the differences between high- and low-status people reflect accidental, and perhaps temporary, variations in social relationships. This emphasis on equality was reflected in the introduction of universal suffrage in America long before it came in other nations; in the fairly consistent and extensive support for a public school system so that all might have a common educational background; and in the pervasive antagonism to domination by any elite in culture, politics, or economics.

The value we have attributed to achievement is a corollary to our belief in equality. For people to be equal, they need a chance to become equal. Success, therefore, should be attainable by all, no matter what the accidents of birth, class, or race. Achievement is a function of equality of opportunity. That this emphasis on achievement must lead us to new inequalities of status and to the use of corrupt means to secure and maintain high position is the ever recreated and renewed American dilemma.[1]

To some, especially critics from the left as it emerged in the America of the 1960's and 1970's, this is thin stuff. For them, an America teetering between equality and achievement is not egalitarian at all—merely libertarian. For them, America will only merit the former designation when it commits itself to pursuing equality of result.[2] But this has hardly been the majority persuasion. In fact, the combination of several American elements has formed a package of immense attractiveness, of great pulling power, to those who would judge a social order by the prospects it offers for social mobility—the advancing of one's own status beyond that of one's father. Opportunity—perceived and real—has been the key; America's exceptional ability to provide opportunity (as opposed to Europe's and the less developed world's) has been a matter of conviction for many Americans as well as others. "Opportunity" in this sense, however, has only taken on meaning in the context of a range of possible outcomes—some desirable, some undesirable. There has been little emphasis in the American ethos upon equality of results or outcomes. Rather it has always been upon opportunity construed as the absence of prior political, economic, and social conditions which in other societies render the results not only unequal, but predictable.

"The land where the streets are paved with gold"—that is how Europeans traditionally have thought of America, meaning the United States. The allegory had some basis in fact. The expanding continent with its open frontier combined with the impact of the industrial revolution, which could be fully exploited in the absence of an aristocracy with a feudal heritage, to create unheard-of opportunities for economic advancement. After the closing of the frontier itself vast open spaces and a rapidly expanding industrial economy absorbed still larger numbers of immigrants and continued to supply much opportunity for social mobility.[3]

Social mobility in America is the concern of this chapter. Like the rest of this volume, it looks at an aspect of the American experience in a *democratic, capitalist* order. This is, generally, a straight-forward task. The U.S. is a democracy of the constitutional-parliamentary sort. Its economy *is* capitalist, free-market, and remaining decidedly so even in the face of heightened governmental intervention since the New Deal—and nowhere more clearly so than when we compare it with state-socialist economies in the U.S.S.R. or Eastern Europe, "mixed" economies of various kinds, or premodern economies in third world states.

America is neither the only democracy nor the only capitalist country in the world. Its assemblage of these and other characteristics does, however, make it unique—although in a real, if trivial, sense, each capitalist economy is unique. Capitalism is a central concern of this book, yet it is beyond our power to specify exactly what contribution capitalism—or democracy, or any other element—makes to the American pattern of mobility. Two observations, however, can be made. First, the connection between capitalist free-market economies and democracy and individual freedom is not accidental. Not all capitalist economies are in democratic states, but all democratic states have capitalist economies. No state-socialist economy coexists with a free political order. Second, while free enterprise is not the only engine of economic growth and development—factors critical for social mobility—it has nonetheless proven to be an effective one, sustaining fairly high rates of mobility as opposed to other kinds of economies.[4]

Analytically, social mobility can be separated from other properties of societies: the overall level of wealth, for example, or the degree of inequality in the distribution of goods (the distance between social classes, top to bottom). Concretely, however, these are not separate matters. The U.S. is a wealthy country, and the distribution therein of income and wealth is not equal. But how unequal? Unequal compared to what? On such questions, "neoconservatives" and egalitarians of a leftist persuasion will differ; but one consequence is clear. Economic growth and the distribution of its benefits, however unequal, has left the U.S. a "middle-class society," whose lower reaches enjoy significant advantages over those of most other societies. There has been no large and debased lower class to prompt the raising of barriers, the erecting of unbreachable obstacles to their political and economic aspirations.

The poorer a country and the lower the absolute standard of living of the lower classes, the greater the pressure on the upper strata to treat the lower as vulgar, innately inferior, a lower caste beyond the pale of human society. The sharp diffference in the style of living between those at the top and those at the bottom makes this psychologically necessary. Consequently, the upper strata in such a situation tend to regard political rights for the lower strata, particularly the right to share power, as essentially absurd and immoral. The upper strata not only resist democracy themselves; their often arrogant political behavior serves to intensify extremist reactions on the part of the lower classes.[5]

It is in the perception that the American order conferred extraordinary benefits on the "common man"—either *in situ* through a working-class living standard much higher than that of his counterparts elsewhere, or through opportunities to become owner rather than employee, professional rather than wage-earner—that the U.S. has appeared so attractive. It has been in this spirit that domestic critiques (at least prior to the 1960's) of American performance have been made. Americans have judged their country by sterner standards than those by which they have judged the "old world"—where so many Americans came from, and of which they have expected less. Conversely, an earlier generation of Europeans like Werner Sombart answered the question "Why is there no socialism in the United States?" by citing the opportunities available to American workers, convincing them that American capitalism worked; and by pointing out that fewer opportunities in Europe convinced European workers that capitalism should be replaced by socialism.

Whether these turn-of-the-century perceptions were accurate—whether there really has been greater mobility in the U.S. than in the European democracies—is, to some degree, open to question. But for the moment it is enough to consider that some of these European perceptions had less to do with facts and figures on economic growth and mobility (figures on the latter being nonexistent in the early part of the twentieth century) than with the different "feel" of class relations in America and Europe. The word "deference" captures the gap between the American and the European experience and mind-set.

For there is little deference and much egalitariansim in the relations between classes in the U.S. The absence of feudal history, the rejection of monarchical institutions, and the strength of various forms of native populism have all worked against the development of distance in social relations—as European visitors have remarked for well over a century. While egalitarianism in everyday life is discussed elsewhere in this volume, it is worth noting here that American forms of address are democratic, with little ordering by superiority versus subordination; that claims of elevated status in educational, economic, or occupational terms are not readily honored outside the narrow social contexts where they apply; that even within such contexts (such as between patrons and taxi drivers, waiters, store clerks, and the like) the mode of interaction is comparatively egalitarian. Demands upon a waiter, for instance, which would seem reasonable in many European situations, mark the American diner as arrogant and foolish. The boundaries are drawn in different ways.[6]

This nondeferential behavior has always testified to the American conviction that places were not fixed, that society was fluid, that people might differ much in economic terms but rather less in other things. Not for nothing did the story of Horatio Alger arise in the U.S., where such personal histories were viewed as plausible, and where the absence of older models of correct upper-class behavior—defended staunchly by those with a stake in denying status to "new money"—meant that there was no insurmountable block to raising one's status through one's own exertions and settling comfortably into a higher status once it was achieved. Characteristically, it has been American business, government, and other leaders who boast of humble origins. Europeans in the same position tend to minimize the distance they have traveled.[7]

The emphasis on achievement within an egalitarian, nondeferential value system provided a psychological spur to American mobility. It would be difficult, with such an ethos, to hold out different socially approved goals to members of different social classes—or, more important, to their children. And indeed, as the Horatio Alger ideology dictated, all were *expected* to strive, to take part in the race.[8] Failure to achieve showed personal inadequacy, not the unfairness of the system. This ethos has distorted American realities to some degree, and placed psychological burdens on the ambitious which are different from those endured in Europe. Yet it also allowed new freedom: the American worker, aspiring to make something of himself and pass it along to his children, could think realistically of *individual* advancement. The

European worker, on the other hand, saw the solutions to problems of political status and economic welfare in *collective* terms: European class consciousness (or that of intellectuals concerned with developing it) propelled workers into political activity in order to change the rules of the game. It was in this context that Sombart asked, and answered, the aforementioned question.

For the most part, we have been discussing the past. This is not to suggest that the present differs critically, or that the American view of social mobility in the late twentieth century is somehow sundered from these historical precedents. But there is little systematic data on what actually happened in the period up to mid-century. Reality must, in some measure, be reflected in the American ethos; but beliefs do not totally depend on such validation. The growth of the American economy, the transition from an agrarian to an industrial to a post-industrial nation, implies changes in the work and life of sons versus their fathers, as the occupational structure itself was transformed. This *has* occurred: whether in sufficient degree to justify beliefs about the essentially benign outcomes of democratic capitalism in America is in some ways a matter of perspective. The record we are about to examine will not satisfy those to whom unequal outcomes, however generated, are abhorrent. But then, no concrete society will. A more realistic focus, it seems to me, is on the *supply* of opportunity to move up (and, conversely, the possibility of moving down, due to lack of qualification, enterprise, or even bad luck), rather than the abstract equality of those opportunities, independent of how much space society of economy might afford the enterprising for improving their lot.[9] Abstract equalities motivate few. Opportunities to advance, perceived as concrete, attract many. It is in this light that the performance of democratic capitalism should be judged.

Social Mobility: The American Record

Recording the patterns by which people rise or fall is a complex matter, especially with a view to conveying the meaning of numbers. It will not do to cite some percentage of doctors, lawyers, corporate executives, or academicians born in working-class households, without knowing what share they represent of all born in similar circumstances, and thus how many of their peers remained there. Nor is it sufficient to observe that many farm sons have graduated from their fathers' businesses, because so few are now found in farming. We would like to know how many stayed, how many found blue-collar work, how many rose into the professions, and so forth.

This section offers a resonably systematic look at mobility in this sense, and its correlates: a tracing of the movement of men from their fathers' status, to their own adult status. "Status" is measured here as a composite—not money earned or the raw "prestige" of a job in public opinion, but a combination of the average earnings for a particular job and the education of those who hold it. Grouping jobs closely on these dimensions gives fairly coherent, if general, categories: upper and lower white-collar, upper and lower manual, and farm occupations—five in all. Our record is based on the questionnaire responses of large, naturally representative samples of working adult men: their current jobs, their fathers' jobs when their sons were young, other data, sorted into five categories.

There are, of course, various complications—critical to specialized students of mobility, although less so to the general audience aimed at by this essay. The tables to come are therefore summary—subject to qualifications, the most important of which will be noted in the text. For the most part, they simply trace the "outcomes" for sons of similar-category fathers, in how the sons disperse themselves (reading horizontally across each row). They will tell the reader what percentage of upper white-collar sons wind up in the same category as their fathers; where the rest go; what percentage of all the other-origin sons achieve elevated status, duplicate that of their fathers, and so forth.

Readers perceiving latent sexism here should be advised that our data are limited to males, almost exclusively. The careful study of women's mobility—save from father's status to husband's—and the development of solid trend data await the catching up of social research with women's burgeoning laborforce participation and the expansion of women's opportunities for diverse employment. Only some preliminary indications now exist[10], and the summarization of American women's occupational mobility awaits a later date when some fundamental questions (such as: What is origin—father's occupation? mother's? or a combination? And does this question now apply to men's origin, too? What of mothers not employed outside the home?) are answered.

Compared to that on most other societies, the quantitative data on U.S. mobility are rich. In recent times, these data have been collected and analyzed to a degree of complexity beyond what space, or the concerns of a general readership, will permit us to reproduce or discuss here.

Two large-scale surveys of males in the "experienced civilian labor force," conducted in 1962 (Blau and Duncan, 1967), and in 1973 (Featherman and Hauser, 1978)[11], both yield the most recent national data, and provide the base for discussion.*

Table 1 provides the summary data for both studies. By any reasonable standard, these show the American social order to be marked by substantial mobility. At the "top," a majority of sons of men in the upper white-collar stratum duplicate their fathers' status—but these are small majorities, and almost half descend, a fair percentage of them to the ranks of manual work. Birth and growth in an upper white-collar family do not, clearly, guarantee a free ride to elevated status. Lower white-collar sons in both surveys show substantial upward mobility into this "elite"—more do so than stay in their origin class—but also descend to manual work in significant numbers.

Still, the majority of white-collar sons retain this status. Is this consistent with the notion that the American social ethos and the market capitalist economy permit blue-collar and farm sons to make their way up the social ladder to prestigious occupations?

Evidently so—for the figures show close to a third of sons from the upper manual group of fathers, and almost a quarter of those from the lower manual group (essentially, "skilled" and semi- or unskilled fathers), achieving elite status in each survey; with an additional number entering the lower white-collar ranks. Farm sons achieve more moderately, but still about a quarter enter white-collar work. Sons born below the white/blue-collar line are

---

*By the normal standards of social research methodology, both the 1962 study of "Occupational Changes in a Generation" by Peter Blau and Otis Dudley Duncan, and the replication of the study by David L. Featherman and Robert M. Hauser in 1973, are exceedingly well crafted, and "representative" of the totality of employed males in the age-ranges surveyed. Both were conducted via mail-back questionnaires, with the assistance of the Census Bureau's monthly Current Population Survey—the major governmental effort to monitor demographic processes through large-scale survey sampling between census years. In technical terms, both involved "stratified multistage cluster samples"—constructed to reflect all the diversity of the parent populations, and to minimize the possibility that those surveyed and their mobility experiences were "atypical" of American men. The samples are quite large (20,700 in 1962, representing an 83% response rate among those receiving the questionnaire; 30,228 in 1973, for a response rate of 88%): the total populations to which they refer are, of course, immense: almost 45 million working men aged 20–64 in 1962; 53 million aged 20–65 in 1973. Readers who wish can acquaint themselves with the detailed descriptions of methodology in the original sources; but in general, they may be assured that well-drawn samples of this size can reflect the realities of the experience of millions; and that no other studies of mobility among US men are nearly so comprehensive.

(1) more likely to leave their fathers' stratum than remain, and (2) more likely to improve on their fathers' status than not.

This is far from stagnation—far from a situation wherein it could be said that one's fate is decided by birth and nurture through adolescence in a particular class. Sons are "deployed" across a wide range of social destinations. That there is little difference between the 1962 and 1973 panels should give little cause for concern. About 75% of persons in the 21–64 age range in 1962 were still in it in 1973; the difference in the populations covered is limited to the exit of those in the oldest age cohort in 1962 and the entry of a cohort in 1973 too young for inclusion in 1962. In turn, these figures show a gross similarity to earlier, less complete American studies going back to 1947. Converting our 1962 and 1973 studies, and three earlier ones, into a common 3 × 3 form (white-collar, manual, and farm categories), we find the gross indicators of Table 2, covering a quarter century.

The pattern persists. Americans born in privilege are by no means guaranteed status inheritance. Men from blue-collar families move in significant numbers into nonmanual occupations; and the share of such men grows over the years of the surveys. Farm-origin men move up themselves, most often to blue-collar work but some further, as the outflow of sons from the farm sector continues.

The impact of these patterns is clearer if viewed from the perspective of "inflow": describing the breakdown of current socio-occupational categories by the social origins of the sons now in them. This is simply the alternative way of reporting Table 1 data.

The most striking point is evident in the first column of each panel. Far from being a hereditary monopoly, the upper white-collar category is populated mainly by men of manual origin— 51.6% in 1962, 54.1% in 1973. Add to these the men of lower-nonmanual origin, and only 25–30% of the slots at the top are left for sons who originated in this group. The lower nonmanual categories in both 1962 and 1973 are even more heavily composed of men on the rise, with over two-thirds of their incumbents manual and farm sons. These inflow percentages show the diversity of sources from which American society has drawn its relatively privileged categories.

This, in simple form, is the story, the "what" of occupational and social mobility between generations in the American variant of a democratic capitalist society, recorded in these tables at a fairly high order of generality. Though we will not linger long on comparisons with other societies, we can say that in general no other society records rates consistently like these, or manifests quite these dimensions of upward mobility—especially of the long-distance sort from blue-collar to elite. Held up against traditional definitions of what an "open society" means, and against notions of social justice which abhor the "locking" of offspring into their parents' place; the figures show that American society— for all its deficiencies—fares very well as a real social order in the here and now.

Separate components of the story, however, deserve attention; adding though they must to its complexity. In a gross sense, the rates of mobility recorded here or in any society are affected greatly by two factors: structural change in the economy, which brings about growth in some categories or classes and decline in others, creating and destroying "room" to receive the socially mobile; and differential fertility, which affects the number of offspring from different categories or classes entering the mobility competition. At an individual level, the multiplicity of careers which make up a mobility table is a variety of histories wherein a person begins with his father's education and occupational status as assets or liabilities, achieves a certain advantaging or disadvantaging level of education himself, and enters the labor force (first job) at a certain point or in a certain category or class—all steps toward the current occupation data recorded in 1962 and 1973. These individual dramas are set in different time periods—some men entered the labor force during the Depression's trough, others in the boom of the Eisenhower years. All of these need some discussion, however brief, as elements of the performance of the American order.

Economic growth in twentieth-century America radically altered the shape of the occupational structure, promoting mobility by creating demand in the nonmanual sectors, diminishing the size of the manual strata—especially the unskilled. Technology's advance reduced the percentage of the workforce in farming, while increasing agricultural production beyond the dreams of most other nations. Viewed by analysts, such structural changes are a "cause" of mobility, but not a terribly interesting one—since so many investigations of mobility, especially international comparisons, focus on equality of (mobility) opportunity strictly defined in terms of the chances to rise or fall independent of long-term changes in the occupational structure. Thus, at least until recently[12], analysts have regarded these structural changes as "noise" to be filtered out in comparing mobility patterns in different nations, or in the same nation at different times.

Yet such is not, and should not be, our attitude here. Most mobility in any society is of this structural variety—only a small amount can generally be attributed to "circulatory" movement independent of structural change. The amount of structural mobility which a society generates is an important datum about that society. The American record here is striking. The share of desirable, upper-strata occupations has grown, that of less desirable jobs declined. In 1900, about 45 percent of males worked in farming—by 1970, only about 4 per cent. This advance from a "developed" situation, by the world standards of 1900, to the modernity of a service economy in the 1970's, involved mass mobility out of agriculture—avoiding the problems of rural overpopulation and agricultural underemployment which bedevil many third-world nations. In the "professional, technical, and kindred" component of the upper white-collar stratum, growth has been remarkable: in 1900 one in thirty, in 1970 one in *four*, male workers fell into this category.[13] Structural mobility, born of economic progress, has been a remarkable, and benign, property of American life. (And incidentally, it has reduced the farm sector to the point where those remaining are more or less proprietors or employees of highly capital-intensive agriculture, whose place in the lowest row of a mobility table begins to look more historically than logically justified.)

Fertility differentials—that is, differences in the average number of children born in households of different classes—have also played a role. As some observers have noted, the work of a welfare state is done for it to the degree that the rich, systematically, have more children than the poor (if the work of the welfare state be taken as redistribution). Of course this is not the way the world (or the U.S.) typically works. Generally, farm families have more children than nonfarm, and manual more than nonmanual. But mobility opportunities do not thereby suffer automatically. Economic growth has created new space at the top which is greatly in excess of the supply of children actually born to top-status families. In other words, there are vacancies to fill, even if all the children of privilege were to duplicate their parental status. Higher fertility lower down the ladder is disadvantageous, putting a larger denominator under the already smaller numerator of familial financial resources. But it does create recruits for that empty space at the top, or for the middle space vacated by middle-level sons inching their way up toward the elite.

Thus, it is possible to have more than half of upper white-collar sons duplicate their fathers' status, revealing their advantages, and still find themselves to be a minority among the elite, outnumbered by those who have ascended from below.

None of this means that opportunities are absolutely equal, that all begin the race with an equal start. It is difficult to conceive of a tolerable society that could guarantee such equality, given the degree of control and manipulation over family and schooling that this would require. On the other hand, it remains a real problem, in a society valuing both equality and achievement, that the starts are not, and are never likely to be, equal. Economic progress increases the supply of opportunities, but it is still advisable to "choose one's parents wisely."

How heavily do inequalities of origin resources weigh upon American males? How disadvantaged, for example, is he who is born into a blue-collar family and only finishes high school, as opposed to he who is born into a professional household and completes four years of postsecondary education? What if *both* attend college? What if both are sons of professionals, but one is black and the other white? These "What if" questions are important. To address them we must, in a non-technical and summary way, examine what the mobility data have to tell us about family origin, education, regional, and ethnic factors. On the average, we find no set of specifiable factors which allows us to predict the vast majority of individual mobility outcomes. Mobility, and the way we discuss it, is probabilistic. Granting this focus on large categories, we can still explain less than *half* of how a sample of U.S. males disperses itself across a multiplicity of careers—even when we know father's occupational status, son's education, and son's first job. As Blau and Duncan put it for the 1962 survey:

Social origin, education and career beginning account for somewhat less than half the variance in occupational achievement. One may interpret this result, depending on one's expectations and values, either by emphasizing that these three attributes of young men have nearly as much impact on their subsequent careers as all other factors combined, or by stressing that occupational success in our society depends not even so much on the socioeconomic and educational differences measured, as on other factors.[14]

Values and expectations do, of course, differ: for some, the multiplicity of "other" factors which in the main cannot be specified, speak to the openness of American mobility. For others, the fact that so much of the outcome is unspecified means that the inequality of results, by virtue of its explicable and inexplicable elements, is unjust and indefensible; that only equality of result, therefore, is defensible as morally desirable.[15] (They have not convinced this author.)

What matters most? Blau and Duncan's 1962 study[16] found occupational destinations linked (by zero-order correlations of) .32 to father's education, .40 to father's occupational status, .60 to respondent's own education, and .54 to his first job. In prose, this assigns the greatest effect to education received, the next greatest to first job, and so on. But these coefficients do not cumulate: in other words, each one does not add a share of independently operating advantage or disadvantage. Father's education, for example, does affect a son's later prospects, but that effect disappears when one assembles a group of sons whose fathers had a common occupational status, and who themselves have similar levels of education. Then, knowing the educational level of the fathers tells us nothing *more* about the sons' range of occupational outcomes. Fathers' occupational status has some continuing effect, but it greatly reduces when we control for sons' educations and first jobs.

Education is a critical sorting mechanism in America, but over time, its *locus criticus* has changed. Completion of twelve years of school is now close to universal, and is affected less and less by one's social origins. Examining in the 1973 data those men who did not go beyond high school, we find that men born between 1907 and 1911 completed an average 8.66 years; while those born between 1947 and 1951 averaged 11.3.[17] Thus we can see that while in the past social background played a large role in determining how many years up to twelve one would complete, it now plays a role in conditioning access to college. Even so, more people go to college today than ever before, a fact which reflects not only the expansion of educational facilities, but also broader preparation via the upgrading of fathers' occupational and educational attainments. All in all, the ties between those things "one can do nothing about" and the education one receives, have loosened. Combining an impressive array of variables—including father's occupation and education (familiar already), number of siblings, nurture in an intact or broken home, farm versus nonfarm origin—allows us to explain one-third of the variance in educational attainment for men born prior to World War I, but only about one-fourth for men born during and after World War II.[18]

Career mobility takes us from first job—the second most important determinant, after education—to current occupational status. Table 4 shows the picture in 1973.

Comparing these figures with Table 1, we can see the significance of entry point: essentially 80 per cent of men who entered in upper white-collar status stayed there, exceeding the 59.4 per cent who, in 1973, had duplicated their fathers' status across the whole career thus far. Career mobility has a predominantly upward trend, evident in the movement of those starting in lower white-collar, manual, and farm sectors. As can be seen in Table 5, which outlines the previous step (from father's status to first job), the total career route is complex.

Fathers' advantageous placement does not guarantee sons' "inheritance" at the start, and career beginnings for sons of manual workers are notably more modest than their eventual (1973) attainments.

Overall, these data indicate a society in motion. Comparing 1973 and 1962, and more important, comparing the experience of age cohorts who entered the workforce at different times, the general picture is of lessening dependency of sons' eventual attainments upon fathers' attainments, as well as lessening links between eventual attainments and first jobs.[19] Over time, the opportunity to "make something of oneself" has increased—at least, our ability to explain what one becomes in terms of prior constraint or advantage has decreased.

What of the other palpable divisions in American society, such as Southern origin versus Northern, ethnic versus native? These could be discussed at length, but here we will confine ourselves to recording some indications of their declining significance with regard to affecting mobility outcomes.

On the North-South axis, the tale between 1962 and 1973 is one of gradual convergence. The South is growing more modern and universalistic in the paths it provides for people to strive and succeed upon, although the gap has not closed fully (this is comparing southern and northern whites). In the 1962 study, Blau and Duncan noted that average occupational attainments were lower in the South than in other regions: a less modern industrial structure was reflected in both sons' and fathers' occupational distribution. To an inferior pattern of origins was added generally shorter periods of education, such that even when fathers' origin status was equalized between Southerners and Northerners, the Southerners attained lower occupational status, regardless of whether they left or remained in the South. Indeed, they did better in the latter case, benefiting from "a labor market that is adapted to the educational preparation of the labor force that serves it."[20]

In this more traditional South, education played less of a stratifying role, and paternal origin more, than in the North: matching persons of equal educational attainment, we can see that family origin had more direct influence upon the attainments of Southerners than upon those of Northerners.[21] In the past, travellers have often found the South more traditional, more "Old World" in patterns of interclass relations than the rest of the country. In a sense, this fits with what we expect in societies of recent agrarian heritage and less development[22]; the distinctiveness is implied in a somewhat different manner by Blau and Duncan.

Superior family origins increase a man's chances of attaining superior occupational status in the United States in large part because they help him to obtain a better education, whereas in less industrialized societies the influence of family origin on status does not seem to be primarily mediated by education.[23]

By the early mid-1970's (and, one would assume, through the period since then, which has seen further industrial growth and development in the "Sun Belt"), the lag in attainments and differences in mobility processes had moderated. The South had become less exceptional, less a mixture of modern and traditional qualities. In Featherman and Hauser's words as they reflect on the 1973 findings:

. . .the industrial bases of the North and South had converged in most essential respects, the South undergoing rapid industrialization and "postindustrialization" at the same time. Wage rates and mean levels of earnings among workers in similar occupations and industries were far less distinguishable than in prior decades. However, educational distributions, constrained to a slower pace of change through the inexorable replacement of older cohorts by younger ones, remained substantially different. Overall, the educational characteristics of the adult male population of the South in the 1970s were like those of the North in the early 1960s. Convergence of the regions' industrial bases and the growing similarities in their occupational compositions and wage contours brought increasing similarity to the socioeconomic benefits of education and labor experience that in the past had favored northern workers. Southern men remained less successful than northerners in converting their educational qualifications into current occupations in 1973, and in many respects the general pattern of occupational attainment of southerners was like that of the North during the early 1960's. While in some respects the remaining differences in industrial and occupational compositions of the regions may have limited the opportunities for southern workers to apply their training, it is plausible that the lower average level of southern educational achievement and its putatively lower quality (within the population of adults of prime working age) account for the lesser benefits of southern (versus northern) education within a rapidly changing, (post-) industrializing region. But industrial convergence left fewer remaining differences in economic returns to schooling, occupational status, experience, or weeks of work. In this case it was the changes in the processes of economic achievement within the South that were more substantial.[24]

The "melting pot" image of the United States reflects historical fact: the successful absorption and integration of disparate strands of immigration into the American nationality. The great waves of late-19th-early-20th-century immigration are, however, part of the past (with the partial exception of Mexican-Americans and other Hispanic groups), and the mobility record is largely formed by tracing the progress of native-born Americans of foreign-born parentage as opposed to those whose American heritage goes back further. Here, the data of 1962 and 1973 reveal no great effect of ethnicity *per se*, in the experience of mobility. Blau and Duncan concluded that "the occupational opportunities of white ethnic minorities, on the whole, differ little from those of whites of native parentage."[25] To the degree that father's occupational status, son's education, and first job were controlled, the 1962 figures show equal or slightly better job attainments for the foreign-born than for those of native parentage, and even more advantageous performance for the native-born of foreign parentage—this even for the less "prestigious" ethnic minorities, such as southern and eastern European immigrants who have generally arrived with lesser occupational and educational resources than those from northern and western Europe.[26] Educational performance and opportunity played a large role in this process of excelling and overtaking. The past records evidence of some prejudice against the disfavored minorities—but this disadvantage is, largely, mediated or overcome by educational attainment.

By the 1970's, ethnicity had, in general, declined further as a determinant, to the point where it was "in itself no longer a major dimension along which socioeconomic inequalities are generated."[27] Featherman and Hauser found the ethnic advantages of two groups—"Anglo-Saxons" (hardly ethnics in the accepted sense) and persons of "Russian" parentage or heritage (whom the authors call, perhaps with excessive delicacy, "Russian-Americans," although the vast majority are, of course, from the Ashkenazic Jewish emigration from Russia and "Russian Poland" during the early part of the century)—to be declining. But they also perceived a persistent and problematic gap in the attainments of Mexican-Americans, which was especially marked in the failure of third (second native-born) generation men to close the attainment distance separating them from generationally similar members of other groups.[28]

In general,however, elevated ethnic status by itself buys less, and lower origins cost less, today than in the distant or recent past. In their travels through the network of mobility opportunities and obstacles, the foreign born and their offspring (for the third generation is, in essence, part of the general population), increasingly follow the same paths as the natives.

The Mobility Patterns of Black Americans

Very different, in critical ways, has been the mobility experience of blacks in American society. It cannot be readily assimilated either to that of native whites, or to that of recent or historic ethnic migrants, and it merits more extended discussion. Much is revealed by the figures in Table 6, covering black males in the experienced civilian labor force in 1962 and 1973.

By comparison with the 1962 figures for all males in Table 1, one fact stands out glaringly for blacks in 1962: a black father's occupational status had very little to do with his son's attainment. The risk of falling into lower manual work is virtually as large for sons of upper white-collar fathers as for any other category. This reflects gross, compounded disadvantage. Versus the total population, few black fathers were themselves of upper white-collar status (less than 4 percent of all black fathers, as contrasted with 10.9 percent of the whole population).[29] Only 13.3 per cent of their sons were able to maintain a status similar to the father's—as contrasted with 56.8 per cent for the total 1962 sample.

Nor were blacks' problems simply ones of mobility:

. . .a substantial minority of blacks, particularly those born into nonmanual or white-collar households, *were* occupationally *mobile*—in a *downward* direction. Consequently, blacks did not "inherit" low status—in the sense of low-status origins begetting low-status destinations in some "vicious cycle"—as much as they experienced a perverse form of "opportunity" in which the advantages of birth into a high socioeconomic stratum were of no occupational benefit relative to the occupational destinies of the sons of lower status black families. Because of the restricted range of jobs into which blacks were recruited and the limited vacancies for blacks among nonmanual occupations—the manifestations of racial discrimination in the labor market—black men could not cap-

italize upon even the modest resources that their families had accumulated.[30]

A further exploration of the sources and dynamics of black
disadvantage follows, but it is well to note at the outset that the
picture changes significantly in 1973. The percentage of black
fathers reported as being in the upper white-collar stratum by the
1973 respondents rises. More critically by far, the effect of having
an upper or lower white-collar father makes itself felt in a way
virtually absent in 1962. More than 40 per cent of black upper
white-collar sons duplicate father's status, and more than half stay
above the manual-nonmanual line. The dispersion of blacks in the
1973 panel comes closer to the total dispersion pattern of that year
then did the corresponding panels in 1962.

Something has happened between the two samples of black
males, differentiated only by the exit of the oldest age cohort from
the 1962 study and the inclusion of a new youngest age cohort in
1973. Far from closed, the black-white gap in prospects has definitely narrowed. Something has happened, but what?

Changes have come in educational attainment, both absolutely
and relative to whites. Changes have also occurred in the degree
to which education pays off for blacks—absolutely and relative to
whites. The utility of resources has thus increased, bringing those
who possess them closer to whites possessing similar resources. It
has therefore become more rational to invest effort in acquiring
those resources.

In the age cohorts represented in the 1973 data, black educational progress is notable. The oldest (born 1907–1911) completed
an average of 6.74 years versus 9.87 for all males; while the
youngest (born 1947–1951) almost closed the gap, with 11.88 years
versus 12.81 for all in this age category. Thus we can see that
average educational attainment has increased by over five years
among blacks, and the gap of more than three years in the oldest
cohort has declined to less than one year.[31]

Of course, these increases would mean little if pervasive discrimination remained to block the connection between black educational achievement and job prospects. But this has not been the
case. Education, as opposed to social origin, has grown more
important for *both* blacks and whites as a mobility determinant,
but even more so for blacks. In 1962, each year of education
added for a black male was worth only one third of what it was
worth for a white. By 1973, the same added year yielded 63 per
cent of what it gave whites—a significant narrowing of the gap.

Looking at it from another angle, we can see that between 1962 and 1973, schooling increased its status-conferring power as a variable for whites by 18 per cent, while among blacks, it more than doubled.[32] It is still true, however, that discrimination may continue; only at the level of four-year college graduation (and beyond) do added years yield the same absolute quanta of improvement (in job attainment) across the race line.[33]

Looking back at Table 6, we would do well to recognize that there is an increase in *inequality* of origin-based chances among blacks—and to understand that this is a good thing, indicative of progressive trends. The data indicate that by 1973, upper white-collar fathers could expect that placing their sons at a comparable level would be easier than in 1962. In that earlier year, both black occupational attainment and dollar earnings were confined to a narrower and more disadvantaged "band" than those of the general population. By 1973, this was altered somewhat: while the variances (measures of dispersion, or "spread") in occupation and earnings among whites increased respectively by 6 and 74 per cent 1962–1973, among blacks they grew by 82 and 203 per cent.[34] Thus, it became harder to predict where people would appear on the earnings and occupational status spectra, simply from the fact that they were black.

Not all the socioeconomic problems of the black population can be captured or discussed in the context of mobility data: the fact, for example, that between 1962 and 1973 the percentage of age-eligible black males who were actually in the "experienced civilian labor force" surveyed, declined from 93 to 87 per cent.[35] Still, the prospects are far from bleak. Class and status play a larger, and race a smaller, role in sorting black men from origin to destination. While the decline of the effect of these ascribed "origin" variables among the white population may be greeted with approbation as evidence of further openness of the mobility process, their emergence as stronger in effect among blacks bespeaks progress toward equality of opportunity as well.

Insofar as majority families of all societies attempt to preserve whatever privilege and resources they have acquired, conferring differential advantage to the filial generation and transmitting inequality from generation to generation, the rising correlation of statuses between parental and filial black generations can be regarded as an indication of assimilation. . . . Black occupational careers appear less fragmented and unpredictable for younger cohorts than for their predecessors. Occupational statuses at later stages build more clearly upon earlier attainments, relative earnings grow more diverse among occupational levels at successive points in the life cycle, and the articulation of training—particularly college education—with both occupations and earnings renders a degree of economic regularity and universalism to black careers that they lacked in the past. Seen against the growing variability of occupational and economic attainments by blacks, these indications of more predictable socioeconomic careers suggest a weakening of racial duality in the labor market. . . .[36]

Twentieth-Century Mobility in Perspective

The market economy, by and large, provided rapid economic growth, and with it change in the occupational structure. The farm occupations at the bottom of any society's general stratification scheme have shrunk considerably, while manual jobs outside of farming have grown, later stabilizing, to provide employment alternatives more congenial to most farm-origin men. Above the manual-nonmanual line, relatively sophisticated professional-level white-collar employment has grown apace, more rapidly than lower white-collar employment. This developmental dynamic, interrupted only somewhat by the Depression, has been reflected in changing prospects for each successive age cohort as it has entered the labor force. By and large, as one looks at younger and younger cohorts, one finds the distribution of their first jobs growing more "modern," more weighted toward the upper categories in the tables. Put another way[37], in each age cohort from those born 1907–1911 to those born 1942–56, sons—in taking their first jobs—improved on the average occupational "score" of the cohort before them. And they also—predictably—improved on the average status score of their fathers. The smallest increase in sons' score over fathers' comes in the first jobs of those born 1912–1916, who entered the labor force in large numbers during the Depression. Only the youngest cohort in the 1973 data, born 1947–1951, failed to improve on their fathers' average score; and this is likely an artifact of changed patterns in the transition from schooling to the world of work, rather than an indication of reversal of the trend toward a further upgrading of the occupational structure, and with it the maintenance or increase of mobility opportunities.

The changing composition of the occupational structure both reflects past mobility and facilitates further mobility. A society with, say, 40 per cent of the labor force in the farm category has a large "bottom": populated by people whose resources (social origin, education) for mobility are low. This is *a fortiori* the case with a society with more than half the population in agriculture. Even undergoing very rapid development, such a society will find it hard to empty out the farm sector. Thus, outflow percentages for farm sons into other strata will be modest, even though the new industrial labor force created by that outflow will be for the most part made up of those sons; the inflow figures will be more impressive.[38] Even in 1900, the U.S. was advanced beyond this stage.

Much better prospects for intergenerational mobility exist when the middle strata are large. In America, this came about as the result of growth: large industrial-labor demand created room for farm sons; rapidly expanding white-collar strata created space for working-class sons.

The capitalist, free-market economic order is not the only possible progenitor of such mobility; although it is under capitalism that the U.S., and the West European states with the most modern occupational structures, promoted and experienced it. What may be unique about the U.S. pattern is a matter of some disagreement, and answers may depend on the measure one chooses. In their early formulation, Lipset and Bendix argued that it was American belief in high rates of mobility and the attendant opportunities rather than actual performance that was unique, they found gross rates of mobility across manual-nonmanual lines roughly similar for the U.S. and some other industrial societies (France, Germany, Sweden, Switzerland, and Japan).[39] Since then, mobility research has expanded and deepened, and it is now possible to look more closely at subtypes of mobility across a number of societies, refining our view.

Blau and Duncan, for example, find evidence in their 1962 data (as previously hinted) of America being the exception with regard to the high percentage of manual sons—blue-collar and farm—moving into the elite: the "professional, technical, and kindred" category within the upper white-collar stratum. This high outflow into long-distance upward mobility was *independent* of the rather large size of this elite category in the U.S. (again, an index of room at these rarefied heights). According to Blau and Duncan, the U.S. outperformed eight countries on which parallel data was available in the 1960's:

It is the underprivileged class of manual sons that has exceptional chances for mobility into the elite in this country. There is a grain of truth in the Horatio Alger myth. The high level of popular education in the United States, perhaps reinforced by the lesser emphasis on formal distinctions of social status, has provided the disadvantaged lower strata with outstanding opportunities for long-distance upward mobility.[41]

Still, mobility into the elite is not the whole story. The total American mobility record—held up against those of West European democracies, and those of East European socialist states ostensibly committed, under their sundry adaptations of the "Soviet model," to the engineering of opportunity and equality far surpassing that of the capitalist, bourgeois, feudal past—is altogether impressive.

Table 7 provides a few indicators of that record, focussed on mobility across the manual-nonmanual line, based on national studies whose methodology and quality render them reasonably comparable to the American data. They cover a large span of postwar time—essentially the 1950's through the 1970's—with the attendant difficulty in direct comparison and contrast. But such is the case with most similar comparisons; and to deal with all the complexities would require more space than we have. Suffice it to say, in general, that they provide much better a base than speculation, or no data at all (the interested reader can find a detailed discussion of some of the more technical problems readily enough).[42]

The U.S. is no laggard on the two positive, and the one negative, indexes. The access of farm and blue-collar (manual) sons to white-collar work is high; the reverse, nonmanual to manual, mobility is moderate—reflecting once again the predominantly upward thrust over the long term in the occupational structure, and at the same time the lack of any ironclad guarantee of white-collar inheritance. No evidence can be found here of European-American or East-West contrasts indicating American inferiorities—nothing to give the lie to widespread perceptions that American mobility opportunities are abundant.

Overall, the American experience evidences both an assemblage of initial assets and the development and maintenance of a political and economic order—and social ethos—fitted to take advantage of them. Economic growth has been fuelled by resources of remarkable richness, but not total uniqueness. Much has been made of these resources by a freemarket, capitalist economy whose performance certainly merits Irving Kristol's "two cheers." The burden of proof rests upon those who would argue that some other economic system would have served—or might serve now—better than the market has, in providing mobility opportunities. The structural changes born of economic growth have imparted a strong upward bias to mobility in general, while "circulation mobility" (the flow not directly explicable in structural terms) is also impressive.[43] The trend toward less dependence on occupational outcomes, and on what we can measure about paternal origins, is positive, "progressive," to be welcomed.

Upward mobility is not always comfortable, of course; modern writers have made much of status anxieties, of the pains of success, and so forth. And in a similar vein, old-style conservatives have remarked upon the pain of rootlessness in socially (as well as geographically) mobile societies where the warm and intimate, if confining, bonds of family- and class-based lifestyles are being constantly sundered. Still, these reservations, taken together, seem to miss the point. As Andrew Hacker observes, a conservative community "demands habits of deference found only in individuals who can remain content in a status not of their own making."[44] Judging by history, the share of such men in America has never been large, relative to other societies; and the share of such men in many (if not most) societies today may be on the wane. Rising expectations and aspirations are more common today than ever before, and American society has done quite well, through its resources and its methods of developing and deploying them, at offering opportunity to those who have expected, and aspired, to better their lot.

Liberty, Equality, and Mobility in America

We may take a fair degree of satisfaction in recording what we have on mobility in the U.S. in recent years: no evidence has emerged that America is becoming a static society, more affluent but also more prone to lock people into their birth status because of increasing bureaucratism, for example, or organizational gigantism. If anything, what we know about the dynamics of mobility and economic development, and about the interplay between structural and circulation mobility, leads us to believe that equally high-quality data for, say, 1920 or 1940 would show less mobility, and a stronger tie between sons' inheritance and their attainment. And even if mobility were less impressive than it has been, the generally high standard of living has yielded Americans of even modest circumstances a richer life than that possessed by their categorial counterparts elsewhere, and it is a strong positive element in American performance.[45]

On the record, American capitalism has done well at many of the things even defenders of the capitalist order tend occasionally to concede to their critics. There exists an inclination to concede, for example, that socialist solutions would promise more mobility and equality of result, and to defend capitalism on the basis of its compatibility with a free political system and the affluence it creates and diffuses. Yet with respect to mobility, nothing in the evidence—not even the lagging of blacks behind others in the general picture—justifies such a concession. On equality of result, we enter a different area, where ethical conceptions as well as measurement are involved. (We shall return to this briefly later.)

There is strong evidence of a universalistic, meritocratic (in a positive sense, for "merit" is surely a positive word[46]) thrust in the workings of American mobility. Initial inherited disadvantage can be overcome; it is not something carried with one, regardless of later attainments. Worth noting here is Blau and Duncan's somewhat technical but precise formulation.

. . . a man's career is adversely affected if his father had little education, if his father's occupational status was low, and if he himself has little education. *But these three influences are not cumulative . . .* Father's low education only depresses occupational chances because it is associated with father's low occupational status and with son's low education. Once these two intervening factors that mediate the influence of father's education have been taken into account, father's education exerts no further influence on occupational achievements. The influence of father's occupational status on son's career, in turn, is in large part mediated by education, though not entirely. Given such minimum cumulation, it hardly seems justified to speak of a vicious cycle for the population at large, particularly in view of the fact that *most of the differences in occupational achievements are not the result of differences in social origins* (emphasis added).[47]

The noncumulating, or redundant, effect of most origin variables bespeaks openness, the lack of status hierarchies impervious to a college degree and high qualifications if the bearer should, for example, have the wrong accent, last name, and so forth. Discrimination on such grounds is not totally absent—in any society—but it plays a very moderate role in the U.S.. By and large, it is money, and what money buys, which counts for most in

American status achievement. Some may find the centrality of money distressing, supplanting as it does the criteria of breeding, manners, and so on. But in how many societies are not these qualities disproportionately associated with money? And what modern society allocates honor and prestige on the grounds of virtue, service, simplicity alone? The real world does not contain such utopias. Though income inequality is undeniable, it is also the case that Americans is general, to judge by the survey data, express an ideal range of economic reward similar to the one that actually exists—to the chagrin of those who would politicize the issue of income inequality on the basis of justice.[48]

The counterposing of equality and liberty—both of which are, in more than a tangential sense, linked to social mobility—makes more difficulties for some people than for others. Freedom is not hard to define. P.J.D. Wiles' version will do: "doing what you like, and changing your mind about it, without human restraints."[49] No social order refrains completely from imposing human restraints, obviously. But the measure of freedom preserved in the U.S. is second to none, in political and economic spheres. And it has not been bought at the cost of poverty for the many and advantage for the few, or through the perpetuation of these statuses. In any case, freedom is paramount—a touchstone more crucial than equality of opportunity or result. It has been the American experience to see the preservation of freedom, while at the same time enjoying the substantial and growing measure of equality of opportunity—and quality of result—freedom has provided.

Still, none of this will satisfy those to whom nothing suffices but equality of result, who see in equality of result the only possible confirmation of true equality of opportunity. They are not cheered, but rather more concerned, by the fact that we cannot, with careful measurement, account for even half the diversity of sons' accomplishments by examining the mix of fathers' achievements—the rest being unexplained. To such people the fact that "there are still enormous status differences among people with the same amount of education"; that "there is almost as much income inequality among men from the same socioeconomic background as among men in general" and that finally, even "brothers raised in the same home end up with very different standards of lving"[50]; is evidence of massive unfairness, unjustified and unjustifiable outcomes which demand public intervention—not proof that a myriad of processes and contingencies, good and bad luck, effort and laziness, make the difference without being captured or capturable in mobility research. The state (it is implied) should do what research cannot: deal with the unexplained variance in a decisive way—at least in the area of economic outcomes. Nothing we know of either the world or of attempts to do this suggests any but deplorable results, inimical both to freedom and to the measure of opportunity now afforded to Americans. The temptations of such largescale, pervasive interventions arise, no doubt, with special force at a time of recession and unemployment, of growing discomforts visited upon every stratum, any of controversy over economic policy. Without oversimplifying and of the current issues, we must admit that the evidence herein of the recuperative powers of the American order over a period including the Great Depression, reflected in these many mobility histories, should provide good reasons for resisting such temptations.

TABLE 1

OUTFLOW FROM FATHER'S (OR OTHER FAMILY HEAD'S) BROAD OCCUPATION GROUP TO SON'S CURRENT OCCUPATION GROUP: U.S. MEN IN THE EXPERIENCED CIVILIAN LABOR FORCE AGED 21–64 IN MARCH 1962 and 1973

Father's occupation	Son's current occupation					
	Upper nonmanual	Lower nonmanual	Upper manual	Lower manual	Farm	Total
1962 (N = 10,550)						
Upper nonmanual	56.8%	16.7%	11.5%	13.8%	1.2%	100.0%
Lower nonmanual	43.1	23.7	14.6	17.0	1.7	100.0
Upper manual	24.7	17.0	28.3	28.8	1.2	100.0
Lower manual	17.9	14.8	21.9	43.4	1.9	100.0
Farm	10.3	12.3	19.3	35.9	22.2	100.0
Total	24.5	15.9	20.2	31.7	7.7	100.0
1973 (N = 20,850)						
Upper nonmanual	59.4	11.4	12.8	15.5	0.9	100.0
Lower nonmanual	45.1	16.6	16.4	20.7	1.2	100.0
Upper manual	30.9	12.2	27.7	28.1	1.2	100.0
Lower manual	22.9	12.1	23.9	40.1	1.0	100.0
Farm	16.4	9.0	22.9	37.1	14.5	100.0
Total	31.2	11.8	21.9	31.0	4.1	100.0

Note: Broad occupation groups are upper nonmanual: professional and kindred workers, managers and officials, and non-retail sales workers; lower nonmanual: proprietors, clerical and kindred workers, and retail salesworkers; upper manual: craftsmen, foremen and kindred workers; lower manual: service workers, operatives and kindred workers, and laborers, except farm; farm; farmers and farm managers, farm laborers and foremen.

Source: Featherman and Hauser, *Opportunity and Change*, p. 89.

TABLE 2
INTERGENERATIONAL MOBILITY, BROAD OCCUPATION GROUPS:
FIVE U.S. DATA SETS, 1947–1973

Source, Date, and Father's Occupation	Total	Respondent's Occupation		
		White-Collar	Manual	Farm
OCG, 1973				
White-collar	100	67	32	1
Manual	100	38	61	1
Farm	100	25	60	15
OCG: 1962				
White-collar	100	69	29	2
Manual	100	37	62	2
Farm	100	23	55	22
SRC: 1957				
White-collar	100	67	30	3
Manual	100	30	66	2
Farm	100	22	52	26
SRC: 1952				
White-collar	100	65	34	1
Manual	100	31	67	2
Farm	100	22	44	34
NORC: 1947, Adjusted				
White-collar	100	59	37	4
Manual	100	24	73	3
Farm	100	16	50	34

Sources: 1973 figures compiled from Featherman and Hauser, pp. 89,91; other data adapted from Blau and Duncan, American Occupational Structure, p. 102.

TABLE 3
INFLOW TO SON'S CURRENT OCCUPATION FROM FATHER'S (OR
OTHER FAMILY HEAD'S) OCCUPATION: U.S. MEN IN THE
EXPERIENCED CIVILIAN LABOR FORCE AGED 21–64 IN MARCH
1962 AND 1973

Father's occupation	Son's current occupation					
	Upper nonmanual	Lower nonmanual	Upper manual	Lower manual	Farm	Total
1962 (N = 10,550)						
Upper nonmanual	25.4%	11.6%	6.2%	4.8%	1.7%	11.0%
Lower nonmanual	23.1	19.6	9.5	7.0	2.9	13.1
Upper manual	19.0	20.2	26.3	17.1	2.9	18.8
Lower manual	20.1	25.6	29.7	37.6	6.8	27.4
Farm	12.5	23.0	28.3	33.6	85.7	29.7
Total	100.0	100.0	100.0	100.0	100.0	100.0
1973 (N = 20,850)						
Upper nonmanual	29.3	14.8	9.0	7.7	3.2	15.4
Lower nonmanual	16.7	16.2	8.6	7.7	3.3	11.5
Upper manual	20.2	21.0	25.8	18.5	5.8	20.4
Lower manual	21.8	30.5	32.6	38.5	7.0	29.7
Farm	12.1	17.5	24.0	27.5	80.7	22.9
Total	100.0	100.0	100.0	100.0	100.0	100.0

Source: Featherman and Hauser, p. 91.

TABLE 4
OUTFLOW AND INFLOW PERCENTAGES: MOBILITY FROM FIRST
FULL-TIME CIVILIAN OCCUPATION TO CURRENT OCCUPATION:
U.S. MEN AGED 21–64 IN MARCH 1973

First occupation	Current occupation					
	Upper nonmanual	Lower nonmanual	Upper manual	Lower manual	Farm	Total
Outflow						
Upper nonmanual	79.9	7.6	5.7	6.0	0.7	100.0
Lower nonmanual	38.2	25.2	14.9	20.7	1.0	100.0
Upper manual	17.2	9.1	49.3	23.3	1.1	100.0
Lower manual	13.1	10.5	25.6	48.8	2.0	100.0
Farm	7.4	7.0	21.3	40.2	24.0	100.0
Total	30.9	11.6	22.4	31.2	3.9	100.0
Inflow						
Upper nonmanual	54.6	13.9	5.4	4.1	4.1	21.1
Lower nonmanual	18.6	32.9	10.0	10.0	3.6	15.1
Upper manual	7.1	10.4	29.0	9.8	3.6	13.2
Lower manual	16.8	36.2	45.3	62.1	20.8	12.7
Farm	2.6	6.6	10.3	14.0	67.7	10.9
Total	100.0	100.0	100.0	100.0	100.0	100.0

Source: Featherman and Hauser, p. 116.

TABLE 5

OUTFLOW AND INFLOW PERCENTAGES: MOBILITY FROM
FATHER'S (OR OTHER FAMILY HEAD'S) OCCUPATION TO SON'S
FIRST FULL-TIME CIVILIAN OCCUPATION: U.S. MEN AGED 20–64
IN MARCH 1973

Father's occupation	Son's occupation					
	Upper nonmanual	Lower nonmanual	Upper manual	Lower manual	Farm	Total
Outflow						
Upper nonmanual	48.4	17.8	10.3	22.0	1.4	100.0
Lower nonmanual	32.1	23.3	11.3	31.2	2.1	100.0
Upper manual	19.5	15.9	20.9	41.0	2.6	100.0
Lower manual	12.6	15.2	12.8	55.4	3.9	100.0
Farm	8.8	7.7	9.5	34.6	39.4	100.0
Total	20.6	14.9	13.2	40.0	11.4	100.0
Inflow						
Upper nonmanual	34.5	17.6	11.5	8.1	1.6	14.7
Lower nonmanual	17.7	17.7	9.7	8.8	2.1	11.3
Upper manual	19.5	21.9	32.6	21.1	4.8	20.5
Lower manual	18.4	30.8	29.4	41.8	10.5	30.1
Farm	10.0	12.0	16.8	20.2	80.9	23.4
Total	100.0	100.0	100.0	100.0	100.0	100.0

Source: Featherman and Hauser, p. 66.

TABLE 6
OUTFLOW FROM FATHER'S (OR OTHER FAMILY HEAD'S) BROAD
OCCUPATION GROUP TO SON'S CURRENT OCCUPATION GROUP,
BLACK U.S. MEN IN THE EXPERIENCED CIVILIAN LABOR FORCE
AGED 21–64 IN MARCH 1962 AND 1973

Year and Father's occupation	Son's current occupation					
	Upper nonmanual	Lower nonmanual	Upper manual	Lower manual	Farm	Total
1962						
Upper nonmanual	13.3%	10.0%	13.7%	63.0%	0.0%	100.0%
Lower nonmanual	8.3	14.0	14.0	63.7	0.0	100.0
Upper manual	8.2	10.9	10.9	67.0	3.0	100.0
Lower manual	6.7	9.1	11.1	71.0	2.1	100.0
Farm	1.2	5.4	7.1	66.3	19.9	100.0
Total	4.5	7.7	9.4	67.9	10.5	100.0
1973						
Upper nonmanual	43.9	11.8	8.3	36.0	0.0	100.0
Lower nonmanual	19.5	20.8	13.4	45.5	0.8	100.0
Upper manual	16.3	13.9	15.8	53.7	0.2	100.0
Lower manual	12.1	12.2	13.7	61.0	1.0	100.0
Farm	5.1	6.8	16.5	63.2	8.4	100.0
Total	11.6	10.8	14.7	59.4	3.5	100.0

Source: Featherman and Hauser, p. 326.

TABLE 7
BASIC MOBILITY INDICATORS, BROAD OCCUPATIONAL GROUPS, USA AND OTHER SOCIETIES

	Manual to white-collar	Farm to white-collar	White-collar to manual/farm
USA (1962)	37	23	31
USA (1973)	38	25	33
Australia	31.0	19.0	41.0
France	27.8	17.2	35.0
Italy	24.9	11.8	26.7
Norway	25.8	22.1	35.4
Sweden	29.7	17.7	32.9
West Germany	22.3	18.5	32.3
Bulgaria	22.6	10.1	45.8
Czechoslovakia	35.9	20.6	38.4
Hungary	27.5	10.7	28.7
Poland	27.6	10.3	37.9
Yugoslavia	26.1	17.1	33.7

Sources: USA data as in Table 2, above; other countries, from Connor, *Socialism, Politics, and Equality,* p. 163, and sources cited therein.

NOTES

1. Seymour Martin Lipset, *The First New Nation: The United States in Historical and Comparative Perspective* (Garden City, NY: Anchor Books, 1967), p. 2.

2. See, e.g., Herbert Gans, *More Equality* (New York: Pantheon, 1973), pp. 78, 63–64.

3. Peter Blau and Otis Dudley Duncan, *The American Occupational Structure* (New York: Wiley, 1967), p. 425.

4. For an extended comparative discussion of mobility and other issues of social and political equality, based on the experience of the communist states of Eastern Europe and the USSR, see Walter D. Connor, *Socialism, Politics, and Equality: Hierarchy and Change in Eastern Europe and the USSR* (New York: Columbia University Press, 1979).

5. Seymour Martin Lipset, *Political Man: The Social Bases of Politics* (Garden City, N.Y.: Anchor Books, 1963), p. 51.

6. See C.A.R. Crosland, *The Future of Socialism* (New York: Schocken Books, 1964), p. 174 ff.; also Lipset's works, *op. cit.*

7. Crosland, op. cit., p. 182; also Lipset, *Political Man*, p. 269, and Lipset and Reinhard Bendix, *Social Mobility in Industrial Society* (Berkeley and Los Angeles: University of California Press, 1959), pp. 82–83.

8. Lipset, *First New Nation*, pp. 198–199; also Robert K. Merton, *Social Theory and Social Structure* (New York: Free Press, 1957), pp. 136–139; 166–170.

9. A society where paternal origins had no effect on filial placement would, of course, be a rather strange place. Were it also a society where the occupational structure was relatively traditional and unchanging, it would also be a very *unsatisfactory* place. For some thoughts on such a hypothetical society from a mobility perspective, see Connor, *Socialism, Politics, and Equality*, pp. 115–117.

10. For an interesting sample of such work, see the following pieces, all in *American Sociological Review:* Andrea Tyree and Judith Treas, "The Occupational and Marital Mobility of Women," 39, 3 (June, 1974), pp. 293–302; Norval D. Glenn *et al.,* "Patterns of Intergenerational Mobility of Females Through Marriage," 39, 5 (October, 1974), pp. 683–699; Ivan D. Chase, "A Comparison of Men's and Women's Intergenerational Mobility in the United States," 40, 4 (August, 1975), pp. 483-505; Rachel A. Rosenfeld, "Women's Intergenerational Occupational Mobility," 43, 1 (February, 1978), pp. 36–46.

11. Blau and Duncan, op. cit., for the 1962 study; for 1973, David Featherman and Robert Hauser, *Opportunity and Change* (New York: Academic Press, 1978).

12. See Robert M. Hauser, *et al.,* "Temporal Change in Occupational Mobility: Evidence for Men in the United States," *American Sociological Review* 40, 3 (June, 1975), pp. 295–296, for some comments suggesting a refocusing of analytic attention *to* structural change, and cross-temporal and national comparisons taking it into account.

13. See Featherman and Hauser, pp. 41–62; also Blau and Duncan, pp. 111–113.

14. Blau and Duncan, p. 403.

15. This is the thesis of Christopher Jencks *et al., Inequality: A Reassessment of the Effcts of Family and Schooling in America* (New York: Basic Books, 1972).

16. Blau and Duncan, pp. 402–403.

17. Featherman and Hauser, p. 248.

18. *Ibid.,* p. 241.

19. *Ibid.,* p. 124.

20. See Blau and Duncan, pp. 213–219, esp. 217.

21. Featherman and Hauser, p. 424.

22. See Lipset's works, *op. cit.*, for various comments on the different "feel" of stratification systems from this viewpoint.

23. Blau and Duncan, p. 430.

24. Featherman and Hauser, pp. 424–425.

25. Blau and Duncan, p. 233.

26. *Ibid.*

27. Featherman and Hauser, p. 475.

28. For details on this, see *ibid.*, pp. 462–475.

29. Figures calculated from *ibid.*, p. 533.

30. *Ibid.*,pp. 325–327.

31. *Ibid.*, pp. 231, 321.

32. *Ibid.*,p. 340.

33. *Ibid.*, pp. 343–344.

34. *Ibid.*, p. 322.

35. *Ibid.*, p. 381.

36. *Ibid.*,p. 383.

37. *Ibid.*,p. 273.

38. See Connor, *Socialism, Politics, and Equality*, pp. 170–172.

39. See Lipset and Bendix, *Social Mobility, op. cit.*, pp. 19–21.

40. Blau and Duncan, pp. 433–435.

41. *Ibid.*, p. 435.

42. See Connor, *Socialism, Politics, and Equality*, pp. 161–176.

43. *Ibid.*,pp. 172–175 for a discussion of some indices of comparative rates of circulation mobility.

45. See Lipset, *Political Man*, pp. 49–51, and *passim*.

46. Paul Seabury, "The Idea of Merit," *Commentary*, December 1972, pp. 41–45.

47. Blau and Duncan, p. 404.

48. See Jencks, *et al.*, p. 232 (and source cited, n. 71)

49. P.J.D. Wiles, *Economic Institutions Compared* (New York: Wiley/Halsted Press, 1977), p. 459.

50. Jencks *et al.*, *Inequality,*pp. 191, 215, 219.

Equality and the Corporation

Alan M. Kantrow and
Laura L. Nash

WHETHER MODERN DEMOCRATIC CAPITALISM fosters or impedes the realization of such cherished American values as equality is a question which, in this generation, may be said to draw its urgency not from the hard facts of social misery but from the ideological program of capitalism's opponents. A half century ago—and a half century before that—the uneven record of America's market economy gave that question a degree of intellectual plausibility which, as the companion essays in this volume richly attest, it simply does not enjoy today. Yet the charges against capitalism still hang in the air, their accusatory force undiminished.

Whatever we may think of the polemical commitments or political goals of capitalism's opponents, we must admit that their rhetorical strategy has proven unqualifiedly successful. Given the sheer range and weight of the evidence marshaled against them, we may reasonably ask why their arguments continue to enjoy the credibility they do.

One possible answer is that the attack on capitalist institutions represents in part a displacement onto the artifacts of a secular culture of energies and imperatives that are essentially religious and, by extension, utopian. Since the longings of the spirit for a perfect world are rarely satisfied in the world known to history, the gap between vision and reality provides an inexhaustible source of frustration and, thus, an ever-responsive audience for charges of institutional failure. In the face of so bottomless a hunger for perfection, relative success in improving social conditions all too easily becomes an invisible accomplishment.

To the extent that this analysis is correct, it traces much of today's anti-capitalist animus to a frame of mind altogether inhospitable to the measured, incremental achievement of limited, yet immensely practical ends. For those who would have on earth a heavenly city or nothing—and for those who would cloak less noble goals in these shining images of the millennium—the doggedly pragmatic horizon of capitalist endeavor is an insult. Worse, it is morally repugnant, an exchange of fatuous complacency for ethical purpose.

No wonder that, in this view of things, pragmatism appears a species of wholly corrupt instrumentalism. No wonder, too, that the corporation—that archetypal institutional expression of capitalist pragmatism—appears an agent of social repression. How, after all, can an institution devoted in form and function more explicitly than any other to the achievement of the limited worldly ends of individuals be anything less than the hard-hearted jailor of a society still in chains? How, for that matter, can it not be the very type and emblem, the very agent of social inequality?

II. The Roots of the Corporation

The history of the corporation in America—and, more to the point, the history of its social consequences—would seem to deny out of hand the very premise on which questions like these depend. Although generalizations in such matters are difficult, one fact is unavoidably clear: America's experience with corporate organization represents the relentless push of individuals to arrogate to themselves the most effective instruments of economic activity and social betterment. Put bluntly, Americans took a piece of institutional apparatus initially dedicated to the ends of the state and the established social order and transformed it into an engine of private economic and social advancement. This transformation did not, of course, happen all at once or in any one place. In historical terms, the structures of economic prerogative and social privilege gave way slowly, as thousands of separate pressures and demands battered continually against them from all sides. But once they finally started to crumble, much like an aged dam against which a flood has long been rising, the process quickly gathered irreversible speed. In the later 18th century, the corporation still showed a marked allegiance to its medieval and later mercantilist origins; by the middle of the 19th century, it had lost its communal or statist orientation and had become for all intents and purposes a recognizably modern instrument of private interests and advancement.

Part of the explanation for this pattern of evolution is that the corporation, as a form of business organization, had a mixed parentage. As Edward Mason and others have noted, its first ancestors were those communal groups—ecclesiastical, civil, and craft-based—traditionally granted certain rights of self-government under English law. The right of incorporation, which at the outset was granted solely by the crown and later by Parliament as well, provided the legal basis for the decentralized regulation of affairs at a time when the centralized administrative mechanisms of the state were not yet well enough, or extensively enough, developed to allow for more direct control. Several centuries later, by the 1500s, this first version of the corporation had begun to combine with the joint-stock mode of economic organization to create a form of business entity especially well-suited to the mercantilist purposes, but limited abilities, of the crown. What resulted—a privately managed pooling of risk capital over a sustained period of time—turned out to be, when advantaged by appropriate monopolies and exemptions, an exceptionally powerful agent of royal policy.

Even at the time, however, the corporation's experiential nature and hybrid origins were widely appreciated, and these in turn prompted great caution in the granting and policing of corporate charters. Mobilizing private energies and resources on the crown's behalf was all to the good, but doing so through an institutional device that harnessed ample capital to nascent self-government inevitably threatened to produce a creature only reluctantly answerable to London.

To some extent this built-in tendency toward a fission of interests was counterbalanced, at least during the early years of colonial settlement, by the actual dynamics of corporate self-government. In practice, the management of affairs was not entrusted to the general population of settlers and their parochial interests, but commonly fell into the hands of a few responsible senior men—even in those colonies, like Massachusetts Bay, whose frame of government was provided by the adaptation to civil ends of the corporate charter of a trading company. Though freemen of the commonwealth might, in law and theory, be none other than full members of a chartered corporation, they shared only to a limited extent in the prerogatives of self-government. Much as Samuel Stone, an early minister at Hartford, said of the governance of his congregation, civil direction was supplied by a "speaking aristocracy in the face of a silent democracy."

Yet even the firmest and most well-intentioned hand on a colony's tiller could not guarantee that local and royal purposes would complement each other. In point of fact, experience constantly ran in the other direction, much to the infinite and incessant displeasure of London. Once brought into being, corporations like these might provide resources and raw materials and geographical advantage for the crown, but they constantly threatened to put their own concerns first and, by a kind of reflexive sovereignty, grant charters of their own to local citizens.

With their narrow administrative reach, it did not take colonial governments long to recognize the immense practical rewards to be gained from mobilizing private resources—appropriately advantaged, of course, by monopolies and exemptions—in the service of colony or commonwealth. This lesson, once learned, dictated in no small measure the course of economic activity up to the Revolution and beyond. Extending franchises for the performance of services to benefit the public showed itself every bit as effective a solution to administrative problems in the meetinghouses of colonial government as it had been in the corridors of Whitehall. Thus were new towns formed; mills, bridges, turnpikes, and aqueducts constructed; fisheries and factories encouraged; public services provided; and a medium of exchange supplied.

But it was a fine line indeed that protected a general acquiescence in the granting of these exclusive franchises from a general recognition that such grants conferred substantial private benefit. During the first four decades or so of the 19th century, that line held less and less well against the constant demand for broader private access to legal charters. By the end of that period, incorporation was a status no longer restricted to the privileged few by special acts of state legislatures. It was open on demand to all. The American corporation, then, quickly became—whatever its official standing—the chosen means of private individuals to advance their own ends while keeping, of course, at least a weather eye on the public good. Even where established as a statist instrument, it could not long withstand the centrifugal pull of private interests.

In the 20th century, the corporation has become the representative institution of what Peter Drucker has called our "society

of big, highly organized and managed institutions." In fact, corporations now provide, according to Drucker, "the very fabric of
economically and socially developed societies." They are no
longer small, isolated creatures on the sprawling social landscape;
they dominate it.

III. Implications of structural change

This dominance has not gone unremarked. As the private
corporation became the nation's major provider of goods and
services, its major source of employment, and its major vehicle for
individual investment, questions inevitably arose concerning the
wisdom of concentrating so much economic power in the hands of
such institutions. These questions took on special force by the end
of the 19th century. As efficiencies of production and economies
of scale—and, in some cases, a simple desire to minimize effective
competition—pushed the older units of family capitalism toward
larger organizational scale and what Alfred Chandler has called
the "visible hand" of professional management, many industries
were themselves evolving toward heightened levels of consolidation. This parallel evolution gave public doubts about the effects
of the corporation on the achievement of equality a most convenient focus.

Some industry consolidation took the form of horizontal integration, a formal or informal arrangement among competitors to
keep firm limits on production, to maintain prices, or to do both.
Some of it took the form of vertical integration, an attempt to
increase efficiency by locking in economies of scale at some point
in the production process. As Thomas McCraw has argued, these
two forms of integration had markedly different economic consequences, although they were superficially alike, and an ever-
suspicious public, then and later, was inclined to lump them—as
well as the general increase in corporate size—indiscriminately
together as prima facie evidence of a conspiracy against the public
good.

Now, in McCraw's view it is important not only to define the
precise impulse behind any historical increase in size or concentration but also to recognize the differential likelihood that
various kinds of companies would respond to one or the other
mode of growth. One group of late 19th century companies, those
large organizations in, for example, steel and railroads that Mc-

Craw labels "center firms" usually enjoyed substantial scale economies, possessed elaborate managerial hierarchies, planned
systematically for long-term development, and were relatively
capital intensive. A second group of companies, the "peripheral
firms," were

everything center firms were not. Typically they were small, labor-intensive, managerially thin, and bereft of economies of either scale or speed.
They perforce looked to this year's profits more than to five-year plans.
Peripheral firms were not necessarily unimportant, however. Such industries as textiles, furniture, clothing, food service, building materials,
hotels, and automobile repair were and still are characterized by a large
number of relatively small firms. These firms compete with each other
very much in the fashion of Adam Smith's classical model, which is still
the model of economics textbooks.

Other things being equal, center firms tended toward an
oligopolistic industry structure based on corporate growth
through vertical integration. Some of these firms, of course,
sought horizontal defenses against competition, but they were the
exceptions. This pattern, as McCraw notes, was

not peculiar to the United States but is common to all major capitalist
countries. In Germany, Britain, Japan, Canada, and others, such industries as oil, automobiles, electrical appliances, tires, cigarettes, steel, and
sewing machines are nearly always controlled by only a few firms each;
and these firms are characteristically large and vertically integrated. In
other words, the inherent economic tendencies of center firms seem
more important than legal systems or different national cultures in
determining their relative size and industrial organization. This is a fact
of surpassing importance in assessing the historical record of the evolution of big business in the United States and the reaction to it by (Louis)
Brandeis and like-minded insurgents.

Thus, although the trend toward large-scale corporations and
oligopolistic industries has over the years provided more than its
share of ammunition to consolidation-hating critics, because it is
representative of generic structural developments in all advanced
capitalist economies, the burden of proof must rest with those
who immediately equate all evidence of consolidation with anti-
competitive or other frowned-upon intentions. Said another way,
consolidation at the corporate or industry-wide level is an indif-

ferent fact. It does not by itself indicate a development at odds with the public good or in violation of broad social values. Except for those doctrinaire opponents of capitalism who invariably see in each phase of its historical evolution a set of institutional realities that are socially noxious, no one need view the rise to prominence of the modern corporation as being inflexibly antagonistic to any long-cherished social ideal.

Whether a particular ideal—in this case, the commitment to equality—is threatened or advanced by the workings of corporate capitalism is a question open to empirical study. An obvious—and unavoidable—place to begin that study is with a quick survey of the relevant macroeconomic statistics. Consider, then, the data in Tables 1 and 2 which are taken from the work of Richard Caves on the structure of American industry.

According to the data in Table 1, which divides American industry roughly by the motivation and means of social control that influence its decisions, the period since World War II has seen a relative decline in the size of the unregulated corporate sector, little change in the relative size of the regulated corporate sector, and a substantial increase in the relative size of the nonprofit and government sectors. As Caves notes, these changes are, for the most part, real—that is, they are not the result of reclassifying industries from one sector to another.

Table 2 indicates that, over the same period, the number of different kinds of enterprises has, by and large, kept pace with or outgrown the increase in human population, the effect being most pronounced with corporate forms of organization. At the same time, however, there has been a marked decrease in the real size (receipts in constant dollars) of individual enterprises. Together with the findings summarized in Table 1, these data strongly suggest not only that large corporations—those bogeymen of capitalism's critics—are growing more slowly than other sectors of the economy but also that, to the extent private corporate growth exists, it is primarily taking place among smaller companies.

But is increasing corporate size an inescapable evil where it does exist? Among manufacturing companies, which may serve as convenient surrogates for all nonfinancial corporations, the share of total value added contributed between 1947 and 1972 by the fifty largest companies grew more rapidly than the share of value added accounted for by other firms in the top 200. Contrary to the expectations of many, the rate of increase was at its height just after World War II and has been declining since then. Nonetheless, there is a general trend toward concentration—a trend accompanied, it is worth noting, by disproportionate gains in efficiency and benefits to employees. As Caves argues,

The fifty largest manufacturing companies accounted for 25 percent of all value added in manufacturing in 1972. Their share of the value of factory shipments was almost the same, 24 percent. Their share of payroll to employees was smaller, 22 percent, and their share of all manufacturing employees was smaller still, 17 percent. That is, the fifty largest manufacturing companies use proportionately less labor in their production processes than do smaller companies, but their employees earn higher wages.

The implications of these data are by no means invalidated by the fact that levels of concentration in assets among the top 200 manufacturing companies are greater than levels of concentration in sales, which are in turn greater than levels of concentration in value added. It should come as no surprise that the largest manufacturing enterprises are relatively capital intensive.

If the consolidation of economic power represented by the modern corporation is essentially neutral with regard to the social good broadly construed, how then are the relevant dimensions of corporate performance to be defined, let alone measured? One obvious approach to assess the effect of corporations is to look at the changing composition of the American labor force itself; but here one comes up against a strong interpretive prejudice. Because in recent years these changes have taken place against a backdrop of falling rates of growth in both real wages and labor productivity (see Table 3), many observers have attributed the decline in rates to adjustments in the labor force. On the best current evidence, however, this attribution is incorrect.

In their effects on wage rates and productivity, demographic shifts in the labor force have by and large tended to cancel each other out. For example, as Richard Freeman reports, "the sizable increase in the educated work force in the period (1948–1973), which tends to raise growth, is balanced off by the increase in labor inputs due to fewer hours worked and the changing age-sex composition of employment" (see Table 4). These demographic shifts, however, even if not the cause of productivity decline, remain potentially significant indicators of social change within the employing institutions.

As summarized by Freeman, major labor force changes over the period 1948–1980 include:

1. an increase in the number of workers who are young, female, and educated

2. a decrease in the number of workers who are older and male

3. an increase in the number of workers who are in white-collar and skilled jobs and a corresponding decrease in the number of workers in blue-collar and lower skilled jobs

4. a faster rate of growth in the supply of educated labor than in the supply of skilled jobs requiring that degree of education and, thus by extension, an increase in the 'underemployment' of educated workers

5. a decline in relative earnings among workers who are college educated, young, and male and an increase in the relative earnings of workers who are black, at least some of which improvement can be traced to the existence and operation of federal anti-bias programs.

Tables 5–8 and Figures 1–2 document these summary findings. Although they speak clearly to the concerns of many about the way the American economy is developing overall, they do not, on balance, shed any directly useful light on the social implications of the corporation itself. To get a handle on these implications, we must look within the corporation proper—especially to the various and changing means by which individuals have achieved access to managerial power.

IV. Access to Power in Management

It might well be claimed that the strongest driving force for egalitarianism in American business had its origins in geography, for the establishment of a salaried managerial class first proceeded from a response to geographic necessity. Prior to 1850 most American businesses were single units under the direct control of owner-founders or their heirs; after mid-century, however, the transcontinental railroads developed a need for many highly skilled people to manage the details of each far-flung business enterprise. The simple fact that a railroad system stretched across America in a series of widely separated offices connected by hundreds of miles of track forced owners to take the radical step of relinquishing direct control of operations, thus opening the way for a significant number of non-owners to participate for the first time in the direction and rewards of a major American industry. This participation was a decisive factor in shaping American business as was the technological revolution to which we customarily attribute the industrial transformation of the nineteenth and early twentieth centuries.[4]

Before the railroads, the owner of a business would typically manage all the details of purchasing, sales, and shipping as well as supervise the few male clerks who staffed the office and kept accounts. If overseas trade required a representative of the firm to operate at a distance from the main office, that position was most often filled by a member of the owner's family—his son or son-in-law, a trusted brother, or perhaps a nephew.

This dynastic pattern held true even when industrialization began to broaden substantially the scale of enterprise, as the first fully integrated textile mill in America, constructed outside Boston, Massachusetts, by Francis Cabot Lowell, attests. Lowell had made his fortune as a merchant in partnership with his paternal uncle William: his new partner was brother-in-law Patrick Tracy Jackson. Their engineer, Charles Storer Storrow, himself a direct descendant of the Appleton family, eventually married Jackson's niece, who like Francis Lowell happened to bear the middle name of Cabot.[5] The Lawrence Brothers, already successful as Boston importers, acted as sales agent for the Lowell mills, but did not remain outsiders for long, as later Harvard president Abbott Lawrence Lowell's name indicates.

Many of these first family names survive in American business—especially in financial institutions[6]—but in general business administration today is not synonymous with family ownership. The railroads and to a lesser degree other forms of transportation and communication initiated this real separation of ownership and administration, since their new scale of enterprise and technological complexity required a new class of commercial administrator: the salaried manager. For the first time in American history the broad-based possibility of achieving upward income mobility and job authority was not directly dependent on a prior accumulation of capital through blood tie or marital good fortune.

Even the most entrepreneurial of the nineteenth century's legendary business figures were greatly affected by this revolutionary structure for administrative control. In the Horatio Alger-like career of Andrew Carnegie, for example, lies a balanced report of the opportunities inherent in both the old managerial system and the new. Carnegie began his career as a typical representative of the new class of salaried managers: a poor Scottish immigrant in Allegheny City, Pennsylvania, seventeen year old Carnegie was hired at the Western Division of the Pennsylvania Railroad to be assistant to the first superintendent, Thomas Scott. When Scott was promoted to vice president, Carnegie replaced him, and his (Carnegie's) administrative abilities—particularly in the area of cost control—were of such caliber that his career as manager at the Pennsylvania seemed assured. Carnegie, however, had a strong entrepreneurial streak and used his railroad expertise to organize his own steel company. He appointed several excellent administrators and engineers but, in the style of earlier owner-founders, retained the major decision-making power. His E.T. Works was soon producing a record 31 percent return on equity, a foretaste of the vast personal fortune he would later accumulate from the mass production of steel. Though the success of Carnegie's empire rested on old-fashioned entrepreneurial skill, the talent which created that empire—his ability to organize and manage people and to employ new technology to cut costs and increase scale—had been acquired during his formative period as a professional manager at the railroad.

The extent to which managerial power and operational responsibility had become separated from ownership by the end of the nineteenth century can be seen in a document drafted by Daniel C. McCallum, superintendent of a division of the Erie Railroad, who was then promoted to general superintendent. McCallum's six general principles of administration not only describe the nature of his expertise but also formalize the responsibilities and positions of authority which now accrued to general managers:

(1) A proper division of responsibilities.

(2) Sufficient power conferred to enable the same to be fully carried out, that such responsibilities may be real in their character [that is, authority to be commensurate with responsibility].

(3) The means of knowing whether such responsibilities are faithfully executed.

(4) Great promptness in the report of all derelictions of duty, that evils may be at once corrected.

(5) Such information, to be obtained through a system of daily reports and checks, that will not embarrass principal officers nor lessen their influence with their subordinates.

(6) The adoption of a system, as a whole, which will not only enable the General superintendent to detect errors immediately, but will also point out the delinquent.[7]

Although McCallum's principles clearly demonstrated a new deligation of responsibility in the railroad industry, investors had not forfeited all administrative control. Even though career managers now filled some top corporate slots, the positions of president and treasurer most often remained in the hands of major shareholders, and the other investors who composed the board of directors continued to review all significant policy decisions such as strategies for growth, coordination with other railroad systems, and major capital outlays for maintenance of the line. Despite the continued participation by owners in some important aspects of policy, the appearance of semi-autonomous salaried managers meant that a new and more variegated pattern of power had been devised for business, a power which would now rest on competence as well as inheritance. Chandler has proposed (p. 9 etc.)—and we would agree—that as the corporation continued to increase in size and diversity, the separation of management and ownership became even more pronounced. By the 1920s it had become standard; even the Rockefeller family had relinquished its hold over Standard Oil's management to become relatively "pure" investors who collected dividends and voted at annual meetings.

It was precisely this delicate pattern of joint but discrete responsibility and power—with its unique ability to attract dynastic fortune and talent while also providing incentive and opportunity for new blood—that made and continues to make the American corporation the most egalitarian in the world with regard to access. The management *structure* of the large corporation, however, was eminently hierarchical, and the share of wealth and decision-making power which accrued to each individual was clearly not equal.

The pyramidal management structure certainly favored top management and the handful of investors who comprised the board of directors, but their interests were in constant tension.[8] The railroads of speculator Jay Gould, for instance, were generally poorly managed and badly equipped because Gould used corporate revenues for further acquisition rather than improvement of existing systems. On the other hand, the Pennsylvania, which Gould unsuccessfully tried to take over in 1869, had one of the strongest managements in the industry, and there managers dominated the board.

A survey of publicly-held corporations (both large and small) in America today would generally show a similar split in control between outside investors and salaried management. Although the balance of interests which these two groups represent is unique to each institution, it is clear that the latter group has steadily increased in size and influence over the last century and that the modern business enterprise has provided a permanent alternative to inheritance or marriage as the only means for income mobility. It is not so much the case that a salaried management force suddenly provided the opportunity for every American in the gay '90s to compete with Cornelius Vanderbilt in personal income and power, but rather that the average person now had the chance to achieve some degree of autonomy at work, to be a boss over some aspect of corporate affairs, to receive a steady salary from such activity, to have reasonable expectations of advancement based on performance, and to expect a certain stability of association with the business entity.

V. Education

If geographic expansion severed absolute operational control of the corporation from family ownership, it was professionalism which provided the work gloves with which the salaried manager would pick up the scattered fragments of business responsibility. As the technical and administrative knowledge needed to operate a railroad increased and as investors became more and more dependent on their managers' expertise, railroad officials began to generalize their knowledge and to organize formally into professional associations similar to academic associations.

Although many of the business journals that sprang up in the late nineteenth century centered on the engineering aspects of railroad systems, the idea that administrative techniques could also be described and communicated between managers was quickly accepted, as McCallum's report indicates. In the first decade of the twentieth century, a former chief engineer at the Midvale Steel company, Frederick Winslow Taylor, gained great notice and even notoriety with his intriguing proposition that management could be a science, subject to the rigors of measurement and capable of generating principles and formulae.

Paradoxically, Taylor's theories, sometimes misunderstood as being efficiency studies to sweat more work out of the poor laborer, were a combination of philosophical egalitarianism and intellectual elitism. He demanded that both parties in industry, workers and management (among whom he seems to include investors), revolutionize their thinking:[9] "both sides should take their eyes off the division of the surplus as the all important matter, and together turn their attention toward increasing the size of the surplus until this surplus becomes so large that it is unnecessary to quarrel over how it shall be divided." The way to achieve this goal was through the scientific analysis of various business tasks and structures. The abilities required by scientific management, however, created a class distinction between the two groups which Taylor proposed to revolutionize:

I can say, without the slightest hesitation, that the science of handling pig-iron is so great that the man who is fit to handle pig-iron as his daily work cannot possibly understand that science; . . . . this inability of the man who is fit to work at any particular trade to understand the science of that trade without the kindly help and cooperation of men of a totally different type of education, men whose education is not necessarily higher but a different type from his own.

Although this professionalization of management inherently widened the gap between worker and manager, it further cemented the separation of ownership and control which a salaried management structure had begun. It also created yet another means of access to positions of power in business—namely, the university. Whereas formerly a college education qualified a man for a position in academia, the ministry, law, or medicine, it now qualified him for the world of commerce and industry. To quote Harvard president Charles William Eliot in 1908:

We observed last June that more than half of our senior class, then graduating, went into business, and we also have observed for a good many years past that a large proportion who have gone into business have attained high place, particularly in the corporation industries and the financial institutions of our country.[10]

Most major American universities had been offering courses in engineering and accounting since the mid-nineteenth century, but in the first decade of the twentieth, academic interest in administrative science as a general field began to increase. In 1908 the first professional graduate school of business administration was founded, at Harvard University,[11] and the progression of that program over the past seventy years offers a striking example of the continued enlargement of access to managerial position in America as professional training programs became both more available and more sophisticated.

Harvard University's School of Business Administration was established to offer a "laboratory method of instruction in administration":[12] clearly Frederick Taylor's belief in management science was shared.[13] The School's first class totalled 80 students (40 of whom were Harvard College graduates); and eight years later the Business School was enrolling 232 students from 84 different colleges in its two year program.

The focus at Harvard was simple: to prepare students to assume top management positions, which many of them subsequently did. Their successful leadership and the School's laboratory method of instruction—i.e., of generating teaching material from actual business situations and experiences—attracted the interest and support of many leading businessmen, whose personal contributions to the School's endowment and employment of its students helped assure the opportunity for the advancement of both. George F. Baker, for example, who was then president of the First National Bank of New York, responded to the School's campaign to raise five million dollars in order to build its own campus by offering to donate the entire amount. Baker himself had no formal higher education and had originally been skeptical of the business worth of a university education, but after inquiring extensively into the School's activities he concluded, "I should like to found the first Graduate School, and give a new start to better business standards."[14]

Baker's words are symbolic of the profound change which had occurred in thinking about American business, namely that administrative expertise could be learned through formal education rather than exclusively through entrepreneurial zeal and long first-hand experience. The importance of the support that business gave to the graduate schools of education in America cannot be underemphasized: in the early years it endowed the schools and frequently contributed to their faculties; in later years it not only hired their graduates and set them on upwardly mobile career paths, but also sent even experienced senior executives back to school to learn more about administrative science.

In the post-second world war period, for example, Harvard's business school established its Advanced Management Program to meet the continuing education needs of executives who were about to move into positions of broad responsibility within their firms. In the 1950s a similar middle-level program (called PMD) was added. To judge the egalitarian validity of these programs is to judge the effectiveness of the self-fullfilling prophecy: companies selected people from their organizations who had already demonstrated outstanding managerial capabilities and sent them to Harvard to become even better. Most often their subsequent career did indeed take them to top management positions. For our discussion what is definitive about the executive education programs is how many people in top positions within the corporation today have engaged in some sort of professional training, and that this belief in management education has facilitated entry into and effective performance in top management—even for those people who were not born with silver certificates of corporate ownership in their mouths.

In the 1950s the mushrooming demand for middle managers to administer the booming post-war expansion of American business outstripped the aims and capacities of the business schools, and business responded with the highest form of flattery for professional management education: it created its own training programs for junior executives, frequently staffed in part with business school professors. It was now possible for the highly diverse pool of graduates for whom the GI Bill had made a college education possible to enter a firm directly from college and, without an advanced degree, receive access and preparation for a managerial position.

But was the rise in professionalism truly an egalitarian means of increasing access to higher levels of management or simply a way of legitimizing the elite who could already afford a college education? A complete breakdown of business school classes by ethnic affiliation and income class over time was not available to us. The folk tradition is certainly that at Harvard Business School, at least, only the sons of the wealthy industrialists were admitted. Harvard denies this, and can cite statistics of financial aid to students clear back to its origins; as for family dynasties, out of approximately 950 admissions last year only twenty were children of HBS alumni. Sheer numerical increases in MBA enrollment in the post-war period and again in the late 1970s would also substantiate the claim that professional management has opened its doors to an increasing variety of social groups: between 1967 and 1981 the number of MBA graduates in America leaped from 14,900 to 54,000, with over 450 MBA programs available from a highly diverse range of educational institutions.[15]

What is also clear is that blacks and women have not shared as immediately as white males in the rewards of a professionalized management program. Women were not admitted to Harvard Business School until 1962, and their ability to rise within an organization through internal corporate management training programs was clearly limited. Despite the fact that the number of white married women who work nearly doubled between 1950 and 1977, the opportunity for this advancement seemed to remain closed; until recently the overwhelming majority of women occupied the same cluster of low-level, low pay jobs. American business seemed much more receptive to blacks than women; the number of black males in managerial positions has more than doubled. Though it is too early to predict whether America's social structure and cultural expectations can encourage a lasting advancement of women and minorities to senior positions, business professionalism seems to be producing increasingly egalitarian results in several ways: the professional business degree, which has long secured for men a starting opportunity for corporate leadership, is beginning to overcome traditional barriers to women's entry onto top management career ladders; the 1981 HBS class, for example, showed only a slight difference in starting salaries between its men and women graduates and no discernable difference in status.[16] Surveys of job satisfaction among the American work force have indicated that there is generally a strong increase in importance placed on financial equity—i.e., the chance to obtain the position and pay for which one is qualified.[17] What haunts these apparent trends towards increased opportunity, however, is the less certain proposition that equal opportunity at the managerial entry point will assure egalitarian representation of women, minority groups and white males in top levels of management. So far, such egalitarian results have eluded the corporation, and our insight into how Americans will sort out the recent increase in non-white and/or female managers is singularly murky.

What is clear, however, is that the modes of authority in business are becoming increasingly diversified. A more diverse composition in the top managerial group or even a dissolution of the pyramidal structure would advance egalitarian trends even further. For example, the rash of large-scale mergers and acquisitions, which has raised for many observers the spectre of decreased competition and individual enterpreneurial opportunity, has organized itself in such a way that many of the largest diversified multinationals[18] have in fact increased opportunities for autonomy at very high levels in these vast organizations. For example, many of these companies have evolved into a decentralized divisional structure in part to nourish the individual manager; though subject to the imposition of financial objectives "from above," the divisional president or group vice president in these firms has almost complete operational autonomy and a great deal of financial discretion.

Following what is commonly called the Japanese style of management, other companies are discarding their traditional hierarchies altogether at the operating level in preference to a consensual mode of decision making wherein the expertise of the experienced machinist is given as much consideration as the administrative knowledge of the professional manager. The votes are not in yet as to how far such quality circles will penetrate higher levels of corporate management and whether they will succeed in dissolving the "corporate absolutism" which Louis Brandeis so eloquently attacked over sixty years ago. While it is true that the head of the UAW now sits on the board of Chrysler, he concurrently represents a formal structure in business—the trade union—which is as hierarchical as the largest corporation.

Quality circles have re-defined expertise to loosen its dependency on a formal education, but within business as a whole, professionalization of management has accelerated with supersonic velocity in the last decade. Like the *wissenschaftliche* magnification of the specific which marked professional research and training in the hard and social sciences during the '50s and '60s, business administration has focused its attention on increasingly discrete sub-fields of management science. Whereas in the past, executive education at Harvard (reputedly the most generalized of the top tier of management schools) consisted of two broad programs, (AMP and PMD, mentioned above), in the last eight years the School has added over a dozen shorter programs which offer quite advanced seminars on more specific functional or industrial issues. Other schools have done the same and the professional associations are also sponsoring a rising number of advanced semesters and conferences.

That the corporation would sponsor and participate in this creation of so many experts in so many discrete fields would seem ideologically contradictory to the traditional pyramidal structure of authority—diverse noncomparable expertise must necessarily diversify the power structure of the organization—and it may be that this recent scientification of management will spark a new wave of egalitarian re-organization just as the first introduction of professional business education helped revolutionize business structure and job opportunity. Under this scenario, the corporation abandons neither meritocracy nor egalitarianism: levels of expertise are recognized, but at the top, one top expert is as valuable as another.

Further diffusions of managerial power can be expected as American business continues to increase its reliance on information systems and to upgrade the complexity of its data processing capabilities. If information is power, then we might expect the entire power structure of the corporation to be distributed more widely as managers acquire the ability to call up vast amounts of information on the minicomputer that has been placed at each desk, and that overcomes previous geographic restrictions.

It should be noted in passing, moreover, that severe external pressures have increased the representation within corporations of outside constituencies: many corporate public-affairs departments have grown tremendously since the early '60s in response to the rise in consumer and environmental pressure groups, while boards of directors are increasingly admitting outside directors (i.e. those whose representative powers are not primarily centered on financial or managerial involvement in the company). Both changes further advance our thesis that the history of the modern American corporation—though its power is elusive to quantification in all but the grossest ways—has been a cumulative series of egalitarian gestures: to increase the appropriateness of its managerial structure and the size of its assets, the corporation has repeatedly had to capitalize on every opportunity to open new doors.

VI. Social Benefits of the Corporation

In previous sections of this chapter we have argued that American capitalism has been a significant egalitarian factor in our society both in a direct (mean average income in America) and an indirect (access to employment and advancement) way. Another common measure of egalitarianism, however, namely, the widespread distribution of wealth other than through salary, remains a problem for discussion. How "beneficent" has the corporation been, and to whom, and in what way?

Despite American capitalism's strong belief in allowing unsympathetic market forces to determine survival, the fittest of that same system have always sought ways to redistribute part of the profit to the disadvantaged. Legal and ideological restrictions on the use of corporate funds, however, have often clogged these philanthropical fonts.

In 1868 Andrew Carnegie decided to limit his personal income to $50,000 a year in order to use the surplus for the benefaction of others. Carnegie's philosophy was made explicit some twenty years later in a famous essay, simply entitled "Wealth" which appeared in the *North American Review* and was subsequently reprinted as a penny pamphlet. At the time of publication, Carnegie's fortune was estimated at thirty million dollars, and his annual income $1,850,000:

Poor and restricted are our opportunities in this life; narrow our horizon; our best work most imperfect; but rich men should be thankful for one inestimable boon. They have it in their power during their lives to busy themselves in organizing benefactions from which the masses of their fellows will derive lasting advantage, and thus dignify their own lives. . . . There is no mode of disposing of surplus wealth creditable to thoughtful and earnest men into whose hands it flows save by using it year by year for the general good.

Although Carnegie's philanthropy may have surpassed that of his fellow industrialists, he exhibits two characteristics that were common to the period: the redistribution of capitalism's gains came largely out of private impulse and out of a private income that was by common standards vast. Carnegie Steel was not contributing part of its profits to the general good, but rather in large proportion to Mr. Carnegie. Social responsibility, then, was the duty of the elite, a private rather than corporate obligation—at least with regard to the charitable redistribution of wealth. Carnegie felt it the obligation of wealthy men to supervise and determine personally the best public use of their wealth. In his opinion private charities and government-administered benefactions were totally wasteful and misdirected. But by the turn of the century it was clear that Carnegie's individualism had to be modified: no one person would administer the scale of charity which his wealth made possible.

To answer the problem of responsible administration of surplus income, Carnegie set up a series of perpetual trusts designed to be self-sustaining and to support specified causes which ranged from education to international peace. At about the same time another great philanthropist, John D. Rockefeller, attempted to resolve the problem of administrating charitable funds through a radically different channel, namely, the U.S. Congress. Previously Rockefeller had established several private organizations with a board of carefully selected but independent trustees to administer funds for medical research and education, much of it centering on diseases and educational problems of the South and the southern black. One of those trusts had obtained federal charter of incorporation in 1903, and in 1910 Rockefeller sought to reestablish the same kind of system on a larger scale; he introduced a bill into the U.S. Senate to establish the Rockefeller Foundation as a federally chartered corporation subject to the control of the U.S. Congress, who would supervise the administration of the trust's funds "for the public welfare." After three years of debate, the Taft administration refused Rockefeller's request; public sentiment against the Rockefeller name was high after the recent decision of the Supreme Court to order the dissolution of the Standard Oil Company, and as Taft's Attorney General wrote:

Is it, then, appropriate that, at the moment when the United States through its courts is seeking in a measure to destroy the great combination of wealth which has been built up by Mr. Rockefeller . . . the Congress of the United States should assist in the enactment of a law to create and perpetuate in his name an institution to hold and administer a larger portion of this wealth?[19]

Rockefeller was forced to establish the trust privately, and in his lifetime he gave over $200 million dollars of his own and his wife's money to that institution.

At the time of the establishment of the Rockefeller and Carnegie Trusts the concept of a charitable foundation was quite new—only seven had been formed in the previous century. They quickly gained acceptance in the '20s but remained almost exclusively a channel for the perpetration and distribution of *private* wealth. To some social critics, Carnegie's formulaic obligation to achieve private wealth for the purpose of redistributing it privately to enhance the public good was a mis-directed conception: social welfare and egalitarianism would be better achieved by a direct redistribution of corporate profits among employees of the corporation. As George Bernard Shaw proposed in *Socialism for Millionaires*, "We often give to public objects money that we should devote to raising wages. . . . or to substituting three eight-hour shifts for two twelve-hour ones."

To one wealthy industrialist of the day, however, Shaw's version of social responsibility held great validity. In 1914, Henry Ford raised the daily wage of his workers from $2.34 to $5.00, and two years later he opened a trade school which favored the applications of the neediest. Over the next decade Ford continued to use the opportunities for employment to aid the disadvantaged by establishing a policy to hire the mentally and physically disabled, as well as blacks. Ford began to create his own utopia, providing language instruction for immigrants, discount grocery stores for workers, and in 1918 a limited profit-sharing system.

Throughout the nineteenth and early twentieth century these two forms of beneficent re-distribution of profits—the massive donation of private wealth by owners of the corporation, and the internal distribution of monetary and non-monetary benefits to workers within the corporation—remained for the most part individually motivated. The one notable exception was the railroad industry's support of the YMCA, whereby Y facilities for the hostelry of railroad workers were created out of corporate contributions and maintained by YMCA personnel, many of whom were on railroad payrolls. This early instance of corporatewide, systematic philanthropy could accurately be called symbiotic charity, for it solved the problem of housing the necessarily transient railroad worker while providing a captive audience for the Y's missionary zeal.

But once corporate self-interest was not as immediately apparent as in the YMCA hostels, and/or company ownership spread over a larger constituency, the idea of a corporate charitable contribution presented business—or at least its legal counsellors—certain difficulty. The first large-scale cross industry giving appears to have occurred at the outset of the First World War, when the American National Red Cross enlisted the aid of Y administrators to solicit private and corporate aid for their relief work. In order to avoid charges by shareholders of improper appropriation of corporate funds, many corporations offered a Red Cross Dividend, whereby shareholders were solicited on an individual basis to authorize the corporation to pay the amount of their dividend to the Red Cross. By the time of the second Red Cross drive in May 1918 several states had already passed legislation allowing corporations to contribute directly to war charities. As the war continued, corporations increased their contributions to various relief efforts, usually through a united appeal within a city. The United War Work Campaign of 1918 was conducted under the joint leadership of the seven major charitable organizations in America, who seized upon the concept of corporate quotas—in some areas up to 2½ percent of estimated net earnings—to meet their goals. United States Steel Corporation donated $5 million to this drive, while Standard Oil Company (New Jersey) offered $1 million.

Out of the war effort a general pattern of corporate giving was established: namely, the creation of an umbrella agency through which a single appeal for contributions could be made to the corporations and through which funds could be distributed to serve various community needs. While the charitable effectiveness of such organizations as the Community Chest has received widespread criticism since Carnegie's day, American business has continued to participate in united fund appeals; United Way, for example, raised $1.3 billion in 1980.

The problem of whether corporate contributions are motivated by self-interest or genuine concern for the disadvantaged is not unlike an exploration of the private motivations for altruism, but in the first case the question becomes at least operatively important, for the charitable distribution of funds in that legal tradition seemed firmly in violation of shareholder rights under contract. Although corporate giving to community chests continued after the First World War, it was not until 1950, when the state of New Jersey allowed a small manufacturing firm (A. P. Smith) to donate $1,500 to Princeton University, that the precedent for a broad application of corporate contributions was set. The argument advanced by presiding Judge J. C. Stein was one of self-interest:

I cannot conceive of any greater benefit to corporations in this country than to build, and continue to build, respect for and adherence to a system of free enterprise and democratic government. . . . Nothing that aids or promotes the growth and service of the American university or college in respect of the matters here discussed can possibly be anything short of direct benefit to every corporation in the land.[20]

Immediately following the Smith decision, corporate giving increased dramatically, from which it might be argued that corporations had long been willing to redistribute a certain portion of their profits to nonshareholders, but had had no legal channel for doing so. As reported to the Bureau of Internal Revenue, business "gifts and contributions" grew from $30 million in 1936, to a plateau of a little over $200 million each year between 1944–1950 and then jumped to over $300 million in 1951.[21] By another estimate (see Table 9), it can be seen that corporate giving increased by 50% again by the end of the 1950s.[22]

Despite the legal reconciliation of profitmaking and almsgiving that accelerated corporate donations from the '50s onward, until recently charity has continued to remain largely a private impulse in America. As the social claim on "obscene profits" continues to rise with the fall of individual buying power, however, the private-corporate ratio of relative beneficence has reversed: in 1979 corporate philanthropy surpassed that of private giving (including private foundations) for the first time, as companies chipped 2.3

billion dollars into the non-profit cash flow.[23] Even so, most corporations have fallen far short of the 5 percent limit Congress first placed in 1935 on corporate donations of pre-tax earnings—the mean average is just under 1 percent—and it is not at all clear that a substantial increase in giving would survive the legal scrutiny of those shareholders who are more interested in their own largess than the indirect benefit to corporate resources that donations to non-profit causes might secure.

Has business then offered self-interest as a decoy to investors, as a rational base to support the philanthropic impulses of its directors? Or have corporations had social responsibility thrust upon them, as it were, by an increasingly hostile public environment? Either way one holds the telescope, it is clear that corporate responsiveness to basically egalitarian demands for a wider distribution of wealth has existed for a long time and appears to have increased in recent years in terms of income distribution and charitable contributions.

Moreover, just as the monetary extent to which the American corporation is redistributing its profits to support charitable or nonprofit endeavours has increased, so too has the corporation widened its role as social benefactor to its internal constituency, particularly since the Second World War. While earlier attempts to ensure employment stability, compensation insurance, and old-age pension schemes through corporate and personal donations had failed—the most notable was the proposal of General Electric's Gerard Swope in 1931—in the 1950s corporations were beginning to offer many of these benefits as a matter of course: by 1959 the number of companies making basic medical plans available to their employees had doubled since the beginning of the decade, medical insurance plans had been added, and private pension plans were growing so rapidly that it was feared these funds would upset the money markets.

In recent years the demands on the corporation to support social service systems for its employees continue to increase. As Rosabeth Moss Kanter concludes from worker satisfaction surveys, the more we have, the more we expect as a right: maternity leave, paternity leave, dental care, flexible hours, reduced hours, and child care are among today's claims on corporate earning.[24] Whether one sees these benefits as unproductive drains on corporate resources or legitimate egalitarian solutions to ensuring everyone's right to meaningful work and fair compensation, it is clear that the American perception of redistribution of wealth has moved further and further away from the private control legitimated by ownership, which it once enjoyed, toward a corporate assumption of social responsibility.

Since the 1950s the demand for corporate responsibility has become far more public, and with that increase in public accountability the corporation's social benefactions have become one of the chief indicators of cultural values in America today: in the 1960s the beneficent corporation was most likely to address the problems of racial discrimination and poverty; in the early 1970s programs such as the National Alliance of Businessmen, designed to promote minority employment and minority businesses, were widely adopted in the corporate world, only to give way to environmental and consumer issues as the primary concern of the "responsible" corporation.

One fascinating insight into the way business has shifted its understanding of its responsibilities would be to compare the welcoming speeches of Harvard Business School deans over the past thirty years. In 1951, Donald K. David set a tone of patriotic commitment to America's new global leadership:

. . . You are coming to this School at a time in which our society needs as perhaps never before an increasing supply of competent administrators in business, in government, in our Armed Forces and in our academic and philanthropic institutions. This need has been created by the dynamic growth of our economy and by our country's acceptance of new responsibilities in the leadership of civilization. . . . We cannot afford to be weak either in the quality of our arms and government or in the skill of the management of the millions of civilian organizations—business and otherwise—which are the basis of our strength. By choosing to come to this School you have assumed the responsibility of doing your utmost to participate in the management of your country's affairs.[25]

In 1964 Acting Dean George P. Baker sounded the Business and Society clarion that would precede such movements as the social audit for business:

. . . . The United States is a business society and the business administrator has had a key role in its development. . . . The developing economic strength of the country has made possible the winning of two World Wars and has given us the ability to face the USSR with a formidable national defense. In large measure this has been brought about by the professional manager working in combination with other elements in our society. . . . Business will be expanding and reaching out to feed, clothe, house, and provide transportation, recreation, and a myriad other things for a population that may exceed 300 million in the United States and 7 billion in the world at the beginning of the twenty-first century. All the while competition with Communism, economic as well as political and military, will be a critical, paramount fact of life, and the business man must act constructively in the preserving of that degree of freedom of business action so essential to national progress, as well as in the preserving of our freedom as a nation . . .[26]

In 1981 one can see a generally individualistic thrust to America's understanding of corporate responsibility in such movements as the right to meaningful work, the restructuring of management away from pyramidal hierarchy, and in the "business ethics" demand that corporate behavior not compromise the individual morality of its employees.

This new individualism in the corporation underscores a fundamental tension in American business which is at the heart of the various forms of egalitarianism described in this essay: the cultivation and rewarding of individual strength together with the maintenance of a universal right to well-being. To keep this tension between private and social improvement constructive, the corporation has had to create and sustain an increasingly wider access to its power and profits while yet preserving the rewards and status system of a meritocracy. In short, the modern corporation has been a system that is at once widely egalitarian and sternly individualistic. The premium placed on both values can be seen in the welcoming address of Dean John H. McArthur to the MBA class of 1983, and it is a philosophy upon which we believe most corporations' success depends today:

. . . . It is my deep conviction that what you bring with you as you *enter* the MBA program will be far more important over your lifetime than what you will take away from your experience here. I am convinced, of course, that the broad approach to problem solving, action and managing people and organizations that is the core of what we do here will serve you well. Even more important, though, will be luck, good physical and mental health, and a happy and stable personal and family life. These are all things that demand constant attention and care on the part of each of us. In addition to these things, there are the fundamental personal qualities that the Admissions Board was searching for when you were admitted to the program. These qualities include honesty, integrity in your relations with others, self-discipline, loyalty, a capacity to make commitments to others, a willingness to help and lead others, and a

strong set of personal social and moral values. All of us in this great
university understand as well the crucial importance for those destined
to leadership roles of a broad sense of history and culture. These are
largely the personal qualities and background you bring with you to the
School. They comprise the truly important dimensions of socially and
morally conscious leaders who can act wisely in managing cooperative
human endeavor and organizations.

TABLE 1

AMOUNT AND PERCENTAGE DISTRIBUTION OF NATIONAL
INCOME ORIGINATING FROM SECTORS DISTINGUISHED BY
MOTIVATION AND SOCIAL CONTROL, SELECTED YEARS, 1950–75

Sector		1950	1955	1960	1965	1970	1975
Investor-owned,	Amount[a]	186.6	249.2	306.0	407.8	554.4	847.8
unregulated	Percentage	77.8	75.7	73.6	73.0	69.3	68.7
Investor-owned,	Amount	25.8	35.9	47.3	60.8	88.5	141.7
regulated	Percentage	10.8	10.9	11.4	10.9	11.1	11.5
Nonprofit enterprise[b]	Amount	3.9	6.0	9.5	14.4	29.5	44.7
	Percentage	1.6	1.8	2.3	2.6	3.7	3.6
Government and government	Amount	23.6	38.1	52.7	75.4	127.4	199.9
enterprise	Percentage	9.8	11.6	12.7	13.5	15.9	16.2
Total national income of	Amount	239.9	329.2	415.5	558.4	799.8	1234.1
domestic origin	Percentage[c]	100.0	100.0	100.0	100.0	100.0	100.0

Source: U.S. Bureau of the Census, *Statistical Abstract of the United States, 1973* (Washington, D.C.: Government Printing
Office, 1973), p. 325; ibid., *1978*, p. 446. U.S. Bureau of Economic Analysis, *The National Income and Product Accounts of the
United States, 1929–74; Statistical Tables* (Washington, D.C.: Government Printing Office, 1977), tables 1.14 and 6.5; *Survey
of Current Buisiness* 59 (July 1979): 31, 54.

[a] In billions of current dollars.

[b] Secured by subtracting compensation of employees in private households (table 6.5 of National Income and Product
Accounts) from national income originating in households and institutions (table 1.14). It is assumed that none of these
non-profit organizations are in the regulated sector.

[c] Percentages may not add to 100.0 because of rounding errors.

TABLE 2
TRENDS IN ENTERPRISE STRUCTURE OF THE UNITED STATES ECONOMY, SELECTED YEARS, 1940–75

Type and Characteristics of Enterprise	1940	1945	1950	1955	1960	1965	1970	1975
Proprietorships								
Total number (thousands)	2,018	5,689	6,865	8,239	9,090	9,078	9,400	10,882
Number per thousand persons	15.2	40.5	45.1	49.7	50.3	46.7	45.9	51.0
Total receipts (billions of dollars)	31	79	n.a.	139	171	199	238	339
Receipts per proprietorship (thousands of 1958 dollars)	31	23	n.a.	19	18	20	19	17
Partnerships								
Total number (thousands)	271[a]	627	n.a.	n.a.	941	914	936	1,073
Number per thousand persons	2.1[a]	4.5	n.a.	n.a.	5.2	4.7	4.6	5.0
Total receipts (billions of dollars)	13	47	n.a.	n.a.	74	75	93	146
Receipts per partnership (thousands of 1958 dollars)	111	126	n.a.	n.a.	76	74	73	72
Corporations								
Total number (thousands)	473	421	629	807	1,141	1,424	1,665	2,024
Number per thousand persons	3.6	3.0	4.1	4.9	6.3	7.3	8.1	9.5
Total receipts (billions of dollars)	148	255	458	642	849	1,195	1,751	3,199
Receipts per corporation (thousands of 1958 dollars)	635	1,105	908	875	720	757	778	840

Sources: U.S. Bureau of the Census, *Historical Statistics of the United States, Colonial Times to 1970* (Washington, D.C.: Government printing Office, 1975), part 1, p. 197, and part 2, p. 911; U.S. Bureau of the Census, *Statistical Abstract of the United States, 1978* (Washington, D.C.: Government Printing Office, 1978), pp. 6, 483, 561.

[a] Data pertain to 1939.

TABLE 3
RETARDATION IN THE RATE OF GROWTH OF PRODUCTIVITY
AND REAL EARNINGS

	Compound Annual Rates of Change (in Percentages)		
	1900–66	1947–66	1966–78
Productivity			
1. Output per man-hour (NBER)	2.40	3.39	—
2. Private business sector output per hour of all persons (BLS)	—	3.30	1.83
Real Earnings			
3. Annual earnings	2.14	2.90	—
4. Compensation per man-hour	—	3.30	1.71
5. Average hourly earnings, private industry	—	2.36	0.84

Sources: Line 1—U.S. Bureau of the Census, *Historical Statistics, Part I*, Series D–683, Washington, D.C.: GPO, 1975, p. 162.

Line 2: BLS 1979c, table 79, p. 229, with 1978 from *Monthly Labor Review* 102 (August 1979): 103, table 31 (1947–66 based on hours worked concept from labor force data with 1978 estimated from 1977–78 from change in output per hour using established data.)

Line 3: U.S. Bureau of the Census, *Historical Statistics, Part I* (1975), Series D–726, p. 164 for 1900–60; Series D–722, p. 164, deflated by E–135, p. 210. I calculated the growth rate from 1900–60, then from 1960–66, and used the final figure to calculate 1900–66. A similar procedure was used to get 1947–66.

Line 4: BLS 1979c, table 80, pp. 231–32 with update from *Monthly Labor Review*, August 1979, table 31, p. 103. Because of slight inconsistencies among the series, I used the percentage change from 1977–78 in the *Monthly Labor Review* to update the series.

Line 5: Monthly Labor Review, August 1979, p. 81 for average hourly earnings and p. 89 for consumer price index deflator in 1978 with earlier figures taken from BLS 1979c, table 118, p. 399.

TABLE 4
NATIONAL INCOME PER PERSON EMPLOYED IN
NONRESIDENTIAL BUSINESS: GROWTH RATE AND SOURCES OF
GROWTH 1948–73 AND 1973–76

	1948–73	1973–76	Change
Growth Rate	2.43	−0.54	−2.97
Contributions to growth rate in percentage points			
Total factor input:			
Changes in workers' hours and attributes:			
hours	−.24	−.54	−.30
age-sex composition	−.17	−.25	−.08
education	.52	.88	.36
Changes in capital and land per person employed:			
inventories	.10	.02	−.08
nonresidential structures and equipment	.29	.25	−.04
land	−.04	−.03	.01
Output per unit of input[a]			
Improved allocation of resources[b]	.37	.01	−.38
Changes in the legal and human environment[c]	−.04	−.44	−.40
Economies of scale	.41	.24	−.17
Irregular factors	−.18	.09	.27
Advances in knowledge and miscellaneous determinants[d]	1.41	−.75	−2.16

Source: Edward F. Denison, *Accounting for Slower Economic Growth: The United States in the 1970s,* The Brookings Institution, 1979, table 17–3.

[a] Contributions to the growth rate shown in subsequent lines are restricted to effects upon output per unit of input.

[b] Includes only gains resulting from the reallocation of labor out of farming and out of self-employment and unpaid family labor in small nonfarm enterprises.

[c] Includes only the effects on output per unit of input costs incurred to protect the physical environment and the safety and health of workers, and of costs of dishonesty and crime.

TABLE 5
RATIOS OF NONWHITE TO WHITE: ECONOMIC POSITION AND
ANNUAL CHANGES IN RATIOS 1949–64 AND 1946–76

	Year			Annual Change	
				Before After	
Males	1949/50	1964	1976	1964	1964
Median wages and salaries:					
all workers:	.50	.59	.73	0.6	1.2
full-time, year-round workers:	.64*	.65	.77	0.1	1.0
Median income: Professionals	.57	.69	.84	1.1	2.1
Relative number of:					
professionals	.39	.45	.65	0.4	1.8
managers	.22	.22	.41	0.0	1.7
Females					
Median wages and salaries	.40	.58	.97	1.8	3.5
All workers:					
Full-time, year-round workers:	.57*	.69	.99	1.3	2.3
Relative number of:					
professionals	.47	.60	.83	0.9	2.1
clericals	.15	.33	.69	1.3	3.3

Source: Incomes from U.S. Bureau of Census, *Current Population Reports,* Consumer Income Series P–60. Employment from Census of Population, 1950 and U.S. Department of Labor, *Handbook of Labor Statistics,* 1977.
*1955.

TABLE 6
PERCENTAGE DISTRIBUTION OF OCCUPATIONS OF EMPLOYED
COLLEGE GRADUATES, 1968–78

| | Men | | | Women | | |
Occupations	1968	1978	Δ	1968	1978	Δ
Professional and technical	60.6	52.1	− 8.5	81.1	65.0	− 16.1
Managers and administrators	22.2	24.5	1.8	4.1	8.7	4.6
Sales workers	6.8	8.9	2.1	1.2	4.6	3.4
Clerical workers	4.4	4.7	0.3	10.6	15.4	4.8
Craft workers	2.2	3.9	1.7	1.2	1.9	0.7
Other blue-collar workers	1.3	2.7	1.4	1.2	1.9	0.7
Service workers	1.1	2.1	1.0	1.5	3.8	2.3
Farm workers	0.9	1.2	0.3	0.3	0.5	0.2

Source: Brown, (1979), p. 58, table 5.

TABLE 7
CHANGES IN THE STRUCTURE OF EARNINGS
IN THE UNITED STATES

	Ratios of Earnings	
	1968	1975–79
Education[a]		
College/high school men		
all	1.53	
25–34	1.38	1.16[b]
Age		
Men 25–34/men 45–54		
all	.85	.79[c]
college	.72	.61[c]
Industry		
Mining/all private	1.11	1.28[d]
Construction/all private	1.53	1.32[d]
Specific Skills Group		
R&D doctorate women/all full-time workers	2.68	2.47[e]
Professors/all full-time workers	2.50[e]	2.47[e]
Professors/all full-time workers	2.50[e]	2.20[f]

Sources: R. Freeman, "Effect of Demographic Factors on Age-Earnings Profile," *Journal of Human Resources,* vol. 14 (Summer 1979), table 2; ———. "The Facts About the Declining Economic Value of College," *Journal of Human Resources,* vol. 15 (Winter 1980), table 1; U.S. Department of Labor, *Employment and Training Report of the President 1977,* Washington, D.C.: GPO, 1978, table C-3, and *Monthly Labor Review,* vol. 102 (August 1979), table 14.

[a] Education data for 1977 has been adjusted for change in imputation procedure in 1975.

[b] 1977.

[c] 1975.

[d] 1979.

[e] 1969–70.

[f] 1975–76.

TABLE 8
NEW PERSONNEL PRACTICES RESULTING FROM EEO

Company Programs and Regulations	Percentage of Companies
1. Have *Formal* EEO Programs	86
Including Affirmative Action Plan	
(of those subject to OFCCP regulations)	96
2. Have Had Investigation or Other Action under Title VII	63
3. Have Made Changes in Selection Procedures for	
EEOC Reasons:	60
in testing procedures	39
in revised job qualifications	31
in application forms	20
in recruiting techniques	19
4. Have Instituted Special Recruiting Programs:	
for all minority workers	69
for minorities in professional/managerial positions	58
5. Have Instituted Programs to Insure EEO Policies	
are Implemented	95
communications on EEO policy	95
follow-up personnel or EEO office	85
training sessions on EEO	67
periodic publications of EEO results	48
EEO achievements included in performance appraisals	33
6. Have Instituted Special Training Programs	
for entry-level jobs	16
for upgrading	24
for management positions	16

Source: Bureau of National Affairs Personnel Policies Forum, *Equal Employment Opportunity: Programs and Results,* PPF Survey No. 112, March 1976 *(lines 1–2;* table 9, p. 15; *line 3:* table 3, p. 4; *line 4:* table 1, p. 9; *line 5:* table 6, p. 9; *line 6:* table 5, p. 8).

TABLE 9
GIFTS BY CORPORATIONS AND PRIVATE INDIVIDUALS, 1929 AND 1959

	$ million		% GNP	
	1929	1959	1929	1959
Gifts by business corporations— tax deductible:	32	482	.03	.10
Total private giving:	2,221	14,930	2.13	3.09

Source: Frank G. Dickinson, *The Changing Position of Philanthropy in the American Economy,* National Bureau of Economic Research, Columbia University Press (1970).

Figure 1
Employment Distribution, 1947-1978

Percentage White-Collar

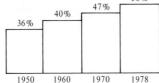

Percentage Professional

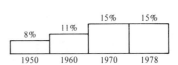

Percentage of Nonagricultural Work Force in South and Southwest

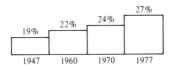

Percentage Government of Total Employment

Sources: Data for 1950-70 white-collar and professional employment from U.S. Bureau of Census 1975, p. 139; for 1978 white-collar and professional employment from Bureau of Labor Statistics 1979a pp.172, 174; government data from Bureau of Labor Statistics 1979c table 50 with the total employment from table 1, regional data from table 52, with total nonagricultural employment from table 42. South and Southwest defined as regions IV and VI and Arizona and Nevada from region IX. See table 52, p. 159 for precise definition of regions.

Figure 2
Fractions of Work Force, 1947-1977

Percentage Female

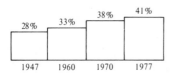

Percentage Less Than 35 Years Old

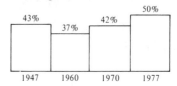

Percentage College Graduates

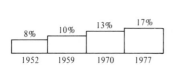

Percentage High School
Graduates or More

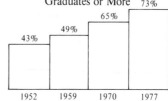

Labor Force Participation of Workers

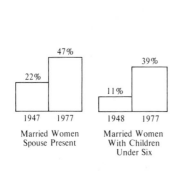

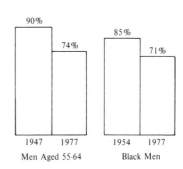

Source: Bureau of Labor Statistics 1979c, table 1 (percentage female), table 3 (age data), table 4 (male participation rate), table 12 (education data) and table 4 (female participation rate).

176

REFERENCES

1. Thomas K. McCraw, "Louis D. Brandeis and the 'Curse of Bigness': Esthetics over Economics," a paper delivered at Public Policy History Conference at Harvard Business School, 24 and 25 October, 1980, p. 32.

2. Richard E. Caves, "The Structure of Industry" in Martin Feldstein (ed.), *The American Economy in Transition*, University of Chicago Press (1980), p. 511.

3. Richard B. Freeman, "The Evolution of the American Labor Market, 1948–80" in Feldstein (ed.), *The American Economy in Transition*, p. 353.

4. The following section has depended largely on Alfred D. Chandler's *The Visible Hand*, Harvard University Press (1977), for historical data.

5. E. Digby Baltzell, *Puritan Boston and Quaker Philadelphia*, Free Press (1979), pp. 220f. Cf *V.H.*, p. 59.

6. Robert Lenzner, Boston's Money Managers, Boston Globe 1972 (supplement).

7. Reprinted from *The Visible Hand*, p. 102.

8. Chandler, op.cit., pp. 237–8, notes that mass retailing was a notable exception to this pattern, and that in that industry top management remained in the control of the founding family for a very long time.

9. Frederick Winslow Taylor, *Hearings Before the Special Committee of the House of Representatives to Investigate the Taylor and Other Systems of Shop Management Under the Authority of House Resolution 90* (1912), III, 1377–1508.

10. Melvin T. Copeland, *And Mark an Era*, (Little, Brown and Co. (1958), p. 16.

11. The Amos Tuck School of Business Administration at Dartmouth College is older (founded in 1900), but its original program was partially undergraduate in nature.

12. Dean Edwin Francis Gay, Harvard Business School "Preliminary Announcement," April 22, 1908.

13. Taylor subsequently served on the Harvard faculty.

14. William Lawrence, *Memories of a Happy Life*, Houghton Mifflin (1972), pp. 420f.

15. 1981–82 *Guide to Graduate Management Education;* financial aid programs support diversity as well: there are now many foundations which actively recruit students to qualify for their loans, and under one federal program an MBA student may borrow up to $25,000 to complete his or her professional education.

16. The exact extent and nature of the discrepancies (i.e. a comparison of technical background etc.) has not been explored.

17. For sixties graduates and past readers of *Ramparts* read "conglomerates."

18. Rosabeth Moss Kanter, "Work in America," *A New America?*, ed. Stephen R. Graubard, W.W. Norton (1978), pp. 60f.

19. Raymond B. Fosdick, *The Story of the Rockefeller Foundation*, Harper Brothers (1952), p. 19.

20. Clarence C. Walton, *Corporate Social Responsiveness*, Wadsworth Publishing Co. Inc. (1967), p. 50.

21. F. Emerson Andrews, *Corporation Giving*, Russel Sage Foundation, (1952), p. 15.

22. Frank G. Dickinson, *The Changing Position of Philanthropy in the American Economy*, National Bureau of Economic Research, Columbia University Press (1970).

23. Ibid.

24. Kanter, p. 50.
25. Reprinted in *The Harbus News*, XLL, 20 September 8, 1981.
26. Ibid.

SOURCES FOR THE TABLES AND FIGURES

A. TABLES

1. Richard E. Caves, "The Structure of Industry" in Martin Feldstein (ed.), *The American Economy in Transition*, University of Chicago Press (1980), p. 504.
2. Ibid., p. 509.
3. Richard B. Freeman, "The Evolution of the American Labor Market, 1948–80" in Feldstein (ed.), *The American Economy in Transition*, p. 352.
4. Ibid., p. 354.
5. Ibid., p. 378.
6. Ibid., p. 365.
7. Ibid., p. 382.
8. Ibid., p. 377.

B. FIGURES

1. Ibid., p. 364.
2. Ibid., p. 358.

Equality in Everyday Life

Richard John Neuhaus

EVERYDAY LIFE is disaggregating. It happens in the plural of everyday lives. In fact, the term "everyday life" may mislead if it is implied that everyday life is the aggregate of everyday lives. There is no "it" about everyday life, there are only myriad actors acting. We are inclined to assume that the significance of an observation—whether about equality, sexuality or redheaded-ness—is keyed to its level of generalization. That is understandable, believing as we do that significance is somehow related to truth and that truth is generally, even universally, true. The bias in intellectual discussion is to move as quickly as possible from the particular to the general. The concept of research supposes that the particular is for the sake of the general. The generalization—rule, principle, theory, hypothesis—is the payoff that justifies bothering with the particular. All of the above is a generalization. It is a generalization that is a traitor to its class, since it urges us to attend to the particular. Discussions of subjects as potentially ethereal as "equality" tend to become a trade in generalities.

Among educated people it is deemed more important to know a general theory about behavior than a specific instance of behaving. Otherwise there is little point in being educated, since any and everybody's life is filled with specific instances. The appeal from ideas to experience, from the theoretical to the practical, is the frequent ploy of anti-intellectuals. Better prepared intellectuals, however, have anticipated the ploy. They nurture a robust skepticism toward generalizations and are ever eager to check

179

them out against "the evidence." As admirable as this scientific posture may be, it still falls short of what is intended by an everyday life consideration of human behavior and attitudes. Specifics are not mere fodder for the statement of general truths; cumulative evidence conceals particular instances; the whole may not be greater than, but may simply distort, the sum of its parts.

Specific happenings are always unequal. Were that not so, they would be identical and therefore not specific. It follows that an everyday life reflection on equality is substantively different from what is ordinarily meant by survey research. Such a reflection assumes the inequality of specifics. The truth about a thing— about attitudes and behavior with respect to equality, for example—may be disclosed in the rare, or even in the eccentric, moment. For instance, how one really feels about one's marriage or life's work may be revealed in a fugitive remark or gesture never to be repeated. Survey research is premised upon the design of generalized responses into which specifics are to be fitted, always leaving a loophole of "none of the above." As useful as such research can be, most people, when really pressed on matters that matter to them, turn out to live the most important dimensions of their lives in "none of the above."

An everyday life approach to equality is not a substitute for any other kind of approach to the subject. It is short on scientific controls and in that respect more accurately reflects the human behavior we would understand. The generalizations that emerge from everyday observation are of necessity incomplete and in part idiosyncratic. Whether we think these characteristics are flaws or virtues depends upon the interests of our discipline, our disposition toward uncertainty and, most probably, on how we think the world works. An everyday life study has a heuristic value at least. Pointing out this and then the other thing about how people act and talk about equality, it suggests the specifics which disclose a truth, if not the truth, about the matter. The suggestion is not falsifiable and therefore is not verifiable in any rigorous sense of the term. It is enough that it be suggestive—informing and tempering alternative approaches and, most important, inviting others to attend to specifics in thinking about equality in American life.

The first section of this chapter deals with popular ideas about equality as they relate to various social policies and proposals. The second addresses the acting out of equalities and inequalities in American "manners." In the first section we examine everyday attitudes and behavior which connect with the distribution of wealth, notions of opportunity, and conflicting views of what should be done for or about "the poor." This section concludes by underscoring reasons for the disjunction between some traditional social policies and everyday attitudes about equality. The second section focuses less on wealth and more on status, especially as the latter bears on "regions of social performance" (Goffman). Here we look at such sundry phenomena as forms of address, occupational interactions, and basic distinctions such as that between children and adults. The suggestion throughout is that equality is essentially a moral idea that is both imprecise and pervasive in American life. It is more clearly related to the dignity of persons than to the design of policies. The idea of equality does not lend itself readily to rational application, it is of limited utility as an explanatory concept for understanding everyday behavior, and yet it cannot be avoided, for it appears to affect everything.

Imagining America is Peter Conrad's account of how British visitors have perceived America, from Charles Dickens to Aldous Huxley. Noting the often contradictory perceptions, Conrad writes, "In America's vast emptiness (which John Locke likened to the amiably receptive infantile mind) there are truths to sustain any fiction." We may question in what ways America is or is not empty, but on American attitudes toward equality, as toward most anything else, there are many truths to be told—some of them complementary and some in conflict. This is even more the case when we disaggregate everyday life, recognizing that we all live in specific groupings and only marginally in societal summations. "I'm as good as you are!" and its corollary, "You're as good as I am" (usually without the exclamation mark) take on quite different meanings in different contexts.

"I'm as good as you are!" is a fundamental, if somewhat aggressive, egalitarian proposition. When stated so baldly, the proposition has probably been thrown into doubt. Children typically put it that way. We are embarrassed for adults who feel the need to be so direct. As we were embarrassed for Richard Nixon when he declared, "Your president is not a crook." It ought not have to be said. The proposition that I'm as good as you are or as good as anyone else is, when asserted by sensible people, sharply qualified relative to anything I may be good for or good at. I am not good for a million dollars, as some people are, and I'm not good at tennis, as some people are. "I'm as good as you are!" is not then a descriptive or functional statement, it is not a principle upon which it is proposed that society should be reorganized; it is a statement of belief. The belief is that I am entitled to some basic acknowledgment of my worth "as a person."

The acknowledgment must be at a high enough level to entangle others in a substantial degree of accountability to me. That logically requires a measure of mutual entitlement and account-ability, although, human nature being as it is, that logical extension is somewhat muted in popular culture. In the operative values of American society, it might be argued, the belief is not simply that we are all equal in the sense that all of us are entitled. It is not simply, as the social contract theorists would have it, that we strike a deal about mutual obligations. "I'm as good as you are!" is not true because it is agreed upon, it is agreed upon because it is thought to be true. Stripped of "incidentals"—such as wealth, power, status and sexual prowess—we really are equal. We are equal before God, say some, or before the judgment of history, or before the law, say others. This is a key part of the American creed. That creed is sometimes called the civil religion or the public piety of American life. G. K. Chesterton's observation that America is a nation with the soul of a church means that our public discourse is marked by a certain moral pretension. Moral pretension is closely related to hypocrisy. As one preacher has put it, the aim is to get the hypocrites off the street and into the church where they belong. Most Americans do not have to be recruited to the church of egalitarian faith. They were born there.

To be sure, in everyday life we do not ordinarily relate to one another in terms of absolute worth, stripped of the incidentals of whether someone is good for a million dollars or good at tennis. Similarly, the precepts affirmed in church and synagogue are somewhat battered during the course of the week. But the egalitarian proposition is our sabbath faith, the source of aspira-tion and, more frequently, of bad conscience. Somehow, it is suggested, everday life should approximate the egalitarian ideal. More modestly, everyday life should not egregiously violate the suspected truth that ultimately, perhaps metaphysically, we are equal. The Declaration of Independence and its confidence in "Nature and Nature's God" may not be self-evident to many today, but it seems that most Americans still believe, or want to believe, in a transcendently grounded equality of the human condition.

Among those who have combined attention to specifics with brilliant generalization, few, if any, equal Alexis de Tocqueville's observations of American life. 150 years ago he underscored the connections between religion and civil values such as equality and liberty. Among Americans, he noted, religion "must be regarded as the first of their political institutions." "It may fairly be be-lieved," he acknowledged, "that a certain number of Americans pursue a peculiar form of worship from habit more than from conviction. In the United States the sovereign authority is religious, and consequently hypocrisy must be common." This hypocrisy, or at least this disharmony, about the equality we profess and the inequalities we practice continues to make the subject of equality such a vexing moral issue in American life.

Religion in American life today is institutionally much stronger than it was when Tocqueville wrote. All indices suggest that church membership and participation in religious activities are much more pervasive now than then. And yet it may be questioned whether religion is today the "political institution" that it was in the 1830s. The Puritan consensus which then provided a sovereign public ethic has been shattered, and religion has largely receded into the privatism of our society's moral cacophony, which we style pluralism. There is today, in Daniel Bell's terminology, a sharper disjunction between religiously-based belief in equality and everyday experience. There has also been significant change in economic realities, or at least in the perception of those realities. Tocqueville typically and confidently spoke of "equality of condition" as being characteristic of American society. Both great wealth and severe poverty he viewed as being so deviant as to be worthy of only passing notice. At least among those who write about American life, that is not the characteristic perception today.

As religion has been privatized, so the notion of equality has tended to lose its empirical and economic referents. Equality has tended to be spiritualized and psychologized into notions of personal dignity and potential for self-fulfillment. Among those who would translate belief in equality into social policy, the notion has been secularized in a variety of socialist or quasi-socialist proposals. And yet it is still the case that language about equality is unmistakably moral language; and it is still, perhaps increasingly, the case that moral language is for the great majority of Americans inextricably tied to religious faith.

Another difference today is that equality is no longer related to belief in a great moral cause. In Tocqueville's America that cause was democracy. "The gradual development of the principle of equality is a providential fact. It has all the chief characteristics of such a fact: it is universal, it is durable, it constantly eludes all human interference, and all events as well as all men contribute to its progress . . . Can it be believed that the democracy which has overthrown the feudal system and vanquished kings will retreat before tradesmen and capitalists?" Yes, it can be believed and is in fact today very widely believed. Not only in the jeremiads of the Robert Heilbroners but also in popular culture there seems to be little confidence in the universal prospects of democracy.

The language of equality speaks no longer of the motor force of great and promising historical change. There are no doubt a number of reasons for this. 150 years later we have been sobered by the perverse egalitarianism of the Gulag Archipelago. (Although it should be noted that Tocqueville had criticized most severely a similar perversion in the French Revolution.) Then there is the more widely perceived disparity between rich and poor and a sharp division of opinion over whether that disparity can be or should be challenged. In addition, the privatization of religious belief which has transferred equality, as an article of faith, from the realm of public polity to that of personal satisfaction.

In everday American life now, it might be argued, the notion of equality is not as vibrant as it appeared to Tocqueville. While there are a few whose belief in equality mandates a radical reordering of society, popular opinion would seem to side with the "equality of opportunity" rather than the "equality of condition" argument. And equality of opportunity is not generally advocated in terms of a moral ideal in the service of a grand movement such as democracy. It is commonly advocated less in moral than in instrumental terms, the main point being that equal opportunity facilitates prosperity and attendant personal satisfactions. Another and perhaps more common occasion for talk about equality is related to entitlement. Language about equality has become the language of rights, injury and grievance, the language of complaint against supposedly unfair treatment. Disconnected as it is from a compelling vision of world-historical change, it is little wonder that everyday reference to equality is now less vibrant and less ennobling. The idea of equality does not fare well when forced to stand on its own.

It may be objected that the above is too dour a picture of the current status of equality as an idea in American life. After all, have not the proponents of equality of opportunity linked the idea of equality to a larger notion of liberty? They have gone farther than linking the two concepts, they have made them functionally interchangeable: to have equality of opportunity is to be free, and to be free is to have equality of opportunity. In this way, it might be argued, the disjunction is not so severe as was suggested; equality is still in the service, as Tocqueville thought, of an ennobling vision. But the conflation of the concepts of equality and freedom does violence to both.

Students of the subject who have tried to keep these concepts clear have traditionally assumed that between equality and liberty there is a tension, perhaps even a trade-off. The more realistic, such as Tocqueville, have suspected that most people, forced to choose, prefer equality. "Political liberty," Tocqueville writes, "bestows exalted pleasures from time to time upon a certain number of citizens. Equality every day confers a number of small enjoyments on every man . . . The pleasures of equality are self-proffered; each of the petty incidents of life seems to occasion them, and in order to taste them, nothing is required but to live." Freedom defined as equality of opportunity, combined with open-ended prospects for prosperity, can indefinitely put off a forcing of the choice between freedom and equality. In this way the choice is not forced but it is badly fudged. That is to say, the concepts of freedom and of equality are reduced to purely economic terms, are devoid of the qualities of virtue and therefore without moral status. The concept of freedom is invoked chiefly in the service of greed and the concept of equality chiefly in the service of grievance. Tocqueville's "providential fact" of democracy, from which freedom and equality received their moral dignity, is no longer in the picture. America as a "lively experiment for the ages" has been reduced to a "system" that offers a good deal.

This debasement of our public language, including the language of equality, is pervasive at all levels of everyday life in America. The collectivists who would force a choice between equality and liberty and the market theorists who would equate equality and freedom are both responsible for that debasement. Indeed those true believers in the market who tend toward libertarianism may be the more culpable in that, by encompassing everything under the rubric of economics, they have precluded moral critique altogether. In this respect, paradoxically, they are the mirror images of their Marxist opponents.

A British business leader recently visiting in the United States summarized what he believes is the difference between the British and the American worker's approach to equality. "If the British worker sees that the boss has something he doesn't have, he concludes that the boss shouldn't have it. The American worker in the same situation determines that he's going to get it too." As a description of the general posture of organized labor in the U.S. and Great Britain, the point is a valid one. From the viewpoint of economic efficiency and civil peace, the American worker's attitude is to be preferred. The British worker's approach engages equality as a moral idea. The specific inequality of possessions between himself and his boss violates his idea of what ought to be, of what is *just*. For the American, the same inequality is a spur to further productivity and acquisition. Pressing this contrast of stereotypes further, it is noted that the British concept of equality is substantive while the American worker's is purely procedural. The second is, in the traditional sense, liberal while what is depicted as the British worker's attitude contains a distinctly unliberal distributive ethic.

The two notions of equality may be equally moral in that both are responsive to the clearly moral notion of what is fair. In the American case, however, the moral notion of fairness has, precisely speaking, little or nothing to do with equality. At least it is unrelated to the distributive ethic appropriate to the idea of equality of condition. If what the boss has is a new Cadillac, the worker might aspire to get one of those. If the thing in question is a twelve-room summer home in East Hampton, such an aspiration is not likely to be compelling. In this sense, the worker is not comparing himself with or competing with the boss. He neither doubts nor protests that once he has gotten the thing that only the boss had before, the boss is still in the position to get other things and thus maintain his relative advantage. The point of reference relevant to the worker's motivation is finally not what the boss has but what he, the worker, had and his chance to improve upon what he had. His attitude is attuned not to the external world of the actual distribution of goods in society but to his subworld of what he believes to be reasonable expectations for improving his condition. In that subworld, the condition of bosses and, probably more forcefully, the condition of peers, are stimulants to continued effort. The issue in the mind of this worker is not equalization at all, it is improvement by whatever definition of improvement he embraces. Were he to protest something as a "moral issue," it would be the violation of fairness in the denial of the chance to pursue that improvement. To be sure, these two workers are ideal types and do not accord exactly with what we encounter in everyday life, but the contrast is nonetheless instructive.

Equality in the sense of reducing or eliminating disparities of material condition is a relatively weak moral passion in American life. That was true in the early 19th century because, if Tocqueville and others are to be credited, the disparities were not conspicuous and, where they did appear, they were thought to be impermanent, with everybody having a more or less equal chance to benefit from the next turn of the wheel of fortune. To the students of equality today, inequalities seem both conspicuous and distressingly permanent. But theirs is a specialized perception and, as often as not, a cultivated discontent with social inequities.

Joan Didion is a non-specialized but extremely acute observer. In *Slouching Toward Bethlehem* she reflects on her early thirties when she was living and working in Manhattan. "At that time making a living seemed a game to me, with arbitrary but quite inflexible rules. And except on a certain kind of winter evening— six-thirty in the Seventies, say, already dark and bitter with a wind off the river, when I would be walking very fast toward a bus and would look in the bright windows of brownstones and see cooks working in clean kitchens and imagine women lighting candles on the floor above and beautiful children being bathed on the floor above that—except on nights like those, I never felt poor; I had the feeling that if I needed money I could always get it. I could write a syndicated column for teenagers under the name 'Debbi Lynn' or I could smuggle gold into India or I could become a $100 call girl, and none of it would matter."

Didion was young then and perhaps not typical in her casual approach to ways to make a dollar, but the above reflection does suggest attitudes typical of everyday life in America. One such attitude is that, while there are rules for "getting ahead," they are somewhat arbitrary and one can elect not to play the game or at least not to play very hard. Finally—in terms of personal worth and fulfillment—"none of it would matter." Arbitrariness, contingency, luck, choice—all of these are the enemies of that *ressentiment* which fuels thought about equality in other societies, and in some sectors of our society. Resentment thrives on the perception of injustice by design.

Most revealing in the Didion quotation, however, is this: "except on nights like those, I never felt poor." One suspects that most Americans have to be reminded to feel poor. In American reminiscences it as a commonplace for people who were poor in their childhood to exclaim upon the fact that they never *felt* poor. This surprisingly frequent assertion in conversation and memoirs can no doubt be explained in many ways. It may be a sop thrown to the presently poor, assuring them that their state is understood and it really isn't so bad; if only they follow the rules, they too will get ahead. Or it may be a sop that the rich offer themselves, assuring themselves that their prosperity has not changed their essential character, which they nostalgically recall from the past. The wit who observed that he'd been poor and he'd been rich and discovered it is better to be rich evokes a chuckle of self-recognition from the prosperous who are uneasy about the obvious.

Tocqueville thought that a certain uneasiness with prosperity was natural in a democracy where "all stations appear doubtful." He remarked that most Americans he met had at one time been poor and, far from hiding it, almost boasted of it as a badge of membership in the fraternity of the common man. Tocqueville implies that the remembrance of poverty may be a way of hedging bets—in a democracy where fortunes rotate so rapidly one may be poor again, and it is reassuring to believe that "none of it would matter." In a culture alleged to be obsessively acquisitive, Americans profess a remarkable insouciance toward wealth. Whether well fed or remembering leaner days, they profess, sincerely or otherwise, to believe that man does not live by bread alone. (In the 1981 Connecticut Mutual Life Report on American Values, 91% of the general public agrees and 6% disagree with the proposition that "it is better to work at a lower paying job that one enjoys than at a higher paying job that is not satisfying." 95% of the religiously most committed agree, as do 94% of female respondents. Whether because they are consoling themselves or because they have in fact acted upon their professed values, 95% of those earning under $12,000 agree while only 90% of those earning above $25,000 agree.)

My childhood was spent in a lumbering and light manufacturing town of 15,000. In a family of ten children in the 1940s we sometimes ate potato soup four evenings in a row because there was no more money for food. We undoubtedly were poor and, yes, we never felt poor. It is a curious phenomenon. Today one of the first things I would say about such a family is that it is poor. Then, although we were frequently told that we could not afford things we wanted, we apparently didn't want them that badly. Certainly there was no sense of being underprivileged and it was never said, nor would it have occurred to us to say, that we were poor. Our friends were, for the most part, drawn from the lower working class. We were well aware that some people were rich. Each day we walked to school through the wealthier East End, which we called, without either resentment or awe, "snob hill." We knew they were rich, but we did not draw the inference that we were poor. There was no articulated class consciousness, no strong sense of them and us. We let them play in our games and, when at age twelve Clark went with his parents to England one summer, that was hardly as worthy of discussion as the summer on the Biesenthal farm and what Susan Panke let us do one afternoon behind the barn.

One resists drawing too idyllic a picture. There were frustrations, fears and hostilities, of course, but not along anything that could remotely be defined as class conflict. In overhearing adult discussions, there were discontents and even anger expressed about things that bosses said or did at work. But in discussions with childhood friends now of how it was then, nobody remembers the suggestion ever being made that there was anything like a systemic injustice in the distribution of wealth in that town. It would seem that more or less the same situation prevails today. Although people are, or feel they are, better off relative to their condition thirty years ago, there is no evidence that the distribution of wealth is more equitable. Of course these people and others with a similar story to tell may be the victims of a massive exercise of false consciousness. But to say they were and are deluding themselves is simply to impose an understanding of their situation that is different from their own. To attend to everyday life means to respect, although not necessarily to agree with, the feel, the texture, and the substance of their self-understanding.

The weakness of equality as a moral passion depends in large part upon the weakness, or even the absence, of a sense of deprivation, especially of deprivation by unjust design. There are several reasons why we then did not think of ourselves as poor. One reason is that there was an onus attached to being poor; poverty was associated with dependence, mismanagement or laziness. At least one supposes that was the case, although I and those with whom I've discussed the matter do not recall that being said. Poverty was not a significant category of understanding. Another reason we did not think of ourselves as poor is that we were aware of others who really were poor. The children in China would love to have that potato soup I didn't finish. More immediately, there were the people in a shack town, which we called "Hollywood," on the edge of town. They were really poor, but, again, poverty was not the category employed in understanding their situation. Their problem, as we understood it, was that they were dirty, unmannerly, not very bright, and frequently dishonest. Some of them too were included in our games and only in the occasional angry taunt were they reminded that they lived in Hollywood. Finally, poverty did not have the feeling of being poor because the future was open; everything seemed quite up for grabs. Whatever the drawbacks in the existing situation, it was not seen as the result of anything systemic, structured or inevitable. Although it was not the subject of much conversation, of course one could be rich, if it mattered that much.

This sense of a changing and malleable world also struck Tocqueville as a characteristic of the democratic ethos. "Continual changes are then every instant occurring under the observations of every man . . . His reverses teach him that none have discovered absolute good; his success stimulates him to the never ending pursuit of it." A sailor told Tocqueville that American ships were built to last only a few years because, given the rate of progress, they would soon be obsolete. "In these words, which fell accidentally, and on a particular subject, from an uninstructed man, I recognize the general and systematic idea upon which a great people direct all their concerns."

This general and systematic idea of progressive change further dissipates the moral power of the notion of equality. Presumably the American ships were in fact unequal to those of England and France in terms of craftsmanship, appointments, and durability. But the American sailor, if these inequalities are pointed out to him, rejoins that the longevity of the European ships is their handicap, they are stuck in the past. Only if the future is not open, only if reality itself is somehow stuck in the past, does such longevity become an advantage. Inequality as a moral passion is strengthened by a frozen time-frame. Outrage and indignation cannot get up a head of steam if the occasion of discontent is seen as momentary and passing. In the large context, this is the criticism of religion's distractions made by Marxists and others. But, short of the question of eternal life, and within the context of everyday life, this notion of transitoriness enervates the revolutionary potential in the idea of equality. Outrage about inequalities requires a still shot of reality, while American life is the first screening of a motion picture at which the audience suspects that the next sequence is, as likely as not, to present a quite different view of things. Morally charged egalitarianism, in order to effect significant change, requires the stationary targets that American life adroitly declines to supply.

A decade and more ago those who desired a radical reconstruction of American life resorted to ingenious explanations for the elusiveness of the villains against whom the forces of change could be mobilized. We heard much about "cooptation" and Herbert Marcuse's notion of "repressive tolerance" gained considerable currency. The absence of a clear design for injustice and inequality, it was argued, merely reveals the subtlety of the designers. The pervasiveness of this injustice was alleged to be such that everybody had to be its victim. Thus we witnessed a competition for victim status, for lowest place in the hierarchy of inequalities. Blacks, women, students, gays were variously identified in revolutionary scenarios as the proletariat.

For a brief time the most privileged were self-identified as the victims. Their manifesto, Charles Reich's *The Greening of America,* was countered by Brigitte and Peter Berger's "The Blueing of America." The latter argued that, if the privileged declined their reserved places in American life, those places would readily be filled by the sons and daughters of blue-collar America. Since the privileged, with few exceptions, have decided it is better to be rich than to be poor, neither recoloration of America has happened. That period of cultural convulsions revealed, however, how weak and indeterminate is the notion of equality in American life. The phantasmagorical manipulation of the idea of equality by certain radicalisms further besmirched, in the popular mind, proposals for the redistribution of wealth, power and status in American society.

At the same time, however, we may be witnessing some more long-lasting changes in attitudes toward equality. For Tocqueville's Americans, the poisonous resentments that accompany conspicuous inequalities were neutralized by an unbounded confidence in an open and promising future. That confidence is challenged and undercut today by sundry economic and ecological theories resulting in a "no-growth" worldview. More ominously, it is countered by the perceived probability of nuclear war. Various surveys suggest that from one-half to two-thirds of high school students in America believe they will die in a nuclear war. Whatever the precise figures, this widespread expectation also has a strong bearing on the idea of equality in everyday life.

At one level, a no-growth worldview suggests the need for an ethic of distributive justice that aims at a more egalitarian America in a more egalitarian world. The imminence of nuclear apocalypse, however, tends to trivialize any such distributive project. In the face of the End Time, all programs of social transformation seem pointless. There are those who would get on with the business of justice, putting nuclear warfare into parentheses, as it were. It may be that there are more who believe that nuclear warfare puts everything else into parentheses. It is a question of what parenthesizes what.

Irving Kristol has written that the loss of belief in eternal life is the most important political fact of the last two centuries. Among millions of Americans, and especially young Americans, involved in the evangelical-fundamentalist revivals, however, there has been no such loss. Indeed the resurgence of apocalypticism, dispensationalism, and millennialism has raised to fever pitch the concern about eternal destiny. The current shape of this concern does not serve Kristol's interest in sustaining the belief that values and historical progress have transcendent consequences. Nor, although it embraces much of the no-growth ideology, does it serve the redistributionists' interest in a more egalitarian society. The message of the electronic church and of Hal Lindsey's *The Late Great Planet Earth* have a quite different import. The message is to get while the getting is good, in the constant and pious awareness that—Joan Didion's phrase but with different intent—it all doesn't matter that much.

These several developments have obvious consequences for the idea of equality, morally and otherwise. Tocqueville's confidence that equality is the engine of world-historical change toward a democratic future is almost never voiced in the communications media, school textbooks, or everyday conversations of either rich or poor. When equality is treated, it is usually in redistributionist terms which suggest that equality must be pursued at the expense of democratic liberty. Neither is the confidence of Tocqueville's sailor in an open future very commonly encountered. The belief that the future is closing, if it is not already closed, has its secular variant in no-growth ideology and its religious variant in apocalypticism that is frequently combined with no-growth ideology. Little wonder then, that in terms of political and economic change, equality is a weak moral passion in American life today. This picture is not changed by the fact that there are those who vigorously expound the merits of equality of opportunity, for, as we have seen, in that advocacy the idea of equality is almost entirely subsumed under the idea of liberty.

Unless people "feel poor" and are outraged by that feeling, the idea of equality is not a potent instrument for redistributionist change. I have suggested that that feeling is not general in our everyday life. But it might be objected that this is not the case among the very poor, for example, the poorest of urban black America. For seventeen years I was pastor of a large congregation of black Americans in the Williamsburg and Bedford-Stuyvestant sections of Brooklyn. Approximately half of the families were partially or entirely on welfare. With respect to acknowledging a feeling of being poor, the situation was not much different from that which prevailed in my childhood town described earlier, although these people of Brooklyn were by objective economic criteria very poor indeed. Their frequent criticism of visiting bishops and politicians who spoke sympathetically of these people as being victims of injustice was that these visitors were condescending to them. "I may be poor but it's none of their business to tell me I'm poor," declared Charlie Williams in a most commonly expressed sentiment. Again, the reasons for this resistance to feeling, or to acknowledging that one feels, poor are no doubt complex. Dr. Martin Luther King understood that complexity, and his themes in the movement for racial justice regularly emphasized that the movement was not grasping for what others have but was proffering to white America the promise of both greater humanity and greater prosperity. (In the view of some, notably a Marxist biographer David Lewis, 1968 marked a turn toward a redistributionist ethic in Dr. King's thought and strategy. That year was to be "The Poor Peoples' Campaign," which was aimed at "rights in life as well as rights in law." It was a campaign Dr. King did not live to lead, and therefore we know neither whether such a turn was envisioned nor what its consequences might have been.)

The case of the very poor, for whom black urban America is the most effective symbol in popular consciousness, is important to a consideration of the moral status of the idea of equality. In fact, in his very popular *More Equality,* Herbert Gans declares that their existence *is* the moral case for egalitarian social policies: "[This book] does not make a moral case for more equality. This case has been made by others . . . Besides, one has only to visit the slums and low-income neighborhoods of this allegedly affluent country to come away with sufficient moral grounds for more equality." One notes that the moral proposal here is not that the poor should have more wealth but the *way in which* the poor should obtain more wealth, namely, through more equality. Gans leaves no doubt that equality means a more "fair" redistribution of the society's goods.

Admittedly, it is a long way from the theories of Herbert Gans and his egalitarian cohorts to attitudes about equality in everyday life, including everyday life among the poor. But the logic employed by Gans is pervasive, if often inarticulate, in our everyday experience when the subject turns to those who are poorer than we. It is reliably reported that in the mid-70s Nelson Rockefeller was addressing a meeting of community leaders in a Southern city and was asked by a clergyman how, in a world of deprivation, he could square his immense wealth with his conscience. In a moment of candor that was not so rare with him, he is said to have replied, "I have always thought that that was the nub of our problem, this damn Judeo-Christain morality that says everything belongs to God and therefore everything belongs to everybody."

In church and synagogue Americans affirm that "the earth is the Lord's and the fulness thereof" (Psalm 24) but few infer from that a program for economic change. Yet Rockefeller was surely right that the radical egalitarianism of biblical faith is a source of a generalized bad conscience. The obligatory mention of the less privileged at the Thanksgiving Day table is significant. It can mean, "There, but for the grace of God, go I" or it can have a somewhat more guilt-tinged implication that the food is ours to eat only by undeserved luck, by pointless fluke, or by virtue of an injustice perpetrated. "The coat in your closet at home belongs to a poor man," declared the late Dorothy Day of Catholic Worker fame, and surprising numbers of the well-to-do responded with rapturous agreement and, in instances so rare as to be dramatic, with their coats.

As a moral idea in everyday life, then, equality suggests not so much a program for change as a spectral presence at the banquet table. In the interaction between religion and civil piety there have been frequent efforts to translate biblical faith into economic theory. The American "social gospel movement" (1870–1930) married a theological understanding of equality to vaguely socialist schemes of a non-Marxist variety. With a much stronger hold on the popular mind, Bruce Barton depicted the Man from Nazareth as history's premier business organizer in *The Man Nobody Knows* (1925). Today in some churches there is a strong emphasis upon "liberation theology," an approach which joins a literalistic reading of the economics of biblical times with a Marxist interpretation of contemporary reality. In reaction to that and similar developments, there are small but significant stirrings aimed at constructing religious legitimations for, even theologies of, capitalism.

But in the religiously-based values of most Americans it is safe to assume that there is a sharp disjunction between their economic behavior and whatever may be biblical directions about justice as equality. For some, this is because an apocalyptic expectation relegates economics, along with everything else, to being of only momentary importance (which in no way discourages them from raking in all the blessings available at the moment). For others, the disjunction between economic behavior and biblical precept is understood as a necessary consequence of the radical evil of human nature and of history short of the Messianic Age. In this more classic vein, utopian communities and religious orders premised upon radical egalitarianism are a matter of "special vocation" for those called to such ventures. Such communities are understood not primarily as models for social reconstruction but as prophetic reminders of the limitations of social life prior to history's ultimate consummation. In 1982 millions of Christians celebrated the 800th anniversary of the birth of St. Francis of Assisi. Innumerable homilies held up for admiration his rigorous abandonment of wealth in identifying with the poorest of the poor. For admiration, and sometimes for individual imitation, but, with some exceptions, Francis' understanding of equality is not proposed as a design for a more just society.

Equality as a moral idea, then, results in a bad conscience for those who agree with—although they might not express it so directly—Nelson Rockefeller that the Judeo-Christian ethic is out of synch with the real world. For such people, it is a bothersome ideal, and one has done one's duty by it in the ritual acknowledgment of undeservedness at the Thanksgiving Day table. Otherwise, in the real world, the public morality (whether religious or secular) is adequately summed up in Samuel Gompers' call for "More!" For more thoughtful believers, the idea of equality is an ultimate promise, a utopian prospect, that illuminates the limits of the present historical moment. In this view, equality is infrequently actualized in lives and communities of special vocation and is valued as a caution against the cardinal sin of greed, but it is not taken as a guide for generalized social policy. Thus it is that, in the religiously-based everyday values of the American people, equality ends up as a weak moral passion with little effect upon social and economic change.

Although the idea of equality does not fuel movements for major social change, it may nonetheless be a major factor influencing the way in which people relate to others, especially to those who are less fortunate. We have noted Herbert Gans' argument that the moral argument for more equality is the existence of the very poor. In that view, poverty is the problem and more equality is the solution. It is worth considering, however, whether that proposition should not be turned around. That is, we begin with a sense of equality that obligates us to respond in some way to the needs of others. In that case, equality is not the proposed solution but the premise underlying a sense of obligation to seek solutions for, or at least ameliorations of, the problems afflicting others. A traditional term reflecting this sense of equality is compassion— the capacity to feel and suffer with others, recognizing that "we" and "they" are mysteriously joined in a web of common moral accountability. And the traditional term for the behavior produced by compassion is charity. Charity is out of fashion in many circles today because it implies condescension which, in turn, makes inequalities explicit. Condescension suggests superiors and subordinates in a hierarchy of privilege and, perhaps, of virtue. Among those who professionally call us to concern for the poor, the preferred and more politicized phrases are variations on "identification" and "solidarity" with the poor. But, as with charity, the core assumption is that there is an ontological equality, a basic identity built into the human condition, which binds rich and poor together.

The charity of the well-to-do used to be called, and sometimes still is called, philanthropy. Philanthropy may be motivated by reasons both noble and base, both altruistic and self-aggrandizing. Whatever the necessary hypocrisies involved, the significant thing is that philanthropy is intended to be perceived as noble and altruistic. The hoped-for perception that prompts the act reinforces the intuition that we, rich and poor, are embroiled in a common web of moral responsibility. The piety that rationalizes the philanthropy of the Carnegies, Mellons, and their contemporary counterparts is one or another variation on Luke 12: "From him to whom much has been given much will be required."

There are significant differences between those who speak of charity and philanthropy and those who speak of identification and solidarity with the poor. The latter terms usually reflect a political interest in creating a more equal (i.e. more just) world. Equality is a project that is in their political, and perhaps their economic, interest to advance. Combined with this is the fact that, if people of this viewpoint are rich, they tend to view their wealth as an injustice secured at the price of depriving others. For those who think in terms of charity and philanthropy, on the other hand, equality is not a project. The equality of the human condition is a troublesome given that is not in their interests, except as they are interested in being and being perceived as moral actors. On balance, they tend to view their good fortune as earned; it is not incompatible with their understanding of justice nor has it closed the door to similar good fortune for others. In terms of their own interests, compassion is not a program for desired change but an inconvenience. Equality—membership in a community of shared mortality and accountability—is an idea of minimum utility. Thus their acting upon that moral sentiment—a sentiment which they have every self-interested reason to deny—is the more precisely a moral act. Again, it is no less a moral act because they may be chiefly interested in being perceived as moral actors. That hoped-for perception itself depends upon a prevailing morality which judges certain actions to be moral. Thus hypocrisy in motivation produces morality in consequence.

Most Americans, it is reasonable to believe, belong to the charity rather than to the solidarity school of response to the poor. Inequalities are not perceived as evil nor is economic equality a project that commands their allegiance. The intuition of an ontological or cosmic equality of the human condition does compel concern for the poor. The level of popular support for ways to meet the needs of the poor fluctuates. Sometimes the ways supported are very ambitious, as in the Johnson Administration's war on poverty, and sometimes they aim at maintaining only a minimal level of decency, as in the current administration's "safety net."

But there is little to suggest that at any time there has been widespread popular support for equality as the goal of social policy.

Egalitarian theorists and social planners who embraced the redistribution of wealth as a goal of social policy today bemoan the abandonment of that principle. But, since the redistributionist principle was never popularly accepted, it cannot be popularly abandoned. In the past, redistributionist programs were sold not in the name of egalitarianism but in the name of "meeting human needs." It could be argued that "more equality" and "meeting human needs" end up being the same thing. That is, if you give someone with no money a welfare check, then that person is more equal to others who have money than he was before. The fact is, however, that the idea of equality did not elicit support for the giving of the welfare check. The popular rejection of mixing the idea of equality with the idea of meeting human needs was manifested in the reaction to George McGovern's much misunderstood one-thousand-dollar-per-person proposal in the presidential campaign of 1972.

Popular disillusionment with redistributionist programs today has many sources. One is the growing perception that the programs did not in fact seem to better the condition of those they were intended to benefit. Another source is the perception that the programs did mainly benefit government planners and administrators whose "needs" have no compelling claim on the popular conscience. But perhaps most damaging to popular support for such programs is the perception that they are in fact redistributionist, that their goal is an equality that would treat unequals equally and is therefore unfair. In this respect the American temper is in tune with the classic understanding of equality advanced by, for example, Aristotle. For Aristotle, the question of injustice comes up when unequals are treated equally, when the distinctions between virtue and vice, industry and laziness, the excellent and the base, are obliterated. A society that distributes rewards in indifference to these distinctions is, in this view, an unjust society.

In everday American life, then, equality continues to be a vibrant idea. But the equality affirmed is an equality of the human condition that is to be recognized, not an equality of economic or social result that is to be achieved. A well-dressed mother outside Bloomingdale's reprimands her five year old boy for laughing at one of the grotesquely costumed "bag ladies" of New York's streets. "You just remember that she's as good as you are!" she tells her son. Because she does not want her son to turn into a snob.

Because she wants her son to share her intuition that we are all, in John Donne's phrase, "a part of the main." Obviously *not* because she intends or thinks she should intend to equalize conditions between herself and the bag lady in question.

As Tocqueville said, in a democracy based upon the intuition of equality "all stations appear doubtful." In this kind of ethos privilege is uneasy. The cultural context of our behavior is haunted by the *anawim* of the Hebrew Bible, the "wretched of the earth" who are, all appearances to the contrary, God's favorites. The reversal of fortunes in the parable of Lazarus and Dives keeps us on edge. Every survey indicates that Americans think of themselves as a good, generous and caring people. And that self-understanding is born out by the billions of dollars given every year through religious and other agencies. That no man is an island is a poetic sentiment but it is also affirmed as a truth on which millions act in their everyday lives. This is the core idea of equality that is relevant to the sharing of resources in our society. Curiously, these same millions react very negatively when that intuition of equality is proposed as a political program for economic change. This demonstrates, according to some, that the professed belief in equality is insincere. To which it may be countered that sincerity is not the question; that this idea of equality is sincerely held but that it is also sincerely held that the idea cannot be politicized without distorting it.

Charity, noblesse oblige, philanthropy—these perceived virtues are based upon an idea of ontological equality while assuming inequalities in empirical fact. One might infer from that statement that it is believed that inequality is the evil necessary for the exercise of the good that is charity. But seldom, if ever, in American life does one encounter the proposition that inequalities should be maintained in order to facilitate the practice of kindness toward the less fortunate. Rather, inequalities are seen to be the inescapable consequence of uneven endowment and effort. The world is out of whack. Or, as it is commonly agreed among Americans, "Life is unfair." Charity aimed at "meeting the needs of the poor" is designed not to rectify but to temper inequalities. In a world out of whack, charity is a practical tribute to the moral idea of equality that is taken to be ultimately true.

"The smallest he that is in England has a life to live as does the greatest he." This classic assertion by Colonel Rainborough during the Cromwellian era reflects the popular American belief in democracy today. "All men are created equal" is its formulation in our civil creed. To the black poor who are aspiring to be less poor, Jesse Jackson puts it this way: "Nobody is a nobody!" Rainborough did not assume that redistribution would obliterate the difference between small he's and great he's. He did assert that the smallest he had rights, had claims to assert, which the greatest he was obligated to respect. Similarly, Jefferson's and Jackson's phrases assume continued differentiation in the possession of social goods. High school sophomores and some adult social scientists delight in pointing out the naiveté of saying that all are created equal, but Jefferson was well aware that his assertion flies in the face of observable social fact. His allusion to Nature and Nature's God is a moral or metaphysical appeal beyond empirical reality.

As a moral statement, some have inferred from the civil creed an imperative to redesign society, bringing it into line with the ultimate equality that the creed affirms. In his own way of life and in his writings, there is no evidence that this was Jefferson's intent. William Ryan, one of the most strident egalitarian theorists today, writes in *Equality* that the fulfillment of the American promise requires that we move away from the concept of "fair play" to that of "fair shares." Yet he recognizes, to his consternation, that, almost without exception, the popular American notion of equality comes down to the side of fair play. Ryan and those of similar mind are impatient and distrustful with respect to moral beliefs. They believe that in their more or less classless society justice will no longer be dependent upon the weak reed of morality. In such a society morality will be replaced by power, since each individual will possess the "fair share" of power—economic and political—to protect his rights. Equality as a moral concept exists in tension with, and aimed to temper, the unequal distribution of social goods. Equality as a social program aims at making morality dispensable. Because Americans, with few exceptions, choose fair play over fair shares, equality remains a moral concept, which is both the weakness and the strength of the idea of equality in everyday life.

If fair play for subordinates is dependent upon morality (and upon the reflection of morality in law), it is of course fragile. That fragility is most dramatically illustrated in the tortuous history of slavery and racial discrimination in America. It might be argued that before the emergence of democratic equality there were other and better ways in which the rights of the poor were protected. John Calhoun and other defenders of the South's "peculiar institution" contended, with some persuasive force, that the lot of slaves would be worsened by liberty. Tocqueville notes that in pre-democratic aristocratic institutions the weak and powerful were "bound to one another by close political ties." "Although the noble held himself to be a different nature from that of his serfs, he nevertheless held that his duty and his honor required him to defend, at the risk of his own life, those who dwelt upon his domains." The interdependence of classes and castes in pre-democratic social orders made mutual protection mandatory. In feudalism the idea of equality was neither present nor necessary; an understanding of mutual interests produced a minimal security also for the poor. In socialist projections of a classless society, the moral idea of equality is not necessary since it will be assured in social fact by a "just" distribution of power. Feudalism and a classless society are alike in that they dispense with dependence upon morality in relations between unequals; in feudalism because such relations are determined by mutual interests; in the classless society because, by definition, the gap between unequals is slight or nonexistent. In a society based upon democratic equality, a heavy burden is placed upon moral belief and its expression in public virtue. Unless it is actually believed that nobody is a nobody, there is little to prevent us from treating others as nobodies.

One could contend that in a society marked by democratic equality there are, as in past aristocratic and projected classless societies, built-in mechanisms to sustain fellow-feelings and compassion for the less fortunate. If that is true, the dependence upon morality and virtue would not be as heavy as has been suggested here. Tocqueville made this argument at points in his *Democracy*: "When all the ranks of a community are nearly equal, as all men think and feel in nearly the same manner, each then may judge in a moment of the sensations of all the others . . . Imagination puts him in their place; something like a personal feeling is mingled with his pity and makes himself suffer while the body of his fellow creature is in torture. . . [Thus] although the Americans have in a manner reduced selfishness to a social and philosophical theory, they are nevertheless extremely open to compassion."

It is hard to repress the suspicion that, in describing Americans as a compassionate and caring people, Tocqueville gives a somewhat idealistic picture of the way it was then. Now, in any case, America is hardly a community in which "all the ranks are nearly equal." Commuters to and from any major city and everybody who is on the receiving end of the communications media are reminded daily of the gross inequities in American life. Of course, if we limit "community" to smaller towns or to mediating structures within larger conglomerates, the dynamics Tocqueville describes may still obtain. But that is not very interesting, since most people care about "their own kind." Tocqueville presumed to be describing something like "the American character" nationally considered. And, especially in the last half century, the question of attitudes toward the poor which engage values such as equality is located at the national level. This development is both a cause and a reflection of the increasing role of the federal government in welfare policies.

At the same time, Tocqueville's suggested connection between fellow-feeling and compassion continues to be relevant to both public policy and everyday life. In an early 1970s episode of "All in the Family," Archie Bunker reflects on the riotous protests of poor blacks. "What's the big deal about being poor?" Archie asks. "I was poor. Everybody was poor one time." The gravamen of that episode, predictably, was the education of poor Archie to understand that the black plight is utterly unique, completely unlike any experience he may have had of being poor. Archie was of course using his original argument to counter black demands for special treatment such as reparations. Such demands seemed to Archie unfair, violating his sense of equal treatment. By persuading the Archie Bunkers of America that their experience of poverty has little or nothing in common with the black experience, the program intended to teach, Americans will recognize the justice of, or at least will be more willing to accept, special treatment for blacks.

Persuading the Archie Bunkers of this proposition, however, might have quite unforeseen consequences. The proposition that blacks (or Puerto Ricans, or Chicanos, or Native Americans, or any other group that has not successfully emulated the majority migration from poverty) are in a situation that is utterly singular shatters Tocqueville's asserted linkage between the fellow-feeling and compassion that results from a recognition of a basic *equality of experience*. The consequence is that compassion for the poor has to rest its full weight upon equality as a moral idea rather than as a shared experience. In social policy it is not wise to put so much strain upon a moral concept that is in tension with, if it does not conflict with, self-interest and everyday perception of reality. To the extent that the Archie Bunkers are convinced that the black experience is utterly alien to their own, some of them may be opened to the need for special treatment not accorded to other groups in society. With many more, one suspects, the cords of fellow-feeling will break. Having been persuaded that the poor are completely "other," they will be quite ready to wash their hands of any further concern for them.

In a society of great inequalities, the claim of the poor upon the non-poor is tenuous. As in feudalism, the claim is reinforced by patterns of interdependence, but only to a small extent. Most taxpaying Americans, it may be assumed, would not think it a bad thing if ten million or more poor people on welfare painlessly disappeared. Unlike the serfs, they are not needed by any plausible definition of need. The attractiveness of such a prospect is regularly made explicit in pro-abortion arguments based upon reducing the number of people on the welfare rolls. As in a putative classless society, the claim of the poor upon the non-poor is reinforced by countervailing power, but, again, only to a small extent. Economically and in politics, both electoral and non-electoral, the power of the very poor can be dismissed with little risk. There is always the power of disruption and insurrection, but, for better or for worse, a repeat of the riotous protests of the 1960s today would not likely meet with the relative tolerance they encountered then. This brings us back to the proposition, then, that the claim of the poor is overwhelmingly, even dangerously, based upon the moral idea of equality. This moral idea is derived from religious belief in our common status as creatures accountable to a Creator and is strengthened powerfully by cultural images, such as that of the Holocaust, which underscore the view that nobody is expendable. Law and behavior based upon the moral idea of equality are enhanced also by the fellow-feeling of those Archie Bunkers who persist in believing that the experience of the poor is not so entirely unlike their own.

For the idea of equality to function in humane relations between the poor and the not-so-poor, it is necessary to sustain the notion of a shared human nature in a commonality of experience. Commonality of experience does not mean that experiences are identical. President Johnson's famed speech at Howard University was in accord with the everyday American understanding of equality. In that speech, Johnson noted that blacks had been historically handicapped at the starting line of life's race. Compensatory action was required, he said, in order to assure a fair start in competition. In this sense, Johnson was not challenging but reinforcing the notion of equality as fair play. With good reason those who advance the idea of fair shares against the idea of fair play are very cool to the metaphor employed by Johnson, a metaphor which informed the Great Society programs when they enjoyed popular support.

"Of all the political effects produced by the equality of conditions," Toqueville wrote, "this love of independence is the first to strike the observing and to alarm the timid." The image of the self-made man is regularly denigrated in social planning circles as a "myth" that must be destroyed in order to address the issues of greater economic equality. All the education in contempt for this notion, however, seems to have had little effect on the stubborn popular belief that, once given a reasonable chance for advancement, people are independent actors who are—allowing for luck both good and bad—responsible for their lives. Exceptions are readily made with respect to individual persons, or with respect to groups that share a debilitating handicap. The most long-standing and non-controversial instance of the latter is the many compensatory programs to benefit the blind. But there is little patience with individuals who claim a right to such compensatory treatment by virtue of belonging to an ethnic or racial grouping.

Interestingly, those theorists who are eager to give blacks, for example, a scientific basis for claiming handicap status by virtue of genetic or hereditary disability are condemned as racist and anti-poor. At this point the idea of equality as fair play creates a quandary for public attitudes and social policy. People of good intention are frustrated in trying to respond to a collective claim to an exemption from the rules of fair play when the group making the claim rejects any collective basis for the claim. In the case of blacks, the reference to slavery as the grounds for victim status inevitably wears thinner with the passing of generations. Slavery as the cause of failure is also made less plausible by the increasing instances of blacks who are "running the race" with conspicuous success. The result is that accepted notions of equality have created a mare's nest of contradictions from which we are not likely to be extricated any time soon. Liberals who want to exempt the black "underclass" from fair play equality are unable or unwilling to give believable grounds for such an exemption. While those who assert alleged grounds for a group disability are viewed as hostile to the interests of the group in question. The unreconstructed Archie Bunkers are simply unwilling to grant such a group exemption, and it may be that their "unenlightened" view represents the best hope for the participation of the poor in equality as fair play. To paraphrase Tocqueville, a high degree of perceived equality of condition is required for the functioning of the moral belief in equality of opportunity.

Terms such as "the deserving poor" and "the truly needy" are frequently condemned as reactionary. If the analysis offered here has any merit, however, discriminating among those who make special claims upon the society is a humane and indeed liberal necessity. If no distinction is made between degrees of need and reasons for need, the claims for exemption become so massive as to invite popular rejection. More important, such an undifferentiated claim undercuts the belief in equality as fair play, a belief which is crucial to the prospects of the poor in particular. As Durkheim masterfully argued, deviance plays the important function of justifying and upholding the normative validity of non-deviant behavior. Without a more or less commonly understood notion of deviance from the idea of equality as fair play—whether the deviance be deliberate or the result of undeserved handicap—the idea of equality as fair play cannot be maintained.

Those who would replace fair play with fair shares are consistent, therefore, in warning against the notion of deviance, whether in departure from "the work ethic" or in the practice of "alternative life-styles." What they do not usually recognize is that in a completely egalitarian society where work and wealth are shared equally, new definitions of deviance would have to be rigorously enforced. In some cases the old definitions would become more rigid. This is true, for example, of the much maligned "work ethic." In a society where all work is shared equally, those who refuse to do their part would have to be quickly punished. The interdependence created by an equality of fair shares cannot tolerate deviance. It is true that the game-like metaphor of equality of fair play assumes certain prescribed rules and bounds, but they are a great deal more flexible than would be the case in a society of fair shares. In a "rationalized" world of fair shares, little indulgence can be shown toward irrationalities, including the putative irrationalities that contribute to remaining poor.

Everyday ideas about equality, then, continue to have a major impact upon social policies. Disillusionment with recent social policies—especially those generally referred to as entitlement and affirmative action programs—can be attributed in large part to a pervasive animus toward equality as redistribution. Admittedly, Proposition 13 and other developments result from people's natural desire to keep more of what they have for themselves. But it is precisely that natural desire which a moral appeal must overcome and, as is evidenced in voluntary giving, does overcome with great frequency. Redistribution, except for redistribution aimed at enhancing equality as fair play, is simply not an effective moral appeal in American life.

There are several other reasons for this disillusionment which deserve brief mention. We have noted that redistributionist programs are not perceived to be benefiting, chiefly or at all, their putative beneficiaries, namely, the poor. Crime, drugs, and the breakdown of the mediating structures in poverty communities are perceived to have increased in pace with programs aimed at reducing them. In addition, there is widespread suspicion about the wisdom and motives of social planners who urge more of the same. Some Americans may have been turned off by the demands of the poor, but it is reasonable to believe that more have been turned off by those who presume to speak for the poor, notably by the designers and administrators who are major beneficiaries of the programs they promote. A late 1960s cartoon in *The New Yorker* has a sleek bureaucrat declaring at a Washington cocktail party, "I used to be in Commerce but now I'm in Poverty."

Especially galling to many working Americans is the contempt which redistributionists manifest toward their achievements in life. Former Mayor John Lindsay of New York would routinely refer with contempt to the "dead-end" jobs available to ghetto youth. Many workers who feel they have done reasonably well began with such "dead-end" jobs. People will not accept a rationalization for helping others that is built upon the ruins of their own self-respect. Again, William Ryan well illustrates the contempt which has contributed mightily to discrediting the redistributionist version of equality: "In America social mobility is an unquestioned fact. But how many sons of illiterate cobblers become physicians, on the one hand, and how many become, at best, literate cobblers? And how many settle for a job on the assembly line or in the sanitation department? And all of those daughters of impoverished immigrants—how many went on to get Ph.D.'s and become professors? Very few." Professor Ryan is indignant that others do not get to be, or maybe even want to be, like him.

A New York Times survey of workers' views on Labor Day, 1981, represents a sharp contrast. Curtis Myers is 54 years old and has been a longshoreman for 30 years. "You have to work hard," says Mr. Myers. "If you don't unload 18 or 20 or 25 containers an hour, the boss isn't making any money. There's an old saying, 'You can't put the heat up if you don't pay the rent.' The gantry pays the rent . . . Our average weekly pay is $464. That's before deductions. Nowadays there are a lot of deductions . . . I live in Uniondale on Long Island. I used to live in Brooklyn. I like New York." Being a longshoreman has "paid off," he says. "My kids are grown up now. I've got a little house. I pay my taxes. I used to tell my mother—she's dead and gone, God bless her soul—I have never done anything I didn't enjoy."

Frank Panasci is 58 and a meatcutter. He is not enthusiastic about living in New York: "I would prefer other places where it's not as congested." He is a union man and thinks the labor movement is "OK." "But there has to be a stop to everything. You can't just keep demanding. I mean, everybody would like to have a world of dreams, but it's got to stop somewhere. When you get a good salary and benefits, I think that should be it."

Evelyn Miranda, 30, is a bank teller and came from Puerto

Rico. "When she was growing up, Mrs. Miranda said, she wanted to be a 'business lady' and now she believes she has achieved that status. 'Professional—that's what I think of myself,' she said."

And so forth, throughout the everyday life of working America. Are these assertive expressions of satisfaction in fact reflective, as Richard Sennett suggests, of the "hidden injuries of class?" Perhaps so, but it hardly seems respectful or necessary to superimpose such a derogatory interpretation. Is the conclusion to be drawn that the peasants are happy and therefore we can all go on with business as usual? Hardly. Measured by their potential for self-fulfillment and social contribution, it may be that some of these people have indeed "settled" for too little. But then one must quickly ask, Who does the measuring? Within the disaggregated subworlds that constitute everyday life—family, work, friendship, church, neighborhood—these people may well be successes far beyond anything experienced by those of us who read and write essays on equality in America. Finally, however, there is no cause for complacency when we remember that millions of Americans are not participating in the process from which these people feel they have benefited. The most important response to that sobering reminder is that those who have succeeded will only be positively concerned about those who have not when the ways of showing concern are consonant with their own experience and self-respect. Social policy that is effective and politically supportable is policy that is respectful of the idea of equality that prevails in everyday American life. The two most relevant parts of that idea are, first, what Tocqueville describes as the recognition of a common human nature and essential condition and, second, the moral notion of justice as fair play.

Having considered everyday attitudes that bear upon social policies relative to equality, we turn to equality and what might more generally be called manners. Here we take up the quesiton of how people relate to one another in their various equalities and inequalities. Even more than in our prior considerations, the subject lends itself to observations rather than to the establishment of rules. Some generalizations are in order, for manners are not entirely arbitrary. Manners are closely related to mores, to those customs and habits of behavior which are taken to have some moral weight. American manners relative to equality are riddled with anomalies and contradictions. They inevitably frustrate the "disinterested observer" who would explain reality by reference to ordered principles. If we would understand the subject, we must see ourselves as being within it, as interested participants watching ourselves and others acting in sundry "regions of social performance."

With respect to everyday manners, the idea of equality has less to do with fairness and more with propriety. The distinction between fairness and propriety is not an absolute dichotomy. An action may be called proper because it is fair and, at least for those who have a strong sense of manners, an action may be thought fair because it is proper. Nonetheless, the distinction is a useful one. Fairness tends to deal explicitly with the ethical and legal. Propriety engages a sense of fitness, or right order. Fairness lends itself to being contested, propriety is noted in its observance or non-observance. Fairness tends to the assertion of explicit rights, propriety is the observance of usually implicit rules.

As manners have to do chiefly with propriety, so also they relate more to status than to either power or wealth. If we accept status, wealth and power as summarizing the three social goods relevant to the discussion of equality, most writing about equality focuses on wealth at the expense of status and power. Indeed one frequently encounters the assumption, articulated or implied, that status and power are but functions of wealth. Status and power increase in proportion to wealth. That is obviously true in many cases. It is just as obviously false in others. Everyday observation and survey research indicate, for instance, the high status of clergy and college teachers, despite these professional groups' distance from the top of the income ladder. Similarly, a millionaire in the construction business in New Jersey or a drug runner almost anywhere has neither status nor power, except among the criminals, police and politicians dependent upon their enterprise. While William Ryan is among those theorists who believe that status and power are functions of wealth, it is revealing that he thinks it would be upward mobility for a shop foreman to give up his higher salary in order to get a Ph.D. and teach college.

As an aside, it may be that redistributionists tend to short-change power as an independent variable, so to speak, because they are uncomfortable with the subject. And perhaps they are uncomfortable because, whether or not they accept theories about "the new class," they cannot help but know that any design for egalitarian redistribution would give enormous power to those who are in charge of the process. That the professed search for justice might be viewed as a search for power cannot help but be discomforting. More particularly is this the case for those egalitarians who subscribe to the proposition that all human behavior is self-interested.

Status has to do with ranking in an order of prestige, and prestige, in turn, is closely related to privilege. Privilege frequently overlaps with power to the point where the two seem to be inseparable. This is the result of the "cash nexus" in which people interact on the basis of power to purchase the goods, services and entertainments associated with high status. Thus there is a chicken-and-egg relationship between status, prestige and power. For a very few Americans, the everyday experience of equality and inequality is trying to maintain these distinctions at the highest level of status. Thus in most larger cities something like a social register is published or informally circulated. This is a policing function designed to protect a certain definition of status against the incursions of the cash nexus. The parvenu and other gate crashers are to be kept out of the circle in which status is, at least in theory, independent from wealth and power. The people within the circle are presumably the best schooled and best connected from the best families, the last factor being the most important part of that equation. Those who police the perimeter see themselves as engaged in "maintaining standards," and, as the phrase suggests, feel somewhat besieged. They are, often admittedly, aristocratic holdouts against the ethos of a democratic society. The keepers of the social registers are chiefly of interest to themselves and to the probably declining number of chroniclers of "high society."

There are alternative social registers in the several worlds of the arts, of letters, and even of finance and business at their upper reaches. These are more flexible and informal than *the* social register, and the most important reason for that is that they are, at least in theory, meritocratic, based upon achievement in a specific field of endeavor. Thus they are not aristocratic but, again in theory, attuned to the idea of democratic equality. In any case, these self-consciously circumscribed groupings of highest status are not of primary concern in our consideration of equality in everyday life.

The base line of equality in everyday behavior is the concept of personal dignity and the respect owing that dignity. A powerful image of the pathetic loser in American culture is Arthur Miller's Willy Loman. The fundamental claim to equality in everyday life is voiced by his wife toward the end of *Death of a Salesman*. Speaking about Willy, she declares, "Attention must be paid." Everybody has a right, it is suggested, to this elementary "attention," or, as some would have it, respect for personhood. This notion of equality in terms of status as a person is pervasive in our society. Its violation in any sphere of life is promptly protested. Whether in sexual encounters or in encounters with the boss or traffic policeman, the complaint of violation is uniformly expressed in the statement, "He (she) didn't treat me as a person."

This sense of inherent personal dignity is the base line but hardly the only line in the picture of equality in everyday life. Other most frequently encountered lines, at least in public, are related to jobs. Self-respect requires that one's job be in some important respect a contribution. We want to be of service but, at the same time, are nervous about being viewed as a servant. More precisely, the egalitarian grain is rubbed the wrong way by the suggestion that one might be a servant to any very specific person or persons. Generalized servanthood is acceptable. At its most generalized, being a "public servant" is eminently respectable. Serving everyone, one is a servant to no one in particular. Pushing a bit farther, an executive might admit without shame to being a servant of a large corporation or enterprise, but he would certainly bridle at the suggestion that he is the servant of E. F. Fuller, the chairman of the board.

It does not violate, but indeed is required by, the notion of equality that one has a job that constitutes a service and is done for pay. In fact, the doing of something for pay, which aristocrats considered beneath their dignity, now approaches being an essential component of personal dignity, as witness current feminist attitudes toward unpaid homemaking. This constitutes a significant reversal in attitudes toward equality and work. Again, Tocqueville caught the newness of this situation in his probably too sanguine description of the American approach: "In America no one is degraded because he works, for everyone about him works also; nor is anyone humiliated by the notion of receiving pay, for the President of the United States also works for pay. He is paid for commanding, other men for obeying orders. In the United States professions are more or less laborious, more or less profitable; but they are never either high or low: every honest calling is honorable." While it remains the case today that every honest calling is honorable, some callings now, and probably then, are more honorable than others.

A young priest recently preached that the church should reach out to prostitutes and other social outcasts. "After all," he said, "what does a prostitute do except sell part of herself for cash? We all do the same when we work for a paycheck." Eddie, who works as a "super" in Lower East Side tenements, protested vigorously in discussion following the mass. "I don't sell myself," he insisted, "not even a part of myself. I'm my own boss and I decide to do something for the landlord and to help the tenants and I get paid for it." Implied in Eddie's protest was that he is free to do something else if he felt his dignity infringed. Since he is over sixty, in bad health, and perilously close to poverty, Eddie probably over-

estimates the choices available to him. But the point is Eddie's
protest against a moral egalitarianism that equates his position
with that of the prostitute, thus erasing the line between deviance
and honor. At the risk of violating the deference customarily
accorded priests, Eddie asked the preacher whether he too did
not receive a paycheck and therefore was not he too a prostitute.
The young preacher clearly was not prepared for this and, after
emphasizing that he works only for the Lord, came around to
allowing as how Eddie too might be working for the Lord in some
sense significantly different from that of the prostitute's work. In
this vignette was recapitulated what historians of ideas have traced
from the Reformation doctrine of "the priesthood of all believers." Thus it might be urged that the force which levels (and
elevates!) all occupations is, as Tocqueville suggests, pay. But it is
also priesthood, the recognition of a common worth of work in
the face of the ultimate. (Tocqueville was very much a Roman
Catholic and one of the least convincing parts of *Democracy* is his
argument that traditional Catholicism is conducive to democracy
because it posits only one inegalitarian distinction, that between
clergy and laity.)

Occupation is the public face of personhood. Without doubt
some occupations are viewed as more demeaning and others as
more elevated. This is an embarrassment in the ethos of democratic equality. In recent decades the embarrassment has been
tempered by euphemisms, the most familiar being the elevation
of garbagemen to sanitationmen and of janitor to maintenance
engineer. Especially suspect in egalitarian society is any job that
explicitly suggests a servant-master relationship, such as that of
waiter. One waiter friend in an elegant restaurant rather gran-
diosely styles himself "an architect of dining pleasure." As he
reaches for the higher status of architect, we might ask how the
architect fashions himself. Certainly not, we may be sure, as a
servant of his client-patrons. More likely, the architect would
describe himself as a creative artist. Although we are past the
hungry-artist-in-the-garret stereotype, it is worth noting that artists, although generally not among the highest paid, maintain a
lofty status. In almost every profession—law, medicine, religion,
teaching—persons feel complimented if perceived as artists in
their work. In survey research of the general population, however, real artists do not rate so high. More consistently at the top
of the list are scientists and clergy, who would seem to represent
quite disparate values and neither of whom, again, are necessarily
associated with wealth.

In addition to the use of euphemism, undemocratic inequalities are also buffered—and sometimes sharpened—by specialization. The more specialized one's region of social performance, the better the protection against invidious comparison. Television technicians in a studio manifest an indifference bordering on contempt for powerful and celebrated people being interviewed on a show. The otherwise high-status person is on their turf where they are finally in control. Being interviewed may be an occasion for the celebrity but not for the cameraman. He has "seen it all" and is not about to be impressed.

In popular mythology, the plumber is probably the king in the manipulation of regions of social performance. The legendary arrogance of plumbers who hold the mighty in abject dependence is more frequently remarked because it seems to turn the tables, since plumbing itself is not thought to be a high-status occupation. The progress of medical doctors over the centuries from barbarous mechanics to demigods is a different and somewhat more interesting case. Plumbers wield power for a moment within their region of performance and then revert to being just plumbers. Medicine combines the power derived from the dependence of others with the high status of science and even of art. In addition, the historic and psychological associations between healing and religion gravitate to the medicine man. Science, art, religion, and the power derived from dependency all come together to make the medical doctor a singular instance of inegalitarianism.

The editor-in-chief of a national journal complains about a first-time visit to a physician. Immediately the doctor called him "Jack." Resenting the familiarity, our editor says he responded by addressing the doctor by his first name. The doctor, taken aback, promptly reverted to "Mr." The editor thought a strong egalitarian principle was at stake and was gratified by his supposed triumph. His behavior might more generally be viewed as a petty protest against implicitly understood roles in American life. Perhaps his egalitarian passion might have been assuaged were there ever occasion, admittedly unlikely, for the medical doctor to enter his region of performance with a manuscript to be published. In that situation he could address the doctor by his first name and would be addressed as "Mr." or, ideally in the European manner, as "Mr. Editor."

In the above instance we are dealing with commonly understood issues of professional status. At other times the indeterminacy or even the reversal of status is more episodic, limited to a brief moment of social awkwardness. A top executive was shopping with his wife in a posh department store. Selecting a number of items, he prepared to pay by check. For some reason the computer into which the clerk put the relevant information would not approve the check. The executive was obviously flustered and in the ensuing exchange several times addressed the young black clerk as "sir," while the clerk's demeanor revealed his surmise that he was dealing with a suspected felon. Finally the check cleared the machine, the executive straightened his tie and composed himself, and the clerk reverted to the usual surliness of a subordinate in a New York department store.

At the opposite end from the episodic reversal is the bureaucratic reversal of status. This needs no elaboration for anyone who has humbled herself before a government bureaucrat in charge of adjudicating a dispute over a parking ticket. The archtypical abasement, of course, is known to anyone who has been called in for an audit by the Internal Revenue Service. In that sharply defined region of social performance, the most junior employee is privileged to treat with condescending incredulity the most solemn asseverations of his betters. It may reasonably be suggested that experience with the tyranny of petty bureaucrats has protected more people from the socialist temptation than have the best reasoned arguments for democratic freedom. The unfair advantage taken by those who have a sharply circumscribed but inescapable region of social performance violates the sense of personhood which is the key intuition about equality in everyday life.

In most instances there is a game-like quality to the flexibility of status in everday life. A sociologist of medicine supplies a pertinent illustration. He consults a doctor who immediately assumes the profession's established manner as superordinate. In brief discussion he discovers his patient is not a mere sociologist but a sociologist of medicine. Exchanging wry smiles, but without a word spoken, a relationship of greater parity is established. It is understood that the examination is now mutual. More recently in American life, status games of "one-upmanship" have taken on a more vicious edge. There has been a rash of books and training seminars promoting sometimes ruthless techniques of intimidation. It is too early to say whether this development is deep or lasting. Perhaps, it might be argued, such promotion is only making explicit what has always been implicit. By popularizing the techniques of intimidation, this movement may simply be democratizing, as it were, the uses of inequalities. Nonetheless, there is an ominous element of nastiness in this development. A belief in equality as shared personal dignity may not be able to survive a close calibration and explicit exploitation of differences.

No essay on everyday life is complete without a reference to the cab driver. Cab drivers turn up so frequently in academic discussions because, one suspects, they are among the only working class folk academics encounter in everyday life. In any case, the cab driver, who occupies a relatively low-status occupation, typically illustrates another compensatory ploy in dealing with inequalities. It may be described as a vicarious compensation. With great frequency, cab drivers will tell passengers about the important people—usually celebrities and politicians—who have ridden in "my cab." Not infrequently, they ask a questioin such as, "Haven't I seen you somewhere? Aren't you on television or something?" The hoped-for answer is obviously Yes, in which case their status has been enhanced once more by contact with status. This should not be confused with the vicarious sense of importance that maids, valets and other servants once reportedly derived from the eminence of their employers. The cab driver is not entering our region of performance, we are entering his. The critical term is "my cab." And, if you are not the celebrity the cabbie hoped you might be, a little of the status of his social space may have rubbed off on you too.

While occupation is the public face of personhood and the major determinant of social placement, it is by no means exhaustive of those factors relevant to equality. Base line equality and the many lines that nuance the notion of equality must take into account the several "selves" comprising the "self" that makes a claim to dignity. For many people occupation is not the primary source of self-esteem or of their claim upon the esteem of others. The more strident egalitarian literature is filled with instances of men in low-status demeaning work who go home to beat up on their wives and children in order to prove they are men of consequence. No matter how few, there are no doubt too many instances of that happening. There are more humane, and surely more common, ways in which people outside their jobs compensate for the lack of, or complement, status.

The waiter mentioned earlier is also a collector of porcelains. Even when acting as an "architect of dining pleasure," it is certain that he is aware of this other self in his identity package. Few, if any, of those whom he serves as waiter could challenge his knowledgeable appreciation of the porcelain offerings at Sotheby's this month. Wilbur C. is a construction worker; not in the elite of the trade, but he says he gets paid well enough and more or less enjoys the work. It is a satisfactory arrangement in which he is paid to work not too hard and which facilitates his real enthusiasm. That is being captain of the Greenpoint bowling team which has two years in a row won the league championship. The team and the league include a good number of people with whom he works, but he has no doubt their most significant association is on bowling nights (Tuesday and Friday). It seems both patronizing and implausible to suggest that Wilbur C.'s bowling is a compensatory strategem for the indignities suffered in his work. It is as least as plausible to say that the suggestion is a compensatory strategem employed by people who need to believe that writing a book on the injuries of class is a more genuine achievement than being the Queens bowling champions for the third year in succession.

Curious dynamics, including what may validly be called compensation, are at work, as we have seen, in the use of forms of address. It seems to be increasingly the case that in America, unlike almost everywhere else, people in social or quasi-social gatherings address one another by their first names upon first meeting. The President of the United States, high court judges, state governors and Roman Catholic bishops appear to be the chief exceptions and are addressed by title. (Even in ecumenical gatherings of religious leaders it is not uncommon for the Catholic bishop to be the only one addressed as "Bishop." Mort Sahl's observation of thirty years ago still holds: "That's the church people mean when people say 'the church.'") Compensation enters the picture not only when someone is trying to achieve status but when others attempt to make up for real or alleged injuries. For instance, at a reception of liberal academics everybody was immediately on a first-name basis, with the single exception of a black woman professor who, a half-hour into the reception, was still being addressed as "Doctor." She finally insisted on being called by her first name, and by virtue of her permission the group's estimate of itself palpably rose.

These curiosities in address sometimes have unintended consequences. Traditionally at Yale and some other schools both faculty and students were addressed as "Mr." In the let-it-all-hang-out sixties, this was thought to be somewhat stuffy. The proposal was that everybody be addressed by their given names. Twelve years later, students are commonly addressed by their first names while faculty, or at least senior faculty, are almost always "Mr." Thus an egalitarian change resulted in an inegalitarian distinction that was not there before. Everyday life perceptions of significant differences keep getting in the way of egalitarian designs.

Among the curiosities of status and address in America are the ways in which black clergy, academics, and other leadership groups interact. When speaking at a black college, a white American is struck by the fact that almost everyone is "Professor,"

"Doctor," or "Dean," even after one has been several days on campus. In black clergy gatherings everyone is "Reverend," "Doctor," or "Bishop," even though the participants have known one another for years and in some cases may be intimate friends. And certainly when lay persons are present titles are never abandoned. This emphasis on titles among black leadership groups may be explained by a need to secure prestige within their own world, a prestige which blacks generally lack in the larger world of American society. A more likely and more winsome explanation is that this is a lingering evidence of Southern courtesy and inclination to "elevated" discourse. Among both whites and blacks in the South there is traditionally a deference of address when speaking to or about "Miss Ella," "Mr. Tom," "Aunt Esther," and "Uncle Bill." Only in the South have "Colonel," "Captain," and "Judge" survived even when the original reason for the title is at best obscure.

Leaving aside forms of address for the moment, there are many other curiosities and contradictions in everyday dealings with equalities and inequalities. In his masterful treatment of envy, Schoeck catalogued numerous ways in which the privileged warded off the resentments of the less privileged. Some of these strategies today might be thought of as protective coloring. For example, in New York and some other cities there are stunning reversals in the status of housing. Working class housing built in the mid-19th century is frequently luxury housing today. In the Bronx, the luxury apartment on the Grand Concourse of sixty years ago is slum housing teetering on the edge of abandonment. In some areas the complete circle has been made from high-status housing, to slum, and back to high status. As interesting as that process of "gentrification" is, even more interesting is the development of high-status housing in what had been the seediest commercial warehouse sections of the city.

A lawyer and his family recently moved into one of these "lofts" in what had been a very tacky warehouse. The developer of the bulding, well pleased with the transformation he had wrought, wanted to dress up the entrance, putting out a fancy canopy that would title the building "Lafayette Towers." The residents protested strongly. They want the building to continue to look as seedy as it and the rest of the area always have looked. The explanation given is that they don't want potential thieves to think there is anything in the building worth burgling. Another reason, one may safely assume, is that there is something fashionable about having done something very clever with so much ugliness. The continued ugliness testifies to the achievement.

The 1950s success of the Volkswagen "bug" gave birth to the

term "reverse one-upmanship." The phenomenon is not new. Sometimes it is more a case of taking on protective coloration, in others it is a fascination with what was called "high camp." In the sixties we witnessed an epidemic, especially among the young and those who would pass as young, of dressing up by dressing down. John Brooks is a current chronicler of the ways in which "downward style" replaces conspicuous consumption as an assertion of status. But this phenomenon need not detain us in a consideration of equality in everyday life. It is only the rich who can afford to compete with one another in conspicuous cheapness about trivia. Only the gratuitously niggardly are deemed stylish. The boast that you got your purse at Sam's Bargain Store only cuts ice if your Gucci shoes give evidence that you didn't need to get it there.

A curiosity that has a stronger bearing on everyday life, and also on public policy, is the effort to be egalitarian in the use of space. One example is the promotion of wilderness space "which belongs to all of us as our common heritage." The promoters of the wilderness mystique are scandalized, however, that so many Americans, and so many of them very common Americans indeed, are claiming their heritage. The result is that we witness a professedly egalitarian wilderness movement engaged in tortured efforts to construct a rationale for limiting access to wilderness which, if access is not limited, will no longer be wilderness. Discrimination by race, color, religion, or country of origin would be as unthinkable as a straightforward discrimination by wealth or the lack thereof. Since it is suggested that not everyone can "appreciate" wilderness, the argument moves toward linking access to a certified capacity for appreciation. Needless to say, exactly how and by whom such certification would be administered has not yet been worked out.

Also in urban America, a commonsensical and everyday perception of significant differences collides with egalitarian theory. Hence the debate over where to locate the "street people" in our cities and where to put low-income housing. The New York Times editorially agonizes over these problems, plus that of single room occupancy (S.R.O.) hotels, with great regularity. Eager to maintain the principle of equal burdens and unwilling to assert frankly the rights of property and its attendant privileges, the Times justifies not putting soup kitchens and methadone clinics on Park Avenue because it is a "showplace for the whole city." In truth the sleazier facilities of urban life will not be put on Park Avenue because the cost of doing so would be forbidding—the financial cost but, more important, the political cost of invoking the wrath of powerful people who would not tolerate it. For the same reason, low-income housing will not be located in Rego Park, Queens—which is equally a "showplace" for the people living there. The case can be made that the everyday idea of equality in American life is not offended—although certain egalitarian theories are—by the practical observance of inescapable inequalities.

A more candid acknowledgment of inequalities and their implications might save the privileged their guilty agonizing and save others the implausible denials of the obvious, namely, that some people have more wealth, power, and status than they do. At the same time, such candor could be socially dangerous. When Chevy Chase, acting as newscaster on "Saturday Night Life," begins with, "Good evening. I'm Chevy Chase, and you're not," it is thought to be funny. It is a humorous deviation from the usual ways in which we try to spare one another's feelings. The mayor of a city would be ill advised to address the citizenry, especially poorer citizens, in like manner. Such are the apparent fudgings, contradictions and dishonesties which Tocqueville understood to be the necessary hypocrisies of democratic equality.

The anomaly that most clearly exposes the gap between egalitarian principle and everyday experience is the enduring distinction between child and adult. To his credit, Herbert Gans is a theorist who acknowledges the problem: "Finally . . . a decision would have to be made regarding the age at which young people are eligible for equality." He suggests that, because kids are getting smarter all the time, maybe adolescence should begin at ten with adulthood following soon after. More intriguing is the suggestion that people become "eligible" for equality. The concepts of eligibility and equality are in tension, if not in conflict. Either all people are equal or they are not. Obviously, they are not, but to state that so baldly is bad manners. The child/adult distinction is an inescapable point at which egalitarian theory hits the dangerous shoals of everyday reality.

The line of adulthood may be variously drawn at 21, 18 or 14 years. For significant segments of the society it is drawn, for all practical purposes, at the mid-twenties, after the completion of graduate school and a couple of years for "finding" oneself. Wherever drawn, the line has the embarrassing appearance of arbitrariness. Yet some of the most significant inequalities in terms of claims and opportunities are determined by that line. The drawing of the line can be rationalized by reference to intelligence or other competencies, but a line drawn by such criteria would exclude a large part of the over-21, and especially of the elderly, population from being "eligible" for equality. Those who feel the need for a rationalized way of drawing the line are often the same people who, if they think incest somehow wrong, develop an elaborate fretwork to justify their opposition to it, lest their inhibition be viewed as primitive prejudice. Other more liberated types, believing that in many cases it might be harmless fun and even therapeutic, campaign to overthrow "the last taboo" against incest. Interestingly, these are often the same people who advocate "children's rights" against parental authority and deplore the incidence of sexual assault within families, especially by fathers and older brothers against young girls. When incest is therapeutic fun and when it is sexual assault apparently depends upon how you do it. But then any attempt to distinguish between acceptably loving and unacceptably aggressive sex is sure to draw fire from the sado-masochist lobby.

This mare's nest of contradictions that interest relatively few people vanishes entirely in the workings of everyday life in America. With the exception of unavoidable dilemmas arising in juvenile and family courts, most people think the answers to the above problems are more or less self-evident. Incest is wrong because it is wrong. Some would add that it is against the teachings of the Bible or "animalistic" (an esthetic criticism that might be lodged against copulation in general), but most people would likely stick by the proposition that it's wrong, and that's that. Of course people might be "educated" out of that prejudice. In recent years many Americans have been educated out of the bias against abortion, a bias which was once assumed to be an unmovable pillar in personal and public morality. And in our century millions of people have acquiesced in programs of genocide which earlier would have been thought unthinkable by those who later countenanced and perpetrated them. Nonetheless, one may be permitted to hope that with incest behavior has reached the outer limits of societal elasticity.

Although the child/adult distinction and its ramifications regularly come up in discussions of equality, in everyday life they have little to do with the idea of equality. Here again, the idea of equality is subordinate to a perceived moral order. That perception is, however insecurely, based in societal mores and manners. The idea of equality is not equal. Except for a few intellectuals, equality is not equal to, and certainly it does not exhaust, the idea of right and wrong, nor of justice.

In egalitarian theory the presumption of equality can only be overriden by devices derived from theories such as utility, social contract, or representative democracy. Parental authority rests on no such theoretical "override," it is just there. "Because I'm your mother, that's why you should do it," she tells the resisting child.

And that, finally, is the only logic that can be offered for this inequality—for so long as it works. The claim is backed up, of course, by economic force: "As long as I'm paying the bills, you'll listen to what I say." *In extremis*, crises regarding parental authority can also be appealed to law. One does not want to leave the impression that parental authority is simply a power play. It should be, and one hopes it usually is, softened by bonds of mutual affection and caring. But in everyday life the structure of this most elementary inequality is untouched by egalitarian theory.

In terms of effective authority in the actual living of our lives, the adult/child relationship is at some point attenuated, but it is not terminated. Except for adolescents, for whose necessary rebellion allowances are made, we would think it very strange were an adult to assert that he is the equal of his mother. In a way that is primordial but perdures into old age, parents continue to possess an authority long after they have lost control over their grown-up children. While indifference to old people is much and justly deplored in our society, it is well to recall that only four to five percent of the over 65 population is in institutional care. With respect to the overwhelming majority of old people, also with respect to those in nursing homes and other institutions, children continue to supply support and care. For most people, no single concern so greatly shapes their life plan and behavior as the care of their own children and of their parents. And all of this on the basis of a nonrational "accident" of family relationship, quite unrelated to theories about equality, thus again pointing up the relative weakness of any systematic idea of equality in everyday life.

A systematic concern for equality must of necessity intensify concern for inequalities. That is, the nonrational or accidental factors that make for inequality must be more carefully calibrated in order to make the compensations demanded by equality. The resulting preoccupation with differentiations is distasteful and socially destabilizing; it offends and disrupts the functionings of everyday life. For example, there is no reasonable doubt that physical appearance has a strong bearing upon life opportunities. Physically attractive people tend to attract favorable attention and are thus reinforced in their self-estimation and potential for success. The instinct in everyday life is to try to take the harsh edge off these "givens" of inequality. One daughter is praised for her beauty, but then it is quickly added for the benefit of her plainer sister, "but you too are very pretty in a different way." A humane society is only possible where differences of physical attractiveness and prowess, of intelligence and personal charm, are not calibrated in order to assure equality of outcome in life. In a paradoxical manner, the popular idea of equality militates against the application of any program aimed at equality. The commonsensical lumping of these very significant differences into the category of "luck" is not an instance of evasiveness but of popular wisdom. The limitations of the idea of equality for understanding society and everyday life within society are underscored by the fact that the most significant differentiations we make in life with respect to how we relate to people are supremely indifferent to the idea of equality.

Perhaps it is true that, as it is said people cannot bear too much freedom, they cannot bear too much equality. Some inequalities are reassuring. The auto mechanic going under the knife in the operating room does not want the surgeon to intimate that the diagnosis indicating a heart by-pass is about on a par with the certainty of the mechanic's estimate that a customer's car needs just a new seal or a whole new transmission. The doctor's status and expertise must be *very* superior to his. Similarly, there is an apparent desire that the President of the United States should manifest a "presidential style," whatever that means (obviously it does not mean wearing cardigan sweaters and carrying your own luggage). At the points in life where people feel things are beyond their control, the symbols of inequality assure them that others are on top of the situation.

It may be assumed that most people have a greater desire for peace than for conflict in their everyday lives. Peace requires the buffering of invidious comparisons. Hence we have, for instance, the peculiar fact that most people want to think of themselves as middle class. Families with incomes of $12,000 per year and those with $65,000 both describe themselves as middle class. There are no doubt many explanations for this phenomenon: it is a question of with whom they compare themselves, of upward status-seeking, in the first case, and of avoiding envy or guilt, in the second. But most basically, one suspects, it reflects an unwillingness to press the issue of inequality. Being in the middle is safe and peaceful— and it is tolerable, if on the bottom level of "middle class" it is assumed that one or at least one's children will likely be moving up. This predilection for the middle can be criticized as the source of pervasive mediocrity in American life or, more convincingly, it can be taken as evidence that Americans who have risen above dire economic necessity desire to transcend mediocrity in myriad ways that are largely unrelated to income. It is very doubtful that Wilbur C. would take a $2,000 raise in place of winning the bowling championship this year. But how about $50,000? It is not a pertinent question. It is probably just as well that Wilbur C., like most of us, is not offered the price for which he would abandon what he most cares about.

Finally with respect to manners and mores relating to equality, there are debilitating as well as humanizing consequences. One consequence that is little remarked is the impact of equality upon the notion of truth and public morality. Nowhere is the pervasiveness of a certain tradition of liberalism more evident than in the everyday attitude toward "tolerance." With respect to what is ultimately true and right, everybody's opinion is deemed to be equal. "You have a right to your own opinion," is perhaps the most characteristic remark in the face of disputes of normative consequence. Every opinion is equal because, it is implicitly assumed, nobody has the truth. At least nobody has the truth in a way that can make a public claim upon others.

Millions of Americans obviously believe they have a hold upon ultimate truths, but these truths are to be asserted only within disaggregated enclaves of religious and philosophical belief safely separated from the public arena. When it comes to public values, we disguise the ethical cacophany by calling it pluralism. Increasingly, what Walter Lippmann termed "the public philosophy" eludes us. On the one hand, this may make for civil peace, precluding wars of religion and explicit conflicts over ultimate beliefs. At the same time, however, such a society is poorly equipped to address those public issues which inescapably engage ultimate issues of justice. Such issues cannot be avoided, as, for example, in the debate over compensations for past injustices perpetrated against sectors of the society, and as, most painfully, in the continuing debate over abortion policy. Without some notion of normative public values, Alasdair MacIntyre has written, "politics becomes civil war carried on by other means." In this light, the idea of the equality of truths reflects not the achievement of tolerance but an ominous emptiness at the heart of our public life. While the gravamen of this essay has been the ambiguity of the idea of equality in the disaggregations of everyday life, the unhappy impact of the idea on public discourse must also be noted. That impact casts a deep shadow over the endurance of the democratic faith which Tocqueville and others have celebrated. Here too, equality, when systematically pressed, ends up being pitted against equality. When all truths are equal, no special status can be secured for the truth of the claim that all people are equal. In that case, the hypocrisies essential to democratic virtue can no longer be sustained.

However confused and unsupported by reasoned consensus,

the idea of equality in American life seems as vibrant today as it seemed to Tocqueville 150 years ago. The basic claim, "I'm as good as you are," cannot be adjudicated satisfactorily in any court of economic, legal, or political reason. Those who advocate a radical redistribution of social goods deplore what Samuel Butler derisively described as "a world in which the poor are respectable and the rich are respected." It is precisely respect, however, which is popularly redefined in an idea of equality that is largely independent of wealth. That respect is contingent upon fair play more than fair shares. The bias in favor of fair play is, in turn, based upon robust skepticism about those who would determine fair shares in the absence of any consensus about fairness.

Equality engages the notions both of fairness and of propriety. Fairness, in the sense of fair play, is sometimes measurable, stated in enprincipled form, and subject to public contestation. Such explicit questions about equality are encountered in the political and legal arenas where, fortunately, most of us do not live our everyday lives. The idea of equality as propriety is soft, intuitive, and largely unconscious until egregiously violated. In the forms both of fairness and of propriety, equality's hard core is the claim to individual respect. "Attention must be paid." Except for some of those whose job it is to theorize about equality, the question of personal dignity is the chief point at which the idea of equality engages the explicit and intense interest of Americans.

The Three Voices of
American Literature

Stephen Miller

"Since becoming a Real American, I can look any man straight in the eye and tell him to go to hell!"

Paul Bunyan

I

MOST AMERICAN WRITERS have implicitly endorsed the idea of equality—believing, as Hector Saint John Crèvecoeur put it, that America is a land free from "the ancient prejudices and manners of the Old World," free from "involuntary idleness, servile dependence, penury, and useless labour."[1] Although many American writers have been critical of American culture, few have argued in favor of racial or class distinctions. Some writers have praised the social hierarchy of the Old South, and some have questioned whether the immigrants streaming into the country from Southern and Eastern Europe were the equal of Anglo-Saxon natives, but most American writers probably would approve of Benjamin Franklin's remark that birth "is a commodity that cannot be carried to a worse market than that of America, where people do not inquire concerning a stranger, What is he? but, What can he do?"[2] Franklin was aware that social distinctions, if not rigid social classes, did exist in eighteenth-century America; and he was aware that the children of the rich were blessed with more opportunity than the children of the poor. Yet even the children of the poor, he thought, could better their condition. Unconstrained by the boundaries of class, Americans were free to make the most of their "talents and enterprize," as Jefferson put it, so that "rank and birth and tinsel aristocracy will finally shrink into insignificance."[3] For Franklin and Jefferson as well as for most Americans of the early years of the Republic, America was a land of equality insofar as it was a society without hereditary privilege. These sentiments have remained basic assumptions of American thought—so basic that after the Revolutionary period few writers even mentioned them.

In the early years of the Republic, many American writers praised Americans for their devotion to equality as well as for other traits that made them superior to the citizenry of European countries. The celebration of distinctively American virtues was commonplace—leading Tocqueville to complain that "no writer, no matter how famous, can escape from this obligation to sprinkle incense over his fellow citizens."[4] Most American writers, however, have been sparing of their incense. They often have criticized Americans for paying homage to the ideal of equality while doing little to ensure its reality. "With what consistency or decency," Thomas Paine asked on the eve of the Revolution, could the colonists "complain so loudly of attempts to enslave them while they hold so many hundred thousand in slavery?"[5]

The more common concern was not the treatment of blacks and Indians but the fate of equality in a predominantly commercial society. Yet it is misleading to imply that many American writers have confronted the question of equality. The best American novelists rarely have taken sides on this question or other questions either; they have taken soundings, plumbing the depths of the American character. Nevertheless, novelists do traffic in ideas—at least in the effect of ideas upon individuals. Moreover, in their essays and letters American novelists at times have ruminated about the question of equality. In order to clarify the idea of equality in American literature, we can speak of three different strains in American writing: the Puritan, individualist, and agrarian. Or, to put it another way, we can speak of three different voices: the voices of Jonathan Edwards, Benjamin Franklin, and Thomas Jefferson.

When American writers lament the decline of communal values and deplore the rise of materialism, they are heirs to the Puritan tradition—imitating the voice of Jonathan Edwards, who was the leading figure of the Great Awakening of the 1740s and 1750s. The Puritans did not argue that commerce was inherently sinful, but they did condemn financial speculation and they often lashed out against men of commerce for becoming excessively preoccupied with material concerns. According to Perry Miller, the literary form in which the Puritan mind found its most appropriate expression was the jeremiad. In countless jeremiads, writers called for a moral and spiritual renewal—asking their readers to rededicate themselves to the original Puritan mission of building "a city upon a hill," a community that would be the earthly equivalent of the heavenly city. Puritan writers continually implied that equality can be preserved only if Americans are animated by a disinterested concern for the health of the community.

A few years after Edwards proclaimed that "the sun of righteousness" then rising in the West would shine forth from America until it regenerated the human race, Franklin composed his influential tract, "The Way to Wealth," in which he praised industry, frugality, and prudence as essential to worldly success. America, Franklin implied, is a community of equals because it is a society of individualists—each man guarding his rights and looking after his interests. When American writers admire the energy, cleverness, and self-reliance of Americans, they are descendants of Franklin.

Finally, when American writers decry the rise of industrialism and attack the rootlessness of urban life, they are speaking in a Jeffersonian vein. Jefferson worried that the rise of manufactures and the growth of cities would undermine individualism by making too many Americans dependent upon others for their livelihood. "Dependence," Jefferson said, "begets subservience and venality, suffocates the germ of virtue, and prepares fit tools for the designs of ambition."[6] Only a nation of yeoman farmers, Jefferson implies, can be a nation of equals. Jefferson himself soon modified his position, recognizing the importance of manufacturing to the new nations, and few American writers have enthusiastically praised the life of a farmer. Nevertheless, many American writers, especially Southern writers, are Jeffersonian insofar as they look with suspicion upon the city and speak with nostalgia about an older pre-industrial order.

The three voices have not been equally influential. The voices of Edwards and Jefferson—of New England Puritans and Southern Agrarians—have predominated; many American writers, from Crèvecoeur to William Carlos Williams, have attacked Franklin. Franklin looked towards the future, hopeful that the enterprise of Americans would lead to technological advances and material progress, but for most American writers the future has meant something lost, not gained—meant the triumph of industrialization, the rape of the land, the rise of an industrial aristocracy, the flourishing of mass culture.

The notion of three voices, however, serves as an adequate guide only to the literary culture in general. The major American writers are not so readily categorized. "A culture," Lionel Trilling said, "is not a flow nor even a confluence; the form of its existence is struggle, or at least debate. . . ."[7] In the work of major American writers, we often see such a struggle taking place—a struggle between the voice of Franklin and the voice of either Edwards or Jefferson. The major American writers often have deplored the crass materialism of the ambitious American, but they also have admired, to quote Tocqueville, the "feverish agitation" of the American mind, "which wonderfully disposes it toward every type of exertion and keeps it, so to say, above the common level of humanity."[8]

Emerson's voice, for example, is a distinctive blend of Franklin's and Edwards'. The relation to Franklin is clear; America's predominantly commercial civilization, Emerson says, nourishes individualism and enables Americans to regard themselves as the equal of any man. On a trip to the West, Emerson remarked: "The people are all kings, and I notice an extraordinary firmness in the face of many a drover, an air of independence. . . ."[9] He also noted in his journals that "we rail at trade, but the historian of the world will see that it was the principle of liberty; that it settled America, and destroyed feudalism, and made peace and keeps peace; that it will abolish slavery."[10] Trade, Emerson suggests, is a positive force because it destroys an old order of class distinctions and racial prejudice; it is a force for equality.

Yet Emerson himself railed against trade. His jeremiads are descended from Edwards', but their central point is very different. For what preoccupied Emerson was not the state of the community but the state of the individual—less his moral self than his imaginative self. His deepest worry was that commerce made a diminished thing of man. "The tradesman," he said, "is ridden by the routine of his craft, and . . . [his] soul is subject to dollars."[11] Americans, Emerson complained, were not making the most of their opportunity to be radical individualists; trade had deflected them from cultivating their "Reason," by which Emerson meant imaginative intuition, not rationality. "The spirit of the American freedman," he said, "is already suspected to be timid, imitative, tame. . . . The mind of this country, taught to aim at low objects, eats upon itself."[12]

What Emerson disliked about the soul of commercial man was its paltriness, not its selfishness. He considered it his task to awaken Americans to the potentiality of equality. All men, he said, are capable of living according to the "dictates of Reason": "that is the equality and the only equality of all men."[13] Emerson regarded the cultivation of "Reason" not only as a way of countering the deadening effects of commerce, he also regarded it as a way for commercial man to steel himself against the hazards of commercial life. Reflecting upon the depression of 1837, Emerson attacks the wisdom of Franklin: "Prudence itself is at her wit's end. Pride and Thrift & Expediency, who jeered and chirped and were so well pleased with themselves. . . . Behold they are all flat and here is the Soul erect and unconquered still."[14] The virtues Franklin praised, Emerson implies, do not guarantee wordly success.

Emerson was not the only writer to worry about what commerce was doing to the soul of man in America. Jeremiads against commerce were commonplace, but some writers did not agree with Emerson's prescription for self-renewal. Hawthorne and Melville were also critical of Franklin, yet they lacked Emerson's faith in the inner light of man. The heart of man, they argued, is full of darkness. Throughout his life Melville wrestled with what he called "the mystery of iniquity," and he praised Hawthorne for the "great power of blackness in him [which] derives its force from its appeal to that Calvinistic sense of Innate Depravity and Original Sin, from whose visitations . . . no deeply thinking mind is always and wholly free."[15] Unlike Franklin and Emerson, who for all their differences often radiate a sense of optimism about the possibilities of life, Hawthorne—according to Melville—had a tragic sense of life. Hawthorne, he said, says "No! in thunder!"[16]

What Melville meant by describing Hawthorne's work in that way was that Hawthorne disliked the millenarian optimism of most Americans—their strong sense that America truly was a brave new world. In "The Celestial Railroad," Hawthorne makes fun of American complacency in the person of a credulous narrator who is impressed by "the wonderful improvements in ethics, religion, and literature," which were made plain "to my comprehension by the ingenious Mr. Smooth-it-away." Hawthorne disliked the innumerable Mr. Smooth-it-always to be found in America, for he thought their optimism about the progress of American civilization did not take into account the dark and refractory side of human nature.

Hawthorne put much less faith than Franklin and Emerson did in the notion that Americans can better their material or spiritual condition by an act of will. Such schemes for self-improvement,

Hawthorne implies in several novels and short stories, amount to very little, for most men are acted upon rather than actors—victims of forces beyond their control, dark forces within themselves that drive them on in ways they cannot completely fathom. So many of Hawthorne's characters seem possessed—enthralled by a nightmare, their will in abeyance. Even those characters who do possess a strong will usually fail at what they set out to do, either because they do not really know what they are doing or because they are forced to contend with wills stronger than their own. Sometimes they fail because their wills collapse. At the end of *The Blithedale Romance*, Hawthorne's novel about his experiences at the utopian community of Brook Farm, we find Hollingsworth—a character who had tried to shape others according to his will—completely broken in spirit. "The powerfully built man showed a self-distrustful weakness, and a childlike or childish tendency to press close, and closer still to the side of the slender woman whose arm was in his." In *The Blithedale Romance*, moreover, Hawthorne implies that human relations are not conducted on a basis of equality—not because of class differences or racial distinctions but because the world is divided into the powerful and the weak, into the wilful and the will-less. Human nature is such, Hawthorne implies, that it is foolish to invest too much hope in any social or political arrangement.

Hawthorne's bleak view of human possibility makes for a certain predictability in his fiction. His characters often seem puppets that rehearse the same dark tale—or, as some critics would say, allegory—of the human condition. Yet at times Hawthorne relents, modulating his point of view. In *The Blithedale Romance* there is one character who stands for the energy and practicality of Yankee individualism. Silas Foster, unlike the main characters, only speaks "to some practical purpose." As the farmer who takes care of Blithedale's economic life, he reminds the members of the community of the need to buy a half dozen pigs, to which the narrator remarks: "Pigs! Good heavens! had we come out from among the swinish multitude for this?" Foster's matter-of-fact attention to such questions serves as a counterpoint to the high-strung impracticality of the major characters. Foster is someone Franklin and Emerson would certainly admire—the Emerson, that is, who said "I like persons who can do things."[17] Emerson and Hawthorne have little in common, yet we find a common thread in their writings: admiration for the resourceful and self-reliant American.

Melville's sensibility has much in common with Hawthorne's. "Now it is that blackness in Hawthorne," he said, "that so fixes and fascinates me."[18] Melville's vision, in fact, is blacker than Hawthorne's; if Hawthorne's characters often endure isolation, Melville's often suffer desolation. To some extent Melville's images of desolation constitute a commentary on the American character, for Melville often implies that Americans practice a destructive brand of individualism. "It is no accident," Melville's biographer has said, "that Ahab, as a whale-hunter, represents one of the great exploitative, wasteful, predatory industries of the nineteenth century."[19]

Certainly Melville's novel, *The Confidence-Man* (1857), can be read as a scathing commentary on American individualism. The novel, which takes place on a steamboat on the Mississippi, is filled with characters who are "constituents of an appalling human world; a radically 'fallen' world, and a splintered one; a wolfish world, wherein the crafty and utterly self-regarding denizens are chiefly intent on fleecing one another."[20] The novel is also a fierce rebuttal to Franklin's notion that in America you are known by what you can do. In *The Confidence-Man*, you are known by what you appear to be. Success comes not from frugality, industry, and diligence; it comes from deception and fraud. The world of the novel is a world filled with schemers and cheaters.

For all his corrosive social satire, however, Melville is not primarily a social or political critic. His main concern was metaphysical; he was preoccupied, as he put it, with "Innate Depravity and Original Sin." He did not attack equality so much as the grand hopes Americans had for a society based on equality. "What he rejects," his biographer says, "is not the profounder moralities of democracy . . . but a cluster of delusions and inessentials that, as he felt, got themselves entangled with the idea of democracy in American minds; the delusion that political and social freedom is an ultimate good, however empty of content; that equality should be a literal fact as well as a spiritual ideal; that physical and moral evil are rapidly receding before the footsteps of Progress."[21] Like Hawthorne, Melville thought there were too many Mr. Smooth-it-aways in America—too many people who did not take into account the obsessive rage of an Ahab, the motiveless malignity of a Claggart (in *Billy Budd*), or the resolute passivity of a Bartleby, who continually says in "Bartleby" that "I would prefer not to." Melville implies that Americans would have a profounder grasp of life if they paid heed to his traveler's tales.

Yet the American reading public did not pay heed to his tales—at least not to those he regarded as his most serious work. The failure to find an audience for his novels bedeviled Melville. "Dollars damn me," he wrote to Hawthorne. "What I feel most moved to write, that is banned—it will not pay. Yet, altogether write the other way, I cannot. So the product is a final hash, and all my books are botches."[22] Melville was disturbed by the gap between the promise of a society based on equality and the limited horizons of democratic man. Yet he could not simply sneer at democratic man, for he had faith in the potentiality of American civilization. In his review of Hawthorne's work, he urged American writers to eschew "literary flunkyism towards England," and he hoped the public would come to appreciate those American writers who "breathe that unshackled, democratic spirit of Christianity in all things. . . ."[23] Unshackled is the key word; American writers, unlike writers in many other countries, can say whatever they want. Praising liberty and equality, Melville said to a friend: "The Declaration of Independence makes a difference."[24] Yet what difference does it make to a writer whose works are not read? Melville praised America's "political supremacy," yet he was often in a state of despair about the taste of democratic man—the taste of a reading public that is devoted, as Hawthorne complained, to "a commonplace prosperity, in broad and simple daylight,"[25] a public that is not interested in works of literature that assess the power of blackness. Given such a reading public, Melville said that "it is my earnest desire to write those sort of books which are said to 'fail.'" But if he welcomed failure as "the true test of greatness," he also became embittered by it. He did not lose faith in equality, but he did lose faith in the taste of democratic man.

Whitman, an exact contemporary of Melville's, did not share Melville's pessimism about American culture. In fact, no writer seems more antithetical in spirit to Melville than Whitman. Melville was preoccupied with "the mystery of iniquity," whereas Whitman was preoccupied with the mystery of creation—with "the procreant urge of the world," as he says in "Song of Myself." Melville's New York is a city of solitude and haunting inactivity—its chief emblem the Tombs, a prison fortress in lower Manhattan where Bartleby spends his last days. Whitman's New York is a "prodigality of locomotion"—its chief emblem the Brooklyn ferry, which takes "countless crowds of passengers" from shore to shore. In both his prose and poetry, Whitman continually speaks of the city as a place one travels to or travels in; he crosses on the Brooklyn ferry, rambles through Central Park, takes a jaunt up the Hudson, rides on the Broadway bus. For Whitman New York is a "vast amplitude" of "never-ending currents"—a city that surges with the energy of American life.

What is distinctive about Whitman is that more than any other

major nineteenth-century American writer he was deeply touched
by the optimistic spirit that infected many Americans—their sense
that America has a "grander future," as Whitman put it, than
Europe in part because of "the complicated business genius (not
least among the geniuses,)" of Americans.[27] In his characteristically grandiloquent manner, Whitman says in *Democratic
Vistas* that "I hail with joy the oceanic, variegated, intense practical
energy, the demand for facts, even the business materialism of the
current age. . . ."[28] Journeying to Boston in 1881, he was impressed by the city's "immense material growth—commerce, finance, commission stores, the plethora of goods, the crowded
streets and sidewalks. . . ."[29]

In his enthusiasm for American commerce, Whitman seems
close in spirit to Franklin. Like Franklin, he admired the in-
ventiveness and industry of the average American. Like Franklin,
he had faith in the American future—a future filled with technological advances. Whitman also had faith in the ability of Americans to appreciate literary excellence. American writing, he says,
has failed to win an audience primarily because it "has never
recognized the People." According to Whitman, "the tendencies
of literature, as hitherto pursued, have been to make mostly
critical and querulous men. It seems as if, so far, there was some
natural repugnance between a literary and professional life, and
the rude rank spirit of the democracies."[30] Whitman's argument is
not very persuasive, but he does at least point to the same problem
Melville had spoken of: the gap between America's literary
culture and its general culture.

There is, however, a dark side to Whitman—a side that does not
in the least resemble Franklin. "The damp of the night," he says in
"Song of Myself," "drives deeper into my soul." Some of Whitman's best prose and poetry are filled with despair about the Civil
War and the death of Lincoln. He also wrote about the dark side
of American cities. In *Democratic Vistas* he describes the American
city as "crowded with petty grotesques, malformations, phantoms,
playing meaningless antics"—a city of "pervading flippancy and
vulgarity, low cunning, infidelity. . . ."[31] In *Democratic Vistas* he
also speaks of "the depravity of the business classes of our country. . . ."[32]

Whitman often contradicts himself, his writing moving from
troughs of despair to waves of optimism. In 1868, when he wrote
most of *Democratic Vistas*, Whitman was disturbed by the sudden
change in spirit from the Civil War to the post-war-era—from a
spirit of sacrifice to one of greed. *Democratic Vistas* is full of contradictions, but it ends on a note of hope: the future will be better

than the present. Despite strong surges of despair, Whitman never lost faith in American democracy. As he said in his notebook: "Though I think I fully comprehend the absence of moral tone in our current politics and business . . . I still do not share the depression and despair on the subject which I find possessing many good people. The advent of America, the history of the past century, has been the first general aperture and opening-up to the average human commonality, on the broadest scale, of the eligibilities to wealth and worldly success and eminence. . . ."[33] The prose is turgid but the thought is clear: America is a land of opportunity because it is a society based on equality.

II

But was the America of the post-war era still a land of opportunity? Most American writers of the post-war era did not think so. In *Democracy in America,* Toqueville had warned of the danger of an industrial aristocracy. "The friends of democracy," he said, "should keep their eyes anxiously fixed in that direction. For if ever again permanent inequality of conditions and aristocracy make their way into the world, it will have been by that door that they entered."[34] According to many post-war American writers, an industrial aristocracy had arisen. Describing the machinations of James Fisk and Jay Gould, Henry Adams said in "The New York Gold Conspiracy" (1870) that the wealth and influence of these financial speculators was "far too great for public safety either in a democracy or in any other form of society," and he warned that the modern corporation, unless checked, "will ultimately succeed in directing government itself."[35] Even Whitman said that the United States is "controlled by a vulgar aristocracy full as bad as anything in the British or European castes, of blood, or the dynasties there of the past."[36]

If Whitman was sanguine that American democracy would survive "the era of incredible rottenness," as Mark Twain described the United States in 1875, other writers were not. Reflecting upon the 1870s, Henry Adams said in his autobiography that "the system of 1789 had broken down, and with it the eighteenth-century fabric of *a priori,* or moral, principles."[37] In the 1870s and 1880s, a host of writers argued that corrupt politicians, in league with financial and industrial capitalists, had made a shambles of representative government. The new industrial aristocracy, they also said, made it very difficult if not impossible for the poor to better their condition. The writers of *Progress and Poverty* (1879), *How The Other Half Lives* (1890), and *Wealth Against Commonwealth* (1894) pointed to the terrible poverty that was commonplace in many American cities, existing in the shadow of enormous wealth, and they argued that unless government made some attempt to control the new aristocracy the oppressed might resort to violent revolution. If in the three decades before the Civil War many writers had worried about the soul of man in a commercial society or bridled at the complacency of American millenarianism, in the post-war era many writers suggested that the new industrial order made a mockery of Franklin's notion that the poor, by being diligent and frugal, can improve their condition in life.

The fear that the system of 1789 had broken down led in the 1880s and 1890s to the publication of more than 150 utopian novels—the most popular being Edward Bellamy's *Looking Backward* (1888). As a reporter for the *Springfield Daily Union,* Bellamy had been appalled by "the inferno of poverty" that the new industrial order had spawned. The problem, Bellamy decided, was not industrialization itself but the power of the industrial aristocracy. In *Looking Backward,* Bellamy describes a new American sociopolitical order in which a technocratic elite manages nationalized industries for the common good. Nationalization, Bellamy argued, would increase society's productive capacity, and it would also transform Americans; instead of pursuing their self-interest, Americans would become disinterested and selfless patriots, working for the common good. Bellamy's new American order is an industrial Sparta, a society of workers organized along military lines. Citizens are compelled to serve in an "industrial army" between the ages of twenty-one and forty-five—rewarded if they perform well with promotions to the managerial elite or disciplined for negligence or disobedience by being placed in solitary confinement on bread and water.

Although *Looking Backward* was praised by many Americans, many viewed Bellamy's prescriptions with distaste. For Bellamy's socio-political order bore no resemblance to republican government. Bellamy spoke of a new egalitarian social order—a society in which people are ranked according to merit—but it was an order in which liberty would be radically curtailed. Most Americans wanted to curb the power of industrial and financial capitalism, but they did not want to be governed by a managerial technocracy, and they did not want to be dragooned into an industrial army in which they would lose the right to vote.

Trying to find remedies for the abuses of the new industrial order, some American intellectuals offered a prescription that had nothing in common with Bellamy's: a return to laissez-faire. E. L. Godkin, the influential editor of *The Nation,* thought the new industrial aristocrats were immoral and irresponsible men who, in their obsession with making money, sought special privileges from government. Godkin also lashed out against labor unions and "labor agitators"—arguing that they wanted a new form of equality: equality of conditions. He warned that the very pursuit of "equality of conditions on which the multitude seems now entering and the elevation of equality of conditions into the rank of the highest political good" would prove fatal to art, science, and law.[38]

Henry James, Henry Adams, Mark Twain, and William Dean Howells—the major prose writers of the post-war era—were probably closer in spirit to Godkin than Bellamy, but we cannot wring economic or political prescriptions from their writings. All four writers attacked the vulgarity and greed of the Gilded Age, yet their writings often betray some admiration for the energy and the cleverness of the parvenu, even if he is a dishonest businessman or a corrupt politician. And they often treat with irony the cultured patricians who complacently regard themselves as morally superior to the businessman or politician.

Nevertheless as the century moved to a close the vision of these writers darkened. They became more pessimistic about the future of American life. The industrial aristocracy, they implied, was not only making it difficult for the poor American to better his condition, it was in its relentless pursuit of wealth destroying the quality of American life. Struck by the way in which Trinity Church is dwarfed by the skyscrapers of Wall Street, James speaks in *The American Scene,* a collection of essays he wrote after returning to the United States in 1904, of "the vast money-making structure quite horribly . . . looming through the weather with an insolent cliff-like sublimity," speaks also of "the consummate monotonous commonness, of the pushing male crowd, moving in its dense mass—with the confusion carried to chaos for any intelligence, any perception; a welter of objects and sounds in which relief, detachment, dignity, meaning, perished utterly and lost all rights."[39] In this Dantesque scene, Wall Street becomes a "heaped industrial battle-field," its sounds and silences signifying for James "the universal will to move—to move, move, move, as an end in itself, an appetite at any price."[40] If the bustle of New York struck Whitman as a sign of the energy of American life, it struck James as a sign of the mad pursuit of wealth—a pursuit that smacks of "pitiless ferocity."

Despite these remarks, it is wrong to regard James, as Leon

Edel does in his introduction to *The American Scene*, as an "out-raged citizen"—wrong to regard James simply as a cultivated expatriate who was appalled by "our vast crude democracy of trade," to quote James himself.[41] Although James castigates America's commercial culture, he was less interested in delivering a verdict on American civilization than in offering his impressions of the American scene. And his impressions were far from uni-form. New York, James says, is a "terrible" city, but by terrible he means awesome as well as horrible—a city that overwhelms him, stuns him, and yet also fascinates him (he had been away from the United States for twenty years). Many passages in *The American Scene* reveal James's fascination with the commercial energy of New York—passages that make James, for all their differences, more akin to Whitman than to his friend, Henry Adams. More-over, James does suggest that in the future New Yorkers might not be so addicted to the pursuit of profit. "As soon as the place begins to spread at ease," he says, "real responsibility of all sorts will begin, and the good-natured feeling must surely be that the civic conscience in her, at such a stage, will fall into step."[42] James does not maintain his "good-natured feeling" throughout *The American Scene*, but in general he is moderately hopeful about the future of American civilization.

In fact, James was more hopeful in many ways than Howells, Twain, and Adams were. As a "restless analyst," which is how he described himself in *The American Scene*, James never remained wedded to any one view of American civilization or any one view of the American man of commerce. Although in his unfinished last novel, *The Ivory Tower*, the man of commerce (Abel Gaw) is a rapacious vulture, in earlier stories and novels James was more inclined to regard the man of commerce as naive rather than rapacious—naive in his belief, as James says of Christopher New-man in *The American*, that "energy and ingenuity can arrange everything." In *The Portrait of a Lady*, moreover, the man of com-merce is morally superior to the man of culture. Caspar Good-wood is a decent if narrow American industrialist, whereas Gilbert Osmond, the cultivated expatriate, is a sinister and repellent fig-ure—a man animated by a fastidious disdain for everyone, a man who reeks with condescension when he asks Goodwood: "Am I assuming too much when I say that I think I've understood from you that your occupations have been—a—commercial?" Even when James describes the American man of commerce as a vulgar parvenu, he often implies that, unlike the man of culture, he possesses energy, toughness, and power. Far from condemning the businessman outright, James often expressed his regret that he knew so little about business. In *The American Scene*, he complains that exploring the world of business to determine "the audibility in it of the human note (so interesting to try for if one but had the warrant) is a line of research closed to me, alas, by my fatally uninitiated state."[43]

James's hopefulness about the American future becomes clearer if we look at his impressions of immigrants. By the mid-1880s many American intellectuals had become alarmed by the vast number of immigrants that were pouring into the country from Eastern and Southern Europe. The immigrants, they thought, would not make good citizens; not only were they easily manipulated by corrupt politicians but they also were infecting American with foreign ideas—especially socialism. In general, they were undermining the social and political order.

Living in Europe, James did not breathe the air of acute pessimism about the future of American civilization that circulated in the drawing rooms of Boston's patrician class. Yet when he returned to America in 1904 he was stunned not only by the "crudity of wealth," but also by the "ceaseless process of the recruiting of our race, of the plenishing of our huge national *pot au feu,* of the introduction of fresh—of perpetually fresh so far it isn't perpetually stale—foreign matter into our heterogeneous system."[44] If *The American Scene* dwells on how the relentless pursuit of wealth has transformed America—especially how it has transformed New York—it also dwells on the ways in which the new immigrants have changed the country.

To say that James was stunned by the new immigrants is an understatement. Taking a trip to Ellis Island, "the first harbour of refuge and stage of patience for the million or so of immigrants annually knocking at our official door," James was shaken, as he says, to the depths of his being by "this visible act of ingurgitation on the part of our body politic and social . . ."[45] The "inconceivable alien," as James puts it, has destroyed his own idea of the American character. "The idea of the country itself underwent something of that profane overhauling through which it appears to suffer the indignity of change." The country, James says, is no longer the country he knew, no longer *his* country. He has been dispossessed, and "this sense of dispossession haunted him . . ." But James, unlike many of his patrician friends, does not luxuriate in a sense of despair about the future of a country that has been so radically transformed by immigration. In order to "recover confidence and regain lost ground," he says, "we must go . . . more than half-way to meet them . . ."[46]

James did go more than half-way to meet the new immigrants.

He wandered the streets of New York, especially those where immigrants lived; he frequented beer-houses and cafes run by immigrants; he had dinner with Yiddish writers. *The American Scene* is thick with discriminating observations of immigrant life in New York, but what stands out in these reflections is James's amazement that the immigrants are "consciously not what they *had* been. . . ."[47] The Italian immigrants, for example, are not like the Italians James had met on his frequent travels to Italy. "The Italians [in New York] meet us, at every turn, only to make us ask what has become of that element of the agreeable address in them which has, from far back, so enhanced for the stranger the interest and pleasure of a visit to their beautiful country."[48] The immigrant, James says, "presents himself . . . as wonderingly conscious that his manners of the other world, that everything you have there known and praised him for, have been a huge mistake."[49]

James prefers the manners of the Old World Italian, but he is less interested in lamenting this loss than in understanding the reason for it. "The great fact," James says of the immigrant Italians, was that "foreign as they might be, newly inducted as they might be, they were at home, really more at home, at the end of their few weeks or months or their year or two, than they had ever in their lives been before. . . ."[50] The immigrants are more at home in America than they ever had been in Italy because they are freed from the class structure of feudal Europe; they are at home because they live in a society based upon what James calls "equality of condition," by which he means a classless society. Their sense of America's equality of condition enables them to cast off their Old World manners as irrelevent to the workings of the New World. "They shed it utterly," James says, speaking of their Old World manners, "after a deep inhalation or two of the clear native air."[51]

Thus James's initial shock at the foreignness of the alien at Ellis Island becomes transformed, some 40 pages later, into amazement at how easily America assimilates the alien. The machinery for assimilation, James says, is "colossal—nothing is more characteristic of the country than the development of this machinery, in the form of the political and social habit, the common school and the newspaper. . . ."[52] but what makes James relinquish the notion that he is dispossessed by the alien is his awareness that both he and the alien exist on the same ground; for America is, after all, a country of aliens. "Who and what is an alien," James asks, "when it comes to that, in a country peopled from the first under the jealous eye of history?—peopled, that is, by migrations at once extremely recent, perfectly traceable and urgently required. They are still, it would appear, urgently required—if we look about far enough for the urgency."[53] James seems to be arguing with his patrician friends who think that the new immigrants are radically different from the previous ones. "Which is the American, by these scant measures?—which is *not* the alien, over a large part of the country at least, and where does one put a finger on the dividing line, or, for that matter, 'spot' and identify any particular phase of the conversion, any one of its successive moments?"[54] The new immigrants are "inconceivable aliens," but the process of assimilation will quickly turn them into Americans, just as the process turned the alien ancestors of James's patrician friends into Americans.

In his notebooks Whitman says that "I like well our polyglot construction-stamp . . . All nations here—a home for every race on earth."[55] In *The American Scene* James is less inclined to celebrate "our polyglot construction-stamp" than to stand in awe of it. "The operation of the immense machine [of assimilation]," he says, "trembles away into mysteries that are beyond our present notation and that reduce us in many a mood to renouncing analysis."[56] The subject is overwhelming; it wears him out—leaves him with mere sensations and impressions rather than opinions. Yet James surely is close to Franklin and Whitman when he speaks of America as "supremely, a field for the unhampered revel, the unchecked *essor*, material and moral, of the 'common man' and the common woman"—exclaiming "How splendidly they were making it all answer for the most part. . . ."[57]

"For the most part": the qualifier makes it clear that James never could give his complete assent to the triumph of the common man. He could recognize America's distinctiveness, even in some ways be exhilirated by it, but he could not celebrate American culture. Writing to Howells in 1880, James attempted to justify being an expatriate. "It is on manners, customs, habits, usages, forms, upon all these things matured and established, that a novelist lives—they are the very stuff his work is made of."[58] James was not appalled, as Dickens was, by the bad manners of Americans. He simply felt that Americans did not have enough manners—meaning by manners what we would call social complexity, social thickness. In his study of Hawthorne, James spoke of the "items of high civilization . . . which are absent from the texture of American life. . . ."[59] In short, America did not sufficiently engage his imagination. Yet if James preferred the complex manners of feudal Europe to "the vast peaceful and prosperous human show" of America, on his trip to America in 1904 he came to realize that the "inconceivable alien," whatever his initial disabilities, quickly becomes assimilated by virtue of the dynamic of equality.

In 1907, the year *The American Scene* appeared, Henry Adams privately published his autobiography, *The Education of Henry Adams*. In the final chapter, which describes Adams' return to New York after a short trip to Europe, Adams begins with a description of New York harbor that closely resembles James's description in *The American Scene*. But there the resemblance ends. James was stunned by New York, even shocked by it, but he was also fascinated by it. Adams found New York appalling. James, moreover, was "quite agreeably baffled" by New York, whereas Adams was quite certain what New York meant; New York stood for the triumph of "a new type of man—a man with ten times the endurance, energy, will and mind of the old type. . . ."[60] For Adams these words were not words of praise; the new man was a barbarian and his triumph was a sign of the unraveling of western civilization. The opening paragraph of the chapter ends on an apocalyptic note: "The two-thousand-years failure of Christianity raced upward from Broadway, and no Constantine was in sight."[61]

James and Adams were good friends, but by the turn of the century James was becoming increasingly exasperated by what he called Adams' "monotonous, disappointed pessimism."[62] Enthralled by his theory of decay, Adams—unlike James—had no desire to go more than half-way to meet the "new man," by which he meant the recent immigrants. As early as 1868, upon returning from a stay of several years in Europe, Adams had come to feel that he was being dispossessed by them. "He had become an estray," he says in *The Education*, "a flotsam or jetsam of wreckage; a belated reveller or a scholar-gypsy like Matthew Arnold's. His world was dead."[63]

As the century moved towards a close, Adams came to single out the Jews as the main reason for the death of his world. In 1895 he wrote John Hay that "after all, that Jew question is really the most serious of our problems. It is capitalist methods run to their logical result."[64] Offering his own brand of self-pitying Social Darwinism, he implied that Jews were more capable of flourishing in the modern age than he—that is, his "race" of patricians—was. After exclaiming that his world was dead, Adams says that "not a Polish Jew fresh from Warsaw or Cracow—not a furtive Yacoob or Ysaac still reeking of the Ghetto, snarling a weird Yiddish to the officers of the customs—but had a keener instinct, an intenser energy, and a freer hand than he—American of Americans, with Heaven knew how many Puritans and Patriots behind him. . . ."[65]

Adams had not always painted Jews in such lurid colors. In his magisterial *History of the United States during the Administrations of Jefferson and Madison,* written during the 1880s, Adams was "quick to catch Jefferson for a scornful reference to Jews."[66] The *History*, moreover, focuses on progress, not decay—the progress that can be expected in a society without class barriers. In the Europe of 1800, Adams says in the *History*, class distinctions "raised from birth barriers which paralyzed half the population. . . . All this might have been borne; but behind this stood aristocracies, sucking their nourishment from industry, producing nothing themselves, employing little or no active capital or intelligent labor, but pressing on the energies and ambition of society with the weight of an incubus."[67] Like the Founding Fathers, Adams thought that the lack of a class structure enables talent to flourish in America, and he pointed out that many American inventors have come from poor or relatively poor families. "All these men," he says, "were the outcome of typical American society, and all their inventions transmuted the democratic instinct into a practical and tangible shape." Expressing sentiments akin to Franklin's and Whitman's, he asks: "Who would undertake to say that there was a limit to the fecundity of this teeming source?"[68]

What caused Adams to turn sour in the 1890s—to convert from a faith in the power of science to promote progress to a conviction that a scientific law (the second law of thermodynamics) doomed civilization to exhaustion, chaos, and eventual collapse? Adams had many reasons for feeling despondent: his wife committed suicide in 1885, his *History* sold poorly; his patrician family had lost ground to a vulgar industrial and financial aristocracy. But the circumstances of Adams' life do not provide an adequate explanation for his cosmic pessimism. It was one thing to question the corruption of the Gilded Age and worry about the effect the new immigrants would have on American life; it was another to assume—as Adams did—that nothing could stop American civilization from unraveling. In the last chapter of *The Education* Adams acknowledges that his theory of history "was profoundly unmoral, and tended to discourage effort."[69] Adams luxuriated in his grandiose theory of historical change in part because it enabled him to ridicule the concerns of Boston's patrician intellectuals—mocking their vague hope that they could reform American life. Reform was impossible, Adams implied; there was nothing to do but savor the decay of civilization.

We see in Adams the flowering of modern cultural conservatism—a world-view ridden with contradictions in that on the one hand it despises all things modern yet on the other often tries to bolster its case by saying that its argument is scientific. Like Adams, modern cultural conservatives—as opposed to what we might call traditional cultural conservatives—have been preoccupied with the power of Jews. Two American expatriates—T.S.

Eliot and Ezra Pound—were close to Adams in this regard. In Eliot's early writings we find disparaging references to Jews; they are rootless, vulgar, and rich. Pound, as we know, became so obsessed with the power of Jews that he became an apologist for Fascism. Yet Eliot and Pound—and Adams as well—go against the American grain; modern cultural conservatism flourished in Europe, not America. Aside from Pound no important American writers—save, perhaps, Theodore Dreiser who was a Communist fellow-traveler—became so disenchanted with American democracy that he called for another kind of regime: feudal, fascist, or Communist.

Nevertheless, towards the close of the nineteenth century disenchantment was rife—less with representative government or the ideal of equality than with the American future. If Mark Train did not possess Adams' cosmic sense of despair, in *A Connecticut Yankee in King Arthur's Court (1889)* he did imply that the American future might be bleak. For Hank Morgan, the entrepreneur who finds himself in Arthurian England after getting cracked in the head with a crowbar, becomes a destructive megalomaniac—bent on using advanced technology to impose his despotic will on a backward society. Morgan's will to power ends in failure, but not before he has succeeded in wreaking death and destruction. Modern technology, Twain implies, may bring with it a new kind of barbarism.

Twain had always been a critic of American society, so *A Connecticut Yankee* is not radically different from his previous work. In *The Gilded Age* (1873), written in collaboration with Charles Dudley Warner, he describes the greed and corruption of Washington during Grant's Administration. And in *Huckleberry Finn* (1884) he offers a devastating attack on slavery—more devastating than countless tracts and moralistic tales because of Twain's masterly handling of Huck's moral dilemma. Yet both *The Gilded Age* and *Huckleberry Finn,* even though they dwell on corruption and slavery, leave us with a sense of the promise of American life. Colonel Sellers, the corrupt huckster who is the central figure of *The Gilded Age,* is an amiable schemer who is far from mean-spirited. And Huck Finn is courageous and clever—surviving the ordeals and escapades that take place on and off the Mississippi River so that at the end of the novel he can "light out for the territory ahead. . . ." By contrast, *A Connecticut Yankee* ends on a note of despair. Having returned to the nineteenth century, Hank Morgan dies in a state of delirium—his dream of fomenting an industrial and political revolution in Arthurian England having turned into a nightmare.

Twain had not planned the novel to be a dark fable about the potential for despotism that lurked within the soul of an American entrepreneur. His notes make it clear that he wanted to write a burlesque of the Middle Ages. His novel would treat as humbug the ideas of those intellectuals who looked back in yearning towards the age of feudalism, chivalry, and faith. The first two-thirds of the novel generally follow Twain's original intention, for Morgan describes how unpleasant daily life is in Arthurian England. And he also describes how a society based on inequality results in an extraordinary waste of talent. The king, nobility, and gentry are idle and unproductive, "acquainted mainly with the arts of wasting and destroying," and the common people are "reduced to a monotonous dead level of patience, resignation, dumb uncomplaining acceptance of whatever might befall them in this life. Their very imagination was dead." Yet in the final third the novel changes from spirited and amusing satire to grim and grotesque farce. Morgan is no longer the engaging—if somewhat complacent—Yankee entrepreneur; he is a vicious tyrant, a man drunk with power. The change is jarring, as if Twain himself changed his view about the American future.

It is difficult to reconcile the two different views of the American future that we find in *A Connecticut Yankee*. For Twain was "capable of sustaining two moods of belief at the same time"[70]— capable of uttering a paean to progress in 1889, on the occasion of Walt Whitman's birthday, when at the same time he was completing *A Connecticut Yankee*. Twain himself was a great American entrepreneur, a man who consorted with plutocrats and provided financial support for as many as one hundred inventions and manufacturing schemes, almost all of them unsuccessful. Perhaps the last third of the novel is suffused with a dark vision of the American future because of Twain's own frustrations with James L. Paige's typesetting machine, an invention that obsessed him—to which he gave so much of his money, time, and energy, to no avail because it was a failure. But perhaps Twain was infected by the general despair about the American future that was current in the 1880s and the 1890s.

Reviewing *A Connecticut Yankee*, William Dean Howells ignored the novel's dark side, calling it a novel that "makes us glad of our republic and our epoch."[71] Yet Howells' own mood at the time was one of increasing despair about the Republic and the epoch. As he confided to Henry James in 1888: "I'm not in a very good humor with America myself. . . . After fifty years of optimistic content with 'civilization' and its ability to come out all right in the end, I now abhor it, and feel that it is coming out all wrong in the end, unless it bases itself anew on a real equality." Howells, however, added a mordant afterthought: "Meantime, I wear a fur-lined overcoat, and I live in all the luxury my money can buy."[72] Howells knew how absurd it was for him—a financial success and a pillar of the literary establishment—to sound as if he were a fervent advocate of radical change, but his remarks betray a sense of frustration that he cannot do anything about the terrible poverty that he saw on his rambles through the streets of New York.

Howells' growing despair about social inequality led him to try his hand at the utopian novel. In *A Traveler from Altruria* (1884), a Mr. Homos describes the past and present of Altruria. Altruria's cities once were "a congeries of millionaires and the wretched creatures who served them and supplied them. Of course, there was everywhere the appearance of enterprise and activity, but it meant final loss for the great mass of businessmen, large and small, and final gain for the millionaires." The description of what Altruria once was like, of course, is a description of what Howells thought America was like during the Gilded Age. There is tremendous energy and bustle in America's cities, Howells suggests, but it all goes for nought; only the plutocrats succeed.

Altruria, however, has been transformed by a peaceful legal revolution, so that now (Mr. Homos relates) it is a commonwealth composed of citizens who do not pursue their self-interest but live for one another in perfect equality. Howells, though, had no illusions that the United States could become an Altruria. The ideal society of Altruria is not a "precise pattern for reform but . . . an animating possibility and informing ideal."[73] Yet it is less a vision of the future than a glimpse of the past—a lament for the passing of an old order: rural, small-town, pre-industrial America. The novel is suffused with nostalgia for a less hurried time in American life—a time when (so Howells assumes) Americans were less frantic about commercial success. Mr. Homos continually emphasizes that in Altruria "there is no hurry."

Howells' despair about the new industrial order was something that slowly built up in him. He did not cultivate his pessimism, as Adams did, nor did he abandon himself to pessimism, as was often the case with Twain. In fact, to some degree he took the side of the "new man." In *The Rise of Silas Lapham* (1885), Howels describes an industrialist (a paint manufacturer) who for all his moral lapses and social gaucheries is a more sympathetic figure than the cultured Boston patricians whose company he so desperately seeks.

By the late 1880s, however, Howells was disturbed not only by the social and economic inequality so evident in New York but also by what the passion for wealth was doing to the American character. Jacob Dryfoos, a central character in *A Hazard of New Fortunes* (1890), was originally a farmer who became a speculator after the discovery of a natural-gas field had brought him an offer of one hundred thousand dollars for his farm. Speculating in real estate and then in the stock market, Dryfoos becomes a millionaire—becomes a man, Howells says, who honors only money, "especially money that had been won suddenly and in large sums," a man moreover who has contempt for "money that had been earned painfully, slowly, and in little amounts. . . ." Recounting the "moral decay" of Dryfoos, Howell implicitly wonders what will become of the Republic if many of those who espouse "good conservative citizenship"—Howells' description of Dryfoos-the-farmer—turn into men who worship at the altar of money. Too many Americans, Howells thought, were engaged in a mad scramble for success. Howells wished the Dryfooses of America would stay on their farms.

III

In the early 1890s, while Howells was writing *A Traveler from Altruria,* Theodore Dreiser, an aspiring journalist, came to New York to look for a job. He too was shocked by the "startling contrasts of wealth and poverty." New York, he would write in *Newspaper Days* (1922), was "difficult and revolting. The police and politicians were a menace; vice was rampant; wealth was shamelessly showy, cold and brutal."[74] But if Dreiser was shocked by New York, he was also dazzled by it. "Here, as one could feel, were huge dreams and lusts and vanities being gratified hourly."[75] And in *A Traveler At Forty* (1913), he says that "All in all, the Atlantic metropolis is the first city in the world to me—first in force, unrivaled in individuality, richer and freer in its spirit than London or Paris, though so often more gauche, more tawdry, more shamblingly inexperienced."[76]

What distinguishes Dreiser from Howells is that for him the 1890s were a time of hope. As a young journalist in Chicago and New York, Dreiser was fascinated by the energy and spirit of the age. America, he recalled, was "in the furnace stage of its existence. Everything was in the making—fortunes, art, its social and commercial life, everything."[77] Although Dreiser dwelled much more than Howells did on the dark and seamy side of life in American cities, he was not primarily a social critic. His novels reveal the social inequality fostered by financial and industrial capitalism, but their main subject is the reality of the American dream—the reality of it as a motivating force. His major characters feel strongly, as Dreiser himself felt, that everything is in the making—feel that they can gain the success they so intensely crave.

Like Franklin, Deiser thought that men of talent and energy could better their condition in America, no matter what their background. Frank Cowperwood, the central character of *The Financier* (1912) and *The Titan* (1914), possesses "magnetism and vision" as well as "dynamic energy." Unlike Franklin, Dreiser thought success has nothing to do with morality. Dreiser regarded conventional morality as an illusion or rationalization. Frank Cowperwood, Dreiser says approvingly, scorns "the conventional mind." Dreiser contrasts him with a powerful Chicago banker who, as a church member and model citizen, "represented a point of view to which Cowperwood would never have stooped." In *An American Tragedy* (1925), Dreiser speaks with obvious disdain of a family that lives in a "petty and highly conventional neighborhood" and contemplates life and conduct "through the lens furnished by a purely sectarian creed."

Dreiser, then, differs from the major writers of the Gilded Age in that he does not attack the immorality of the new industrial order. To see how different Dreiser is from Howells, we need only compare what Howells says about Orville Dryfoos in *A Hazard of New Fortunes* to what Dreiser says about the parents of Roberta Alden (the young woman who drowns) in *An American Tragedy.* Howells laments the moral decay of Dryfoos—the "good conservative mind" of the farmer becoming the crass and immoral mind of the financial speculator. By contrast, Dreiser describes the parents of Alden—"honest, upright, God-fearing and respectable" farmers—as "excellent examples of that native type of Americanism which resists facts and reveres illusions." For Howells the conservative American farmer is the backbone of the Republic; for Dreiser he is either a fool or a hypocrite.

Yet in the world of Dreiser's novels those who scorn conventional morality are not necessarily more enlightened than those who complacently invoke it. If the conventional characters are under the illusion that the world works according to the precepts of morality, the unconventional characters suffer from the delusion that their ruthless pursuit of success will eventually bring them satisfaction. Dreiser admires their lack of conventional morality, admires also their energy and intense craving for success, but he continually—indeed insistently—tells the reader that they are deluded souls. What Dreiser says of Clyde Griffiths, the central character of *An American Tragedy,* applies to all his major characters: "his ideas of luxury were . . . mere wanderings of repressed and unsatisfied fancy." The dreams of these unconventional characters who are driven by "unsatisfied fancy" always end in nightmares of loneliness, dissatisfaction, or outright failure. "I satisfy myself," Cowperwood brags, but Dreiser's major characters never do satisfy themselves. Reality never measures up to their imagination. No matter what level of success they attain, they remain restless and lonely to the end.

Is not, then, Dreiser a social critic insofar as his novels stand as a repudiation of the American dream of success? What is wrong with America, Dreiser implies, is not the inequality fostered by industrial and financial capitalism but the vast number of tawdry dreams American civilization inspires. According to Irving Howe, Dreiser is the chronicler of "the ingrained American delusion" that the craving for success can be assuaged—that the restless imagination can be appeased by worldly success. *An American Tragedy,* Howe says, is "a kind of parable of our national experience. Strip the story to its bare outline, and see how much of American desire it involves. . . ." Clyde Griffiths is the "very image of our culture, hungering with its hungers, empty with its emptiness. . . ."[78] In this view the American dream of success is an *ignis fatuus* that lures people on to their destruction. Equality of condition does not release creative energy but breeds waste. In Clyde Griffiths, Howe says, "is concentrated the tragedy of human waste: energies, talents, affections all unused. . . ."[79]

True, the story of Clyde Grifiths is an *American* tragedy. Moreover, Dreiser continually implies that the dreams of his characters are shaped by the culture they inhabit; their dreams are tawdry because the culture is tawdry. Nevertheless, the origin of these dreams is mysterious. Few people, Dreiser says, are afflicted by a "chemism of dreams"—to use his own pompous pseudo-scientific explanation—that makes them crave success; the craving that gives birth to these dreams cannot be explained by invoking American culture. Dreiser does not have the intellectual depth or the artistic subtlety of the great nineteenth-century French and English novelists, but the yearning his major characters have for worldly success—for a life that suits their own dream of themselves— recalls the yearnings of Becky Sharpe, Emma Bovary, and Julien Sorel. Dreiser's theme crosses national boundaries.

Yet if the loneliness of the dreaming outcast is not an exclusively American theme, Dreiser seems to agree with Tocqueville that American society produces such solitary types in great number.

Dreiser saw himself as a naturalist who charts the complex social forces in America that manipulate these dreamers—saw himself as someone who looks down at his characters from a great height, pitying them for their tawdry American dreams. But if Dreiser wanted to be a scientific novelist, he never lost his romantic fascination with the possibiity of American life. He himself was one of the dreamers; and he never completely assented to the notion that the American dream is a fraud. It is this tension in Dreiser's novels between these two points of view that makes some of his novels, for all their ponderousness and joylessness, compelling.

In 1925, the year *An American Tragedy* appeared, Fitzgerald brought out *The Great Gatsby*—a novel that also centers on a character who dreams huge dreams. Jay Gatsby's dreams are even greater than Clyde Griffiths', for he wants to change the past as well as shape the present and the future. "Oh you want too much," Daisy Buchanan cries to Gatsby when he insists that she never loved her husband, Tom Buchanan. Gatsby, like Griffiths, is deluded—wrong to assume that he can fulfill his extravagant dream. And Gatsby's dream, like Griffiths' dream, is tawdry and vulgar. Yet Fitzgerald celebrates Gatsby more than he pities him.

To be sure, Gatsby's huge dream—a dream, Fitzgerald says, that is larger than his love for Daisy—makes him a figure of pathos, a "poor son-of-a-bitch," as someone says at his funeral. But Gatsby is definitely "great," as the novel's title says. The novel opens with Nick Carraway, the narrator, reflecting upon the phenomenon of Gatsby after the events of the novel have taken place. Gatsby, he says, possessed a "heightened sensitivity to the promises of life," possessed also an "extraordinary gift for hope. . . ." In order to make sure that we see Gatsby as a figure who is larger than life, Fitzgerald never lets us see him up close. We are never privy to his thoughts; and we gain, during the course of the novel, only a vague knowledge of his rise to worldly success. Throughout the novel, he remains somewhat of a mystery—a matter of endless speculation for Nick Carraway and others. Carraway first sees him from afar, as a semi-mythic figure who—standing on the vast lawn of his newly-acquired estate on the North Shore of Long Island—stretches his arms toward the dark water "in a curious way," looking at a "single green light . . . that might have been the end of a dock." The light, we eventually learn, is at the end of Daisy Buchanan's dock; and, at the close of the novel, Carraway recalls the first time he saw Gatsby—thinking of Gatsby's "wonder when he first picked out the green light at the end of Daisy's dock," the light signifying Gatsby's "gift for hope."

Gatsby is great insofar as he is an "extravagantly ambitious" self-

made man who "sprang from his Platonic conception of himself."
By contrast, Tom Buchanan, a child of privilege, is vulgar, mean-
spirited, and purposeless; he stands for a conservatism turned
sour—forever muttering, as Carraway says, "impassioned gib-
berish" about the superiority of the white race. Tom and Daisy,
Carraway says, were "careless people [who] smashed up things
and creatures and then retreated back into their money or their
vast carelessness," and at one point Carraway shouts to Gatsby:
"They're a rotten crowd. You're worth the whole damn bunch put
together."

Like *The Rise of Silas Lapham, The Great Gatsby* is to some degree
a defense of the parvenu against the old order. The Buchanans of
America can play games with life—protecting themselves from
the consequences of these games because they are rich and established. But the novel is less a defense of Gatsby's dream, which
Carraway calls "appallingly sentimental," than a defense of "the
colossal vitality" of that dream. If Dreiser implicitly attacks America for promising what it cannot deliver, Fitzgerald implicitly
praises America for making such huge dreams possible. Gatsby is
worth more than the Buchanans not because he has led an exem-
plary life—Gatsby, Carraway says at the outset, "represented everything for which I have unaffected scorn"—but because he
possesses the capacity for hope and wonder. On the last page of
the novel, Carraway compares Gatsby's wonder to the wonder the
Dutch sailors must have felt when they first came upon the new
world of Long Island.

Did Fitzgerald have a romantic view of the self-made American,
a subject that he returned to in his last novel, *The Last Tycoon?* Not
at all. Gatsby's father shows Carraway that his son had outlined in
a book a daily work schedule and a list of "general resolves" that
bring to mind the list Franklin made in his *Autobiography,* but
Gatsby does not get ahead in life by being industrious and frugal;
he gets ahead, it is implied, by being a ruthless and shady businessman who consorts with gangsters. Moreover, Fitzgerald continually reminds us that if America nourishes huge dreams it also
produces a waste land of failures—those who, like the husband of
Tom Buchanan's girlfriend, lack the talent and energy to make it.
Nevertheless, Fitzgerald was entranced by the promise of American life. And Nick Carraway sounds very much like Walt Whitman when he says that New York, "seen from the Queensborough
Bridge is always the city seen for the first time, in its first wild
promise of all the mystery and the beauty in the world." It is a city,
Carraway thinks, in which ' "anything can happen . . . anything at
all. . . ." '

For all their differences, Dreiser and Fitzgerald have in common a fascination with the self-made American, the man who dreams a huge dream of success. America, they think, is a land of possibility, even if those who strive for success ultimately end up as failures. Most American writers of the last 50 years, however, have regarded America as a place of diminished possibility. They imply that you can better your condition but the price you pay for doing so is high; you lose your individuality, you become an organization man—a "good citizen" like the members of the Good Citizens League of Zenith, whose views Sinclair Lewis describes in *Babbitt* (1920) "all of them perceived that American Democracy did not imply any equality of wealth, but did demand a wholesome sameness of thought, dress, painting, morals, and vocabulary." Tocqueville wrote that "Americans put something heroic into their trading,"[80] but the modern American novelist usually implies that America's men of commerce lead a banal and trivial existence. The everyman of American literature since World War II is probably the man in John Cheever's *Bullet Park* (1969) who rides home on the commuter train "either drunk or weary or both"—humped unconscious over his black dispatch case "in a position that seems desperate and abject." Or it is the other main character, a man who works for "a manufacturing firm that produced a patent floor mop called Moppet, a line of furniture polish called Tudor, and Spang, a mouthwash." In many novels of the post-war period, the main emotion is desperation; the characters feel trapped in America.

The best novels of the period, however, escape these generalizations. Flem Snopes, the central character of Faulkner's *The Hamlet* (1940), is probably the most repulsive man of commerce in American literature—a man who has no natural vices, only a desire for power and money. Snopes clearly is evil, yet he brings out the evil—or at least the greed—in most of the inhabitants of the town he has settled in. It is wrong to regard Faulkner as a defender of the older order of the South against the "Northern" commercial values of the rapacious Snopes. Many of the representatives of the old order in Faulkner's work are not magnanimous and dignified patricians but obsessed and foolhardy egoists, mired in a grandiose vision of themselves and their family's past. If Faulkner's work resists easy categorization, so does the work of other Southern writers of distinction: Flannery O'Connor, Eudora Welty, and Robert Penn Warren. In the work of these writers, as in the work of Vladimir Nabokov, the vulgar parvenu often is treated more sympathetically than those who complacently regard themselves as morally or culturally superior to America's commercial civilization.

The closer we get to the present, the more difficult it is to make generalizations about American literature, yet three novels of the post-war period stand out as complex ruminations on the theme of possibility in America: Ralph Ellison's *Invisible Man* (1951), Saul Bellow's *Seize the Day* (1956), and John Updike's *Rabbit is Rich* (1981).

Graduating from high school, the narrator of Ellison's novel is one of several black youths forced to perform a variety of humiliating antics before an audience of drunken white "big shots"—the leaders of the Southern town in which he lives—after which he is allowed to recite a banal graduation speech. While giving the speech, his mouth filled with blood from the boxing show the youths were compelled to participate in, he says the words "social equality" rather than "social responsibility." The drunken audience grows silent, and a man asks him what he has said, to which he replies in fear, "social responsibility, sir." The man asks: "You sure that about 'equality' was a mistake?" The narrator replies "Oh yes sir," finishes his speech, receiving thunderous applause, and is rewarded with a scholarship to a black college because he is a young man who "will lead his people in the proper paths. . . ."

Thus the opening pages of Ellison's novel introduce us to a virulent racism that degrades and humiliates blacks. The notion of equality is not even honored as an ideal; the very word is taboo. When uttered by the narrator, it signals to the whites that the supposedly "good" black young man does not know his place in society. *Invisible Man*, however, is not primarily an exposé of racism. Although there are several scenes of brutal racial prejudice in the novel, the grotesque and comic adventures of the narrator teach him not the reality of racial prejudice but the reality of his invisibility. No one sees him; no one knows who he is. To the liberal white trustee of the black college he attends, he is an example of the progress of his race. To the white members of the "Brotherhood" (the Brotherhood clearly signifying the Communist Party), he is a valuable recruit who can be used to enlist the masses of Harlem in their cause. To a white woman in New York, he is a fierce and beautiful black lover. To Ras the Destroyer, the leader of a black nationalist group, he is a traitor to the cause of black solidarity. Ellison's novel is a *bildungsroman* in which the narrator is educated by what happens to him in the Deep South and on the streets of New York. He comes to realize that all these people in their different ways refuse "to recognize the beautiful absurdity of their American identity and mine."

The narrator, who remains nameless throughout the novel, does not seek this education. It is thrust upon him. At the college he tries hard to persuade the white trustee that he is a model black, but inadvertently he fails—fails so badly that he is dismissed from the college. He also tries hard to be a good member of the Brotherhood. Again he fails. These identities elude his grasp, but an identity of sorts comes upon him unawares. Trying to avoid Ras the Destroyer and his gang, he puts on green sunglasses and as a result he finds that many people think he is Rineheart, a hipster who is a numbers runner, gambler, pimp, lover, and preacher. Identity, the narrator learns, is a question of appearances. And he also learns that Rineheart's deceptions are for the people of Harlem "a principle of hope"—a way of alleviating the harsh reality of Harlem—whereas the ideologies expounded either by Ras or by the Brotherhood are a form of betrayal, a path out of the wilderness of the black American experience that can only lead to more suffering. Rineheart in all his guises is more in touch with the reality of the black American experience than either Ras or the Brotherhood. Rineheart's world, the narrator comes to the conclusion, "was possibility and he knew it. He was years ahead of me and I was a fool. . . . The world in which we lived was without boundaries. A vast seething, hot world of fluidity, and Rine the rascal was at home. Perhaps *only* Rine the rascal was at home in it."

From Rineheart he learns the need to shape his own identity, not have it thrust upon him. But at first all he is capable of is a negative response—an escape from the identities given to him. The final stage of his education also happens by accident. In the midst of a race riot, he finds himself being pursued by Ras' men as well as by the police. Running in the dark, he falls down into a coal bin. There in the pitch dark, he undergoes a purgation—a renunciation of his quest for an identity. First he refuses to get out, then he burns his identification papers, screams and plunges wildly about, dreams a strange dream, and wakes up "whole," having plunged out of history and arrived at an illusion-less present. He decides to remain "underground," refusing to take on a new identity, savoring the bitter realization that others—both black and white—do not see him.

But the narrator does not want to remain underground—living without an identity. He wants to say yes to something, especially since his grandfather had uttered a cryptic deathbed remark about "agree 'em to death and destruction." In the epilogue he wrestles with this problem, wondering whether his grandfather meant that "we were to affirm the principle on which the country was built and not the men, or at least not the men who did the violence." But he is not sure what his grandfather meant, and finally he decides to escape from the burden of the question—to avoid being either for or against America. "I assign myself no rank or any limit. . . . My world has become one of infinite possibilities." Saying yes to possibility, the narrator implies that everyone—like Rineheart—should create his own definition of himself. But one can only create one's identity out of the materials at hand. "America," the narrator says, "is woven of many strands; I would recognize them and let it so remain." The narrator does say yes to something—yes to the notion of a pluralistic America and a pluralistic self, a self composed of many strands. The narrator's journey towards consciousness of his invisibility has also been a journey towards accepting the "beautiful absurdity" of his American identity. Ellison's novel is an affirmation of possibility—of the American's struggle to create an identity that is his own. As the narrator remembers what a teacher of his said about Joyce's Stephen Daedulus: "Stephen's problem, like ours, was not actually one of creating the uncreated conscience of his race, but of creating the *uncreated features of his face.* Our task is that of making ourselves individuals."

Tommy Wilhelm, the central character of Saul Bellow's *Seize the Day* (1956), also journeys towards acceptance. At the end of the novel he seizes the day by accepting his own failure in life—breaking down and pitying himself, moving "towards the consummation of his heart's ultimate need." Like the narrator of *Invisible Man,* Wilhelm reaches this new understanding of himself by inadvertence. Wandering by accident into a funeral home, he views the open coffin of a stranger and begins to sob, not for the stranger but for himself.

Wilhelm's life has been one failure after another. While in college he had been conned into pursuing a career as a movie actor; it came to nothing because the agent was a charlatan. When the novel opens, Wilhelm is divorced and out of work—living in an apartment hotel on the Upper West Side of Manhattan. Looking for a way to make money quickly, he is conned by a Dr. Tamkin, a quack psychologist who persuades him to invest $700 in commodity futures, all of which he loses. Unlike Silas Lapham, Frank Cowperwood, and Jay Gatsby, Wilhelm lacks entrepreneurial talent; he is a loser from the start, his pursuit of the American dream of success continually ending in failure. Moreover, he is a failure as a son. He fails to persuade his father, a retired doctor who also lives in the apartment hotel, that his plight should be rewarded with fatherly sympathy. The father views the son with contempt as someone who makes too much of his problems. "They ought not to be turned into a career," he says. "Con-

centrate on real troubles—fatal sicknesses, accidents." Wilhelm
never persuades his father that his own problems are real.

What are we to make of Wilhelm, a man who is continually on
the verge of hysteria, a man overwhelmed by the difficulties of
life? Wilhelm, it is clear, is not a failure because an industrial or
financial aristocracy has made it difficult for him to succeed. Nor
is he a failure because he resisted pressures to conform. He wants
to succeed, but he does not know how to go about it. The opportunities of American life confuse him, make him act foolishly. In
some ways Wilhelm is an unsympathetic character—a slob, as his
father says—and we can understand the father's irritation with
him.

And yet the father is also an unsympathetic figure. Obsessed
with his health, all he can offer his son is a cold-hearted brand of
self-reliance: "Carry nobody on your back." Such a notion of self-
reliance leaves losers like Tommy Wilhelm with nothing to fall
back upon, with no one whom they can rely upon in their daily
struggle with the world of appearances that constitutes commercial Amercia. In this sea of confusion, what Wilhelm wants is
straightforward sympathy from his father, but the only sympathy
he gets is from a charlatan psychologist who understands the state
of Wilhelm's psyche. "You see," the psychologist says, "I understand what it is when the lonely person begins to feel like an
animal. When the night comes and he feels like howling from his
window like a wolf." Bellow's novel is not a work of social criticism,
for Bellow never rails at America's commercial civilization. Rather,
he gives us an affecting portrait of an isolated soul who cannot
cope with its complexities—a soul who ends up by howling like a
wolf, lavishing on himself the pity that he sought in vain from his
father.

If Tommy Wilhelm is a failure, Harry (Rabbit) Angstrom, the
central character of John Updike's *Rabbit is Rich* (1981) is a success.
Managing his late father-in-law's Toyota agency, he is making a lot
of money selling fuel-efficient cars during the gas crisis of 1979—
enough money to join a country club, go on a Caribbean vacation,
and buy an elegant stone house in the best suburb of Brewer,
Pennsylvania, the mid-sized industrial city in which he has lived all
his life.

Harry's life definitely has taken a turn for the better. In the two
earlier novels of Updike's trilogy—*Rabbit, Run* (1961) and *Rabbit
Redux* (1971)—Harry's life was more like Tommy Wilhelm's. The
sordid events of those novels often haunt Harry in *Rabbit is Rich*,
but they do not overwhelm him. Updike's novel is thick with the

difficulties of family life, but in *Rabbit is Rich* Harry no longer feels trapped, no longer feels that he wants to run away from the entanglements of family life. At the end of the novel, he prepares to settle down in the new house he has just moved into—feeling exultant that he can afford to move into a better neighborhood.

In the first two novels of the trilogy, Updike tended to look down at Harry, regarding him as a creature to be pitied for his inability to cope with life. In *Rabbit is Rich* Harry is no longer a figure of pathos—a victim. He is someone the reader enjoys if not admires—enjoys because he possesses a "persisting sense of wonder that the world is as it is and that he himself, just as *he* is, is always there to apprehend it."[81] His mind cluttered and curious, Harry is in some ways very much like the Leopold Bloom of Joyce's *Ulysses*.

What is the reader supposed to make of Harry Angstrom? Some critics have argued that Updike is condescending towards his main character—and contemptuous of his vulgar mind and lower-middle-class tastes. According to one critic, "What could be more gratifying [for the reader] than to wallow around in—while carefully keeping one's distance from—a world of tacky people who live in tacky houses filled with tacky furniture, who watch tacky television shows and eat tacky food while thinking tacky thoughts?"[82] No doubt, Updike—in trying to do justice to the "rude rank spirit" of American civilization—at times teeters on the edge of condescension. Yet by and large he views Harry with wonder and detachment as someone who exhibits a zest for life that is very much in the American grain.

That zest is apparent in Harry's attitude towards business. Far from hating commercial life, he is exhilirated by it. Recounting to his son how good a car salesman his father-in-law was, Harry says: "By the time he had sold a car to the customer the poor bozo thought he was robbing old Fred blind when the fact is the deal had angles to it like a spider web." Commercial life, Updike implies, is a game of appearances—a game not for the naive and the gullible—but the entrepreneurial energy that goes into it is impressive. Looking at the new stores and restaurants that have sprouted up in the decayed downtown area of Brewer, Harry reflects: "The world keeps ending but new people too dumb to know it keep showing up as if the fun's just started." Although *Rabbit is Rich* is a flawed novel—weakened by the excessive attention Updike pays to Harry's sex life, weakened also by Updike's penchant for lush prose—it is a comic and moving commentary on the American dream of success.

IV

"Ineptitude," Flaubert said, "consists in wanting to reach conclusions."[83] Novels and poems—even essays and letters—resist being used as building blocks in the construction of a thesis about the idea of equality in American literature. And yet our survey of American literature does push us towards a conclusion of sorts: there is a tension in American literature between the literary culture and the masterpieces of American literature. The masterpieces of American literature often take their stand, so to speak, against the literary culture; they question some of its ruling assumptions, they puncture its complacency.

The literary culture generally speaks with the voice of Edwards or Jefferson; it attacks commerce and industry for destroying an old communal order in which equality prevailed, or it laments that the preoccupation with material success has unleashed an aggressive individualism that has led to a new form of inequality—one based on wealth. To some degree, the masterpieces of American literature reject this view—defending the selfish and crude new order against the refined highmindedness of the old order. In some of the great works of American literature, we hear the voice of Franklin—not so much the Franklin who praises frugality and industriousness but, rather, the Franklin who celebrates the opportunity of American life—the opportunity for men of talent and ambition to make something of themselves, even if what they turn out to be is vulgar and ruthless. We hear this voice intermittently in Emerson, Whitman, James, Twain, Howells, Adams (not the Adams of *The Education*), Dreiser, Fitzgerald, Faulkner, Ellison, Bellow, and Updike. We even hear it sometimes in Hawthorne, but we never hear it in Melville. At times the major American writers say no to complacent visions of progress, but they often say yes to the energy of American life—an energy, Tocqueville suggested, that springs from "the restless ambition born of equality."

And yet this "yes," like Fitzgerald's "yes" to Gatsby, is often rich in melancholy. The major American writers know that the possibility of American life also means the strong possibility that one's huge dreams will be shattered. But American writers also have been half in love with failure because, like Melville, they have thought that in a predominantly commercial society failure is the true test of greatness. For success is a sign of artistic failure—a sign that one's work is appreciated by the masses, who have no taste. In "The Man of Letters as Man of Business," Howells speaks of the "instinctive sense of dishonor that money-purchase does to art."[84] Even those writers who have been fascinated by the possibility of American life have thought that a predominantly commercial society cannot do the serious writer justice, for commerce—they assume—is always at odds with art.

Can we not say, then, that the major American writers have had a lover's quarrel with equality? They praise equality in America insofar as it spawns men of energy and imagination, yet they damn it insofar as it breeds ruthless plutocrats and banal conformists—breeds men whose ambition is paltry and taste is vulgar. Do the major American writers admire the driven and energetic American, for trying to better his condition, or do they condemn him for ruthlessly pursuing his narrow self-interest? The question is often left unanswered. As Fitzgerald said: "The test of a first-rate intelligence is the ability to hold two opposed ideas in the mind at the same time, and still retain the ability to function."[85] In the best works of American literature, we often hear not so much two opposed ideas as two opposing voices—the voice of Franklin struggling with the voice of either Edwards or Jefferson.

NOTES

1. Quoted in A.N. Kaul, *The American Vision* (New Haven: Yale University Press, 1963), p. 20.

2. "Information For Those Who Would Remove to America," *Autobiography And Other Writings*, ed. Russel B. Nye (Boston: Houghton Mifflin, 1958), p. 190.

3. Letter to John Adams, *The Portable Thomas Jefferson*, ed. Merrill D. Peterson (New York: Viking, 1975), p. 539.

4. *Democracy in America*, ed. J. P. Mayer (Garden City: Doubleday Anchor, 1969), Vol. 1, p. 256.

5. Quoted in Eric Foner, "*Common Sense* and Paine's Republicanism," *Early American Literature: A Collection of Critical Essays*, ed. Michael T. Gilmore (Englewood Cliffs: Prentice-Hall, 1980), p. 105.

6. "Notes on the State of Virginia," *The Portable Thomas Jefferson*, p. 217.

7. "Reality in America," *The Liberal Imagination* (Garden City: Doubleday Anchor, 1953), p. 7.

8. *Democracy in America*, Vol. 1, p. 404.

9. Quoted in Larzer Ziff, *Literary Democracy* (New York: Viking, 1981), p. 39.

10. *Selected Prose and Poetry*, ed. Reginald L. Cook (New York: Rinehart, 1955), p. 480.

11. "The American Scholar," *Selected Prose and Poetry*, p. 48.

12. Ibid., p. 67.

13. *Selected Prose and Poetry*, p. 470.

14. Quoted in Ziff, p. 19.

15. "Hawthorne and His Mosses," *Herman Melville: Stories, Poems, and Letters*, ed. R.W.B. Lewis (New York: Dell, 1962), p. 43.

16. Letter to Hawthorne, *Herman Melville: Stories, Poems, and Letters*, p. 43.

19. Newton Arvin, *Herman Melville* (New York: Viking, 1957), p. 180.

20. R.W.B. Lewis, Afterword to *The Confidence-Man* (New York: New American Library, 1964), p. 267.

21. Arvin, p. 97.

22. Letter to Hawthorne, *Herman Melville: Stories, Poems, and Letters*, pp. 60–61.

23. "Hawthorne and His Mosses," *Herman Melville: Stories, Poems, and Letters*, p. 48.

24. Letter to Evert A. Duyckinck, *Herman Melville: Stories, Poems, and Letters*, p. 358.

25. Quoted in Henry Nash Smith, *Democracy and the Novel* (New York: Oxford, 1978), p. 5.

26. *Herman Melville: Stories, Poems, and Letters,*, p. 48.

27. *Walt Whitman: Complete Poetry and Collected Prose* (New York: The Library of America, 1982), p. 939.

28. Ibid., p. 986.

29. Ibid., p. 900.

30. Ibid., p. 944.

31. Ibid., p. 939.

32. Ibid., p. 937.

33. Ibid., p. 1066.

34. *Democracy in America*, Vol. 2, p. 558.

35. *A Henry Adams Reader*, ed. Elizabeth Stevenson (Garden City: Doubleday Anchor, 1959), p. 57 and p. 84.

36. *Whitman*, p. 1068.

37. *The Education of Henry Adams* (New York: Random House, 1931), pp. 280–281.

38. Quoted in J. R. Pole, *The Pursuit of Equality in American History*, (Berkeley: University of California Press, 1978), p. 206.

39. *The American Scene*, ed. Leon Edel (Bloomington: Indiana University Press, 1968), p. 83.

40. Ibid., p. 84.

41. Ibid., p. 67.

42. Ibid., p. 143.

43. Ibid., p. 115.

44. Ibid., p. 64.

45. Ibid., p. 84.

46. Ibid., p. 86.

47. Ibid., p. 126.

48. Ibid., p. 128

49. Ibid., p. 127.

50. Ibid., p. 125.

51. Ibid., p. 128.

52. Ibid., p. 120.

53. Ibid., p. 124.

54. Ibid.

55. *Whitman*, p. 1075.

56. *The American Scene*, p. 124.

57. Ibid., p. 178.

58. Quoted in Leon Edel, *Henry James: The Conquest of London* (New York: Avon Books, 1978), p. 390.

59. Quoted in Edel, p. 388.

60. *The Education of Henry Adams*, p. 499.

61. Ibid., p. 499–500.

62. Quoted in Leon Edel, *Henry James: The Treacherous Years* (New York: Avon Books, 1978), p. 57.

63. *The Education of Henry Adams*, p. 238.

64. Quoted in Morton and Lucia White, *The Intellectual Versus the City* (New York: Menton/New American Library, 1964), p. 76.

65. *The Education of Henry Adams*, p. 238.

66. J.C. Levenson, quoted in William Dusinberre, *Henry Adams: The Myth of Failure* (Charlottesville, The University of Virginia Press, 1980), p. 242.

67. Quoted in Dusinberre, p. 21.

68. Quoted in Dusinberre, p. 119.

69. *The Education of Henry Adams*, p. 501.

70. Justin Kaplan, *Mr. Clemens and Mark Twain* (New York: Simon and Schuster, 1970), p. 280.

71. Quoted in John F. Kasson, *Civilizing the Machine* (New York: Penguin, 1977), p. 214.

72. Quoted in Kasson, pp. 223–224.

73. Kasson, p. 230.

74. Quoted in Morton and Lucia White, p. 139.

75. Quoted in White, p. 137.

76. Quoted in White, p. 142.

77. Quoted in White, p. 133.

78. Afterword to *An American Tragedy* (New York: New American Library, 1964), p. 818 and p. 821.

79. Ibid., p. 822.

80. *Democracy in America*, Vol. 1, p. 403.

81. Thomas R. Edwards, "Updike's Rabbit Trilogy," *The Atlantic* (October, 1981), p. 96.

82. Jonathan Yardley, "'Rabbit' Isn't Rich," *The Washington Post*, April 26, 1982, Section C, p. 9.

83. *The Letters of Gustave Flaubert*, ed. Francis Steegmuller (Cambridge: Harvard University Press, 1980), p.128.

84. *Literature and Life* (New York: Harper & Brothers, 1902), p. 3.

85. "The Crack-Up," *The Bodley Head F. Scott Fitzgerald* (London: Bodley Head, 1960), Vol. 3, p. 388.

The New Egalitarianism

Marc F. Plattner

IT IS UNIVERSALLY AGREED that the decade of the 1960's witnessed a striking resurgence of the egalitarian spirit in American political life. Congressional enactment in the mid-1960's of landmark civil-rights legislation and of the war on poverty bears irrefutable testimony to this fact. It is also widely recognized, however, that in the wake of these legislative triumphs there quickly began to emerge a subtle but profound alteration in the way many Americans interpreted the political meaning of equality. The novelty of this new egalitarianism, and the nature of its departure from the traditional liberal understanding, has been aptly characterized in terms of a shift of focus from equality of opportunity to equality of result.

This shift was most clearly manifested in public policy in the area of so-called "affirmative action" programs. Here what began as an attempt to combat discrimination against minority-group members was gradually transformed in the direction of a quota system for the allocation of jobs. Similarly, with regard to voting rights, the standard of equal access to the ballot began to slide over into a standard of equal representation for minorities by elected officials belonging to their own group. In other areas the new egalitarianism may have been less successful in gaining embodiment in public policy, but it nonetheless came to dominate the "liberal" viewpoint on a whole range of social, political, and economic issues.

During the 1970's, the proponents of the new egalitarianism, especially in the academic and intellectual communities, increasingly turned their attention directly to the issue of economic inequality in our capitalist society. Their proposed remedy for what they regarded as an unacceptable economic "gap" between rich and poor was breathtakingly bold and straightforward: government should simply undertake a redistribution of income, taking money from the rich and giving it to the poor to produce a more equal distribution of economic well-being. Although this policy, in the rather modest form of George McGovern's "Demogrant" proposal, was overwhelmingly rejected by the electorate in the 1972 Presidential campaign, income redistribution remained a centerpiece of the new egalitarian agenda during the remainder of the decade.

Before further analyzing the ideological underpinnings of income redistribution, it is necessary to clear up an important ambiguity about the meaning of this term. Economists often discuss the income redistribution entailed in almost any conceivable set of government tax and spending policies. A tax on cigarettes will have the effect of tilting the post-tax distribution of income in favor of non-smokers. Government expenditures on highways or on libraries will in effect redistribute income in favor of the beneficiaries of these services. As these examples indicate, it is true that modern activist governments inevitably wind up redirecting resources to and from a bewildering variety of cross-cutting and overlapping groups; it is also true, however, that the largely random income effects of such taxing and spending are essentially irrelevant to the kind of income redistribution advocated by the new egalitarians.

It would surely be misleading, though, to suggest that the income effects on rich and poor of federal taxing and spending are meant to be purely random. The progressive income tax is clearly designed to make the rich bear a more than proportionately larger share of the federal tax burden than the poor. And many government spending programs are meant to benefit solely or principally the poor. Although the income effects of *these* taxing and spending policies may not be as large in practice as some might wish, there can be no doubt that they succeed in making the post-fisc distribution of income in America considerably more equal than the pre-fisc distribution.

From this fact, the conclusion has often been drawn—and not merely by some of the new egalitarians, but by economists of all persuasions—that the modern welfare state is properly understood as an instrument for redistributing income from rich to poor. The complaint of the new egalitarians is that the degree of such redistribution has been far too modest, a result that they attribute in large part to the fact that the redistributive purpose of the welfare state has not been made sufficiently explicit. Because the welfare state has been reluctant to acknowledge frankly its redistributive aims, it has resorted to cumbersome and wasteful programs that seek indirectly to raise the incomes of the poor through education and training. Even those programs that more directly augment the income of the poor are needlessly complex and fragmented. According to the new egalitarians, then, our society should openly recognize that it is the business of government to redistribute income to produce greater equality, and the policies of the welfare state should be rationalized so that this goal can be more efficiently pursued.

Although it is often thus presented in the guise of a logical extension of traditional liberal social policy, the redistributionist doctrine in fact represents, on the level of principle, a radical transformation of the welfare state. For the key elements of the welfare state were originally justified in terms that did not at all invoke as their goal the attainment of a more equal distribution of income. The progressive income tax, which in the United States was enacted more than 20 years before the federal social programs brought into being by the New Deal, was generally defended as a method of achieving "equality of sacrifice" among taxpayers rather than as an instrument of redistribution. Indeed, with a maximum rate of 7 per cent, the progressive tax instituted in 1913 could hardly have been expected to have significant redistributive effects. But even when subsequent legislation sharply raised the degree of progressivity, the predominant justification continued to be made in terms of the "ability to pay" of different classes of taxpayers. As Walter J. Blum has noted, "until relatively recent times, almost all the accepted justifications for progression avoided embracing redistribution of economic things: and even the few commentators who supported progression on redistributive grounds invariably stopped short of proposing that the government explicitly increase taxes on the affluent in order to bestow more resources on the poor."

A similar point may be made about the major federal social programs. Not only were these expenditures originally justified on non-redistributive grounds, but they continue to be viewed by the American public as directed toward other purposes. As Martin Feldstein has written, "The actual payments by the government are not regarded as general transfers to achieve greater equality. Rather they are benefits initiated by particular events, by catastrophic conditions, or by the inability of the beneficiary to act on his own behalf. Most of the benefits are regarded as insurance benefits to which rights are earned through the payment of compulsory taxes: unemployment insurance, social security, Medicare, and others. Welfare, Medicaid, and food stamps are seen as reserved for those who are catastrophically poor. And methods of awarding educational grants and places in mental hospitals reflect the agreement that the beneficiaries are incapable of making their own decisions."

With some of the early Great Society programs, it is true, we do begin to find an animating concern with the problem of income inequality, particularly where minority groups are concerned. But even here, the guiding assumption was that the undesirable disparities in the earnings of racial or ethnic groups were the product of unequal opportunity. Hence it was deemed proper for government to take action to enhance the opportunity of those who were unfairly disadvantaged and thus enable them to compete on an equal footing for jobs and income. It was widely hoped that anti-discrimination measures and education programs such as Head Start would improve the earning capacity of their beneficiaries and ultimately reduce income inequalities between the races (and thus perhaps among individuals as well). But such policies in no way called into question the view that income itself, under ordinary circumstances, should not be allocated by the government but rather should be allowed to accrue to individuals in accordance with their own productive accomplishments.

An explicit government policy aimed directly at redistributing income for the sake of greater income equality is a very different matter from progressive taxation, or social insurance, or welfare, or equal opportunity programs. For policies of the latter sort, however one may judge their desirability or effectiveness, are all quite compatible with the basic principle of a liberal capitalist society—namely, that the property of individuals is genuinely private and that they are entitled to keep what they have legally earned, except for that portion of their wealth or earnings which they must contribute in taxes for defraying the cost of public expenses. Income redistribution, by contrast, erodes the dividing line between private and public that is the hallmark of liberalism. If government is empowered to determine the proper distribution of income, individuals can no longer be considered to have a just title to the rewards gained by their own labor; instead, they have a legitimate claim only to those resources which government allots to them (or suffers them to retain). Relieving the poor or enhancing the opportunity of the disadvantaged can, without stretching matters too far, be regarded as serving legitimate public purposes and hence as being proper objects of tax-supported government expenditure. But when government takes money from some and gives it to others simply to attain a desired distribution of income, the concept of a public expense loses all distinctive meaning, and the wealth of the society as a whole has in principle been collectivized.

Although a few of the American proponents of income redistribution have been willing to call themselves socialists, most have not openly proclaimed an opposition to capitalism, portraying themselves rather as liberal reformers. And there is a considerable element of truth in this self-depiction. For even though (as I believe to be the case) the doctrine of income redistribution is fundamentally destructive of liberal capitalism, there can be no question that it derives from a profoundly bourgeois mode of thinking. In this connection, it is well to remember Karl Marx's contempt for those on the Left who "make a fuss about so-called *distribution* and put the principal stress upon it." Marx goes on, in his *Critique of the Gotha Program,* to write: "vulgar socialism (and from it in turn a section of the democracy) has taken over from the bourgeois economists the consideration and treatment of distribution as independent of the mode of production . . ." For Marx himself, of course, it was the mode of production that was the crucial factor, of which the pattern of distribution was merely a derivative feature.

The contemporary champions of income redistribution appear, for the most part, to have no objection at all to the prevailing capitalist mode of production. Not only is there almost no trace of Marxist influence in their thought, but they tend to be thoroughly imbued with the outlook of present-day "bourgeois economics." They are keen admirers of the efficiency of the market. And they are perfectly willing to recognize and endorse the indispensable role of individual incentives in maximizing productivity and wealth. Hence their commitment to economic equality is very far from being absolute. In fact, they are quite ready to compromise it for the sake of avoiding too great a loss in society's economic well-being. This is why the new egalitarians almost all accept in one form or another what Arthur Okun has termed "the big trade-off"—i.e., the need to balance the alleged benefits in economic equality brought by income redistribution against its costs in reduced economic efficiency.

Redistributionism is a curiously hybrid doctrine, one which seeks to preserve the individual liberty and economic efficiency achieved in market societies, but to combine these with a commitment to economic equality generally associated with socialist doc-

trines. From the perspective of genuine socialism or of truly
radical egalitarianism, the redistributionist approach must inevitably appear as a half-measure which remains too attached to
liberalism to be able to fulfill its egalitarian aspirations. Yet from
the perspective of genuine liberalism, redistributionism should be
regarded as a heresy which sacrifices the essential bulwarks of
individual liberty in the name of a misguided conception of equality. I believe that redistributionism is in fact an unstable and
inconsistent theoretical mixture that is vulnerable to the criticism
of both sides. But it is of course the conflict between redistributionism and liberal capitalism that here will be the focus of our
concern.

Although I have characterized redistributionism as a liberal
heresy, it naturally does not appear in this light to its proponents.
They tend to see themselves as the true heritors of the liberal
spirit, striving to repair the inconsistencies within the liberal tradition by returning to first principles. In their eyes, however, the
first principle of liberalism is equality. It was liberalism which
proclaimed the natural equality of men, and which affirmed that
all men equally possess certain inalienable rights. And it is our
liberal democratic Constitution which secures the equal political
rights of all Americans. Yet these same ideas and institutions, the
redistributionists note, have coexisted with an economic system—
capitalism—that not merely tolerates but fosters marked inequalities in income and wealth. Thus we are faced, as Arthur Okun
put it, with the "double standard of capitalist democracy, profess-
ing and pursuing an egalitarian political and social system and
simultaneously generating gaping disparities in economic well-
being."

Is there in fact, as the redistributionists argue, a contradiction
between the equal political rights guaranteed by liberal democracy and the unequal economic outcomes generated by capitalism? Only if one abandons the traditional liberal criterion of
equality of opportunity in order to embrace the standard of
equality of result. Yet even the liberal democratic conception of
equality of *political* rights ultimately makes sense only from the
perspective of equality of opportunity. Consider the right to vote,
the most basic of political rights in a liberal democracy. Although
the right to cast a ballot (as well as the right to run for office) is
distributed equally among the citizenry, this provides no guarantee whatsoever that the outcomes of elections will in any sense be
egalitarian. Indeed it is well known to all, and hardly ever seriously objected to by any, that elected officials in the United States
are much wealthier and more highly educated than the average

citizen. For it is believed that ability to conduct the public's business is a valid consideration in the choice of elected officials, and rarely denied that such ability is, on average, more likely to be found among those who have succeeded in attaining higher income and more years of education. Yet popular election is by no means the only method, and certainly not the most egalitarian method, of determining who shall hold public office. The democracies of ancient Greece, including the Athenian, selected many of their most important public officials by lot. This is surely the method one would choose if one's guiding consideration were equality of result—but (with the exception of the trial jury) it is a method that has been wholly rejected by modern liberal democracy.

The equality of rights that is affirmed by liberalism does not mean equality of results. For the most part, this is still generally taken for granted in the political sphere. If it is increasingly coming to be questioned in the economic sphere, that is because of a marked change that has taken place in the understanding of what constitutes economic rights. Today when people speak of economic rights, as various United Nations documents attest, they are usually referring to the "right" of individuals to be provided with certain economic goods and services (and of the concomitant obligation of governments to see to it that these goods and services are duly provided). Thus Article 25 of the United Nations Universal Declaration on Human Rights, for example, proclaims; "Everyone has the right to a standard of living adequate for the health and well-being of himself and of his family, including food, clothing, housing and medical care and necessary social services, and the right to security in the event of unemployment, sickness, disability, widowhood, old age or other lack of livelihood in circumstances beyond his control." If all people have a basic human right to an "adequate" standard of living, it is hardly unreasonable to argue that other people's income should be redistributed in order to provide it.

Such an understanding of economic rights, however, is utterly foreign to the basic premises of liberalism. The original liberal teaching about economic rights may be encapsulated in a single phrase—the right of property, which was joined with the right to life and the right to liberty to form the three fundamental natural rights in the liberal pantheon. The right of property did not entitle anyone to be provided by other men or by government with economic goods and services. Rather it entitled every man to enjoy in the form of private property those possessions which he had honestly acquired through his own efforts. The barrier which such a right poses to the idea of income redistribution is clearly expressed in the following words of Thomas Jefferson: "To take from one, because it is thought his own industry and that of his fathers has acquired too much, in order to spare to others, who, or whose fathers have not exercised equal industry and skill, is to violate arbitrarily the first principle of association, 'the guarantee to everyone of a free exercise of his industry and the fruits acquired by it.' "

Today, however, the right of property, in theory if not in practice, is unquestionably in eclipse. Although the United Nations Universal Declaration on Human Rights (1948) still recognizes "the right to own property alone as well as in association with others" and not to be "arbitrarily deprived" of one's property, all mention of the right of property has disappeared from more recent United Nations documents on economic rights. Moreover, except for the case of the libertarian Robert Nozick, the revival of teachings based on rights in contemporary political theory has been marked by an imposing silence on the issue of the right of property. Indeed, most of the current proponents of redistribution do not even feel a need to grapple directly with the objections to their viewpoint that would arise from taking seriously the right of property.

Yet the right of property is an absolutely essential element in the original understanding of American liberal democracy. Incontrovertible evidence for this assertion may be found in *Federalist* 10, which is widely and properly regarded as the most authoritative exposition of the political philosophy underlying the Constitution of the United States. In this classic essay, Madison writes: "The diversity in the faculties of men, from which the rights of property originate, is not less an insuperable obstacle to a uniformity of interests. The protection of these faculties is *the first object of government*. From the protection of different and unequal faculties of acquiring property, the possession of different degrees and kinds of property immediately results . . ." (italics mine). This passage makes it clear that the American Founders viewed economic inequality as an inevitable and wholly unobjectionable consequence of the kind of political arrangements they sought to establish. That is to say, a government that is dedicated to protecting individual rights (including, of course, the right of property) will necessarily generate unequal economic outcomes in proportion to the different degrees of industry and skill with which individuals engage in the pursuit of wealth.

The liberal view of property shared by the American Founders had its origins in the political philosophy of John Locke. In the famous chapter "Of Property" in his *Second Treatise of Government,* Locke begins by posing the following problem: if the earth and its natural products have been given (by God) to all mankind in common, how could any individual ever come to have a claim to private property? Indeed, without the consent of all mankind, how could anyone even have a right to consume any of the fruits of the earth? The crucial first step in Locke's answer to these questions is this: "Though the earth and all inferior creatures be common to all men, yet every man has a property in his own person; this nobody has any right to but himself. The labor of his body and the work of his hands, we may say, are properly his." Therefore, in the state of nature, when a man applies his labor to any portion of the great natural commons, it thereby becomes his property. "For this labor being the unquestionable property of the laborer, no man but he can have a right to what that is once joined to, at least where there is enough and as good left in common for others."

Obviously, this natural right of property can no longer apply in undiluted fashion in political societies, where the commons has disappeared, and "the laws regulate the right of property, and the possession of land is determined by positive constitutions." We cannot here explore the complex relationships linking Locke's teaching about natural property and his teaching about civil property. It must suffice to assert that even in political society, "the great foundation of property" remains the fact that man is "master of himself and proprietor of his own person and the actions or labor of it." Moreover, since men naturally exercise "different degrees of industry," and since the invention of money makes it possible for individuals to enlarge their fortunes, it follows as a matter of course that civilized societies will be characterized by considerable inequalities of property.

It is not surprising that those who are opposed to economic inequality would seek to reject the Lockean justification for private property. One might expect them perhaps to place greater weight on the commonness of the earth and its products, or to focus upon the discrepancies in civil society between labor and its rewards, or to emphasize the social rather than individual nature of labor under modern industrial conditions. The contemporary redistributionists, however, tend to attack the Lockean viewpoint at an even more fundamental level by challenging its most basic assertion. That is, they essentially deny the moral legitimacy of the view that "every man has a property in his own person" and that "the labor of his body and the work of his hands . . . are properly his."

This critique, which may be found in some of the more popular redistributionist writers as well, receives its most sophisticated presentation in the most highly acclaimed work of political theory of the 1970s—John Rawls' *A Theory of Justice*. Rawls' book is devoted in considerable part to providing the moral case for redistribution. His celebrated second principle of justice—the "difference principle"—requires that "economic inequalities are to be arranged so that they are . . . to the greatest benefit of the least advantaged." The practical implication of this principle is that society must redistribute income up to the point where the wealth of the poorest part of the population is maximized. In elaborating the difference principle, Rawls explicitly rejects what he calls the conception of "liberal equality"—i.e., political equality and a market economy modified by active government efforts at promoting equality of opportunity. He finds this conception inadequate because it seeks to mitigate *only* those inequalities arising from differences in historical and social circumstances, thereby allowing genuine differences in individual ability and effort to emerge as the determinants of economic success. For Rawls himself, "There is no more reason to permit the distribution of income and wealth to be settled by the distribution of natural assets than by historical and social fortune."

The reasoning behind this extraordinary assertion of Rawls' may be summarized as follows: Individuals cannot in any sense be said to deserve the genetic endowments that they are born with. The distribution of these endowments is "arbitrary from a moral point of view." Moreover, the amount of effort people are willing to make is in large measure influenced by their natural gifts. Therefore, individuals who are more productive because of their greater natural abilities or effort have no moral claim to greater rewards. There could hardly be a more fundamental rejection of the Lockean natural right of property. Individuals are not entitled to enjoy the fruits of their own labor, because the skill and industry that constitute their labor cannot be considered, in a moral sense, to be properly their own.

Accordingly, "the difference principle represents, in effect, an agreement to regard the distribution of natural talents as a *common* asset and to share in the benefits of this distribution whatever it turns out to be." (italics mine). It would be difficult to imagine a more thoroughgoingly collectivist premise. The natural talents of the individual are regarded not as his own property but as the property of the community. Yet Rawls does not follow through toward the full-fledged collectivism his premises seem to imply. For like most contemporary redistributionists, he also accepts wholeheartedly the Lockean, bourgeois goal of maximizing the private wealth of the individual. Indeed, the very aim of the difference principle is to maximize the private wealth of the least advantaged. For the sake of this end, Rawls is led to endorse the utility of market mechanisms and especially the granting of differential economic incentives to spur greater productivity. That is, he recognizes that the gains in economic efficiency secured by permitting at least somewhat greater rewards to accrue to the skillful and industrious will make the poor economically better off in the long run than they would be with a completely equal distribution of income. Rawls thus winds up in the curious position of simultaneously denying that more productive individuals deserve to receive greater rewards and asserting that justice requires that more productive individuals receive greater rewards—a splendid illustration of the contradictory moral tendencies at the core of the redistributionist viewpoint.

Yet whatever its deeper deficiencies, there can be no question that by the 1970s the redistributionist outlook had acquired a considerable degree of superficial plausibility. A great many people found it quite easy to assent to the following propositions:

1) If we believe political equality is a good thing (as we do), then we should also believe that economic equality is a good thing.

2) Therefore, government should take from the rich and give to the poor in order to promote economic equality.

3) Unfortunately, the extent of such transfers must be limited by the practical consideration that redistribution, by impairing people's economic incentives, reduces the wealth of the society as a whole. Hence we can't redistribute as much as our ethical preference for equality would dictate without making everybody economically worse off, including the poor.

4) But (apart from this practical consideration) there is no *moral* reason not to take away the earnings of the better off for the purpose of redistribution.

The degree of acceptance of this final proposition is perhaps the most critical determinant of the progress of the new egalitarianism. The failure of redistributionism to triumph in the political arena thus far reflects the fact that ordinary Americans still generally cling to the belief that people have a moral right to keep what they have legitimately earned. But it is hard to find support for this view in the thought of contemporary intellectuals. Not only has the original liberal idea of a natural right of property long been abandoned, but our economic and moral theorists have come to reject any notion implying that people *deserve* the economic rewards that their honest industry and skill have earned them. And this is true not merely for the new egalitarians but also for some of the most prominent defenders of capitalism.

Indeed, I believe that the vulnerability of liberal capitalism to the redistributionist ideology of the new egalitarianism may in large part be traced to a shift in the ground on which liberal capitalism has been defended. For the leading twentieth-century proponents of a capitalist order, who for the most part have been academic economists, have tended to center their case around the concept of "the free market" rather than the right of property. As a result, their primary emphasis has been on the superior economic *efficiency* of the market and the greater *freedom* which is allowed to the individual when government refrains from intervening in the economy. But in abandoning the language of rights, these thinkers have also rendered themselves unwilling to make any claim whatever for the *justice* of capitalism.

Consider, for example, the discussion of the "ethics of distribution" in Milton Friedman's classic *Capitalism and Freedom*. Here Friedman employs the same basic moral argument as that espoused by John Rawls: "Most differences of status or position or wealth can be regarded as the product of chance at a far enough remove. The man who is hard working and thrifty is to be regarded as 'deserving,' yet those qualities owe much to the genes he was fortunate (or unfortunate?) enough to inherit." On the basis of such considerations, Friedman is led to conclude: "I find it difficult to justify either accepting or rejecting ["the so-called capitalist ethic" (of payment according to product)], or to justify any alternative principle. I am led to the view that it cannot in and of itself be regarded as an ethical principle; that it must be regarded as instrumental or a corollary of some other principle such as freedom." Thus Friedman's opposition to government-directed redistribution is grounded not on justice, but on considerations of freedom and efficiency.

One finds a similar, though lengthier and more sophisticated treatment of this issue in F. A. Hayek's *The Constitution of Liberty*. Hayek too makes the argument that "The inborn as well as the acquired gifts of a person clearly have a value to his fellows which does not depend on any credit due to him for possessing them. . . . A good mind or a fine voice, a beautiful face or a skillful hand, and a ready wit or an attractive personality are in a large measure as independent of a person's efforts as the opportunities or the experiences he has had." But Hayek draws an even sharper conclusion from this line of reasoning than Friedman does. For he not only explicitly denies that capitalism is just in the sense of achieving proportionality of reward to moral merit, but even goes so far as to assert that any attempt to introduce the principle of distributive justice into economic life "would produce a society which in all essential respects would be the opposite of a free society . . ."

It is most revealing in this context to look at a common source for the moral perspective shared by the redistributionist Rawls and free market champions Friedman and Hayek—an essay on "The Ethics of Competition" written in 1923 by University of Chicago economist Frank Knight. This essay is prominently footnoted by Rawls in his discussion of moral desert; it was reprinted in a collection of Knight's essays (under the same title) of which Friedman was a co-editor; and Hayek, in citing another work of Knight's in his own discussion of distributive justice, refers to Knight as "the American economist who has done most to advance our understanding of a free society." Two aspects of "The Ethics of Competition" are particularly striking. First, it presents an almost unrelievedly critical appraisal both of the quality of life of capitalist civilization, and of the justice of the income distribution produced by a free market. Second, its ethical perspective is predominantly and explicitly Christian, though reflecting a modern and somewhat secularized version of Christianity: "It seems fairly clear . . . that it is from Christianity (and from Kant, who merely systematized Christian, or Pauline, principles) that modern common sense derives its conception of what is ethical as stated when the point is explicitly under discussion."

This orientation is apparent in Knight's formulation of the notion that natural ability cannot provide a legitimate moral title to reward: "From the standpoint of absolute ethics most persons will probably agree that inherited capacity represents an obligation to the world rather than a claim upon it." The main burden of Knight's argument is that the human qualities rewarded by capitalism are not the highest human virtues. "But, after all," he asks, "does anyone really contend that 'competence,' as measured by the price system, corresponds to ethical merit? Is it not obvious that 'incompetence' follows just as surely if not quite so commonly from being too good for the world as from being blameworthy in character?"

This suggests that for Knight the most telling indictment of the injustice of the market distribution is that it does not bestow its highest rewards on the Christian saint or the Kantian man of good will. But would a Christian saint or Kantian man of good will want or expect to be rewarded with a high income? And is it reasonable to expect an *economic* system to bestow *economic* rewards in accordance with such unwordly or purely intentional virtues? The critique of the market distribution of income from "the standpoint of absolute ethics"—explicit in Knight and implicit in one form or another in Hayek, Friedman, and Rawls—is the fruit not of moral rigor but of moral confusion. Thinkers like John Locke and Adam Smith never suggested that a commercial society would bring about a correspondence between the attainment of wealth and the exercise of the most sublime spiritual or moral virtues. Their claim was more modest and eminently more sensible. They regarded the attainment of wealth as a just and fitting reward for a much homelier but by no means insignificant class of virtues—prudence, industriousness, sobriety, peaceableness, and the like.

There is another respect in which Knight's essay can be seen to have anticipated or influenced the future course of economic thinking. For at the same time that he so utterly rejects the ethical claims of the market distribution of income, Knight seeks to preserve the case for the superior efficiency of the free market as a mechanism for organizing production: "The argument for individualism, as developed by its advocates from Adam Smith down, may be summarized in a sentence as follows: a freely competitive organization of society tends to place every productive resource in that position in the productive system where it can make the greatest possible addition to the total social dividend as measured in price terms, and tends to reward every participant in production by giving it the increase in the social dividend which its cooperation makes possible. In the writer's opinion such a proposition is entirely sound; but it is not a statement of a sound ethical social ideal, the specification for a Utopia . . . The careful statement of the meaning of individualism falls within the province of the economic theorist rather than that of the ethical critic."

The sharp disjunction that Knight draws between economic theory or science on the one hand, and "absolute ethics" on the other, enables him to endorse the Smithian insight into the economic potency of the free market while apparently jettisoning any moral approval for the capitalist society to which a reliance on free markets gives rise. Thus the way is paved for today's "value-free" science of economics, which may accurately be characterized as pro-market but by no means pro-capitalist. From this perspective, "interventions" in the market which impair its efficiency appear more blameworthy than government policies that threaten the rights of individuals to keep what they have earned. An extreme version of this viewpoint may be found in the writings of Henry Simon, another leading economist of the Chicago school, who rested his case for explicit income redistribution on "the ethical or aesthetic judgment that the prevailing distribution of wealth and income reveals a degree (and/or kind) of inequality which is distinctly evil or unlovely." Writing in 1944, Simons contrasts redistribution through progressive taxation with trade unionism in the following terms: "[P]rogressive taxation is a workable, democratic method of dealing with inequality. The alternative of unionists is to send workers out in packs to exploit and expropriate by devices which resemble those of bandit armies. The one device is inherently orderly, peaceful, gradualist and efficient. It is the device of law. The other is inherently violent, disruptive and wasteful in the extreme. One calls for debate, discussion and political action; the other for fighting and promiscuous expropriation."

A similar tendency to favor redistributive schemes over other forms of government intervention may be seen in the preference of conservative economists for an "income strategy" rather than a "services strategy" for combating poverty. It was Milton Friedman, after all, who fathered the idea of the negative income tax. Dissatisfaction with the bureaucratic inefficiency and wastefulness of services strategies—which often wind up funneling government money primarily to middle-class providers of ineffective services—is, of course, readily understandable and by no means limited to economists. But the alternative of giving cash directly to the poor has its own drawbacks. Friedman himself called attention to perhaps the most fundamental: "The major disadvantage of the proposed negative income tax is its political implications. It establishes a system under which taxes are imposed on some to pay subsidies to others. And presumably, these others have a vote. There is always the danger that instead of being an arrangement under which the great majority tax themselves willingly to help an unfortunate minority, it will be converted into one under which a majority imposes taxes for its own benefit on an unwilling minority. Because this proposal makes the process so explicit, the danger is perhaps greater than with other measures. I see no solution to this problem except to rely on the self-interest and good will of the electorate."

In principle, the negative income tax (and other guaranteed-income plans) could no doubt be justified on non-redistributive grounds. Yet as Friedman recognizes, this is a distinction that would be difficult to maintain. Friedman and other conservative economists are led to favor replacing the existing welter of social programs (welfare, social security, health, housing, employment, etc.) with a single cash transfer program precisely because the latter would provide more resources to the poor at lower overall cost and with less interference with the market. But whereas the existing social programs can plausibly be perceived as intending to serve a variety of public purposes, a single cash transfer program would surely look like a policy designed to increase the private resources of some citizens at the expense of other citizens. The attempt to "rationalize" the welfare state from the point of view of economic efficiency leads toward the legitimation of income redistribution.

Although redistribution can also pose economic dangers to a capitalist society, its most potent and distinctive threat to liberal democracy lies in the moral and political realms. For redistribution undermines the autonomy of the private sphere which is at the very heart of liberalism. A policy of explicit redistribution involves the implied collectivization of all private property. What an individual is allowed to acquire and to keep comes to depend not on his own individual talents and efforts, but on a political decision. Consequently, the power of government over the private life of the individual is vastly augmented.

Can one rely on the "self-restraint and good will of the electorate" (which Milton Friedman invokes) as grounds for hope that this power would not be abused? Although the American electorate may not have been a model of self-restraint over the past two decades, it is true that it has proven resistant to much of the redistributionist agenda. But I would argue that this relative moderation can in large part be attributed precisely to the fact that most Americans still cling to the belief that people have a just claim to what they have legitimately earned, and thus continue to view taxation as an unpleasant but necessary means of meeting public expenses rather than as a mechanism for reducing inequality. If these beliefs are eroded, there is a real danger that democratic politics would deteriorate into an unrestrained struggle to use the power of government to improve the economic position of some groups at the expense of others.

But even if the electorate maintains its resistance to the redistributionist ideology, the fact that so many intellectuals and opinion leaders have ceased to believe in the justice of the capitalist distribution of income must have damaging effects on the health of our liberal political order. Conservative economists and others of a "pragmatic" cast of mind may be willing to defend capitalism even if they do not regard it as just, but it is unlikely that their arguments will, in the long run, prevail against egalitarians passionately committed to eliminating what they regard as the unjust inequalities generated by capitalism. The widely observed loss of self-confidence on the part of liberal democratic elites no doubt stems from a variety of causes, but surely an important factor is their declining sense of the justice of their own economic predominance. It is hard to imagine a free society being long maintained if its leading thinkers and its upper and upper-middle classes no longer believe that the inevitable economic equalities of such a society can be defended as just.

The economic dangers of redistribution—that it will diminish incentives, thereby reducing overall economic output—are much more generally acknowledged. Even the supporters of redistribution admit them in principle, though in practice, they usually argue that the magnitude of such effects will be much less than their opponents believe. These harmful economic effects, however, are not unique to explicit redistribution for the purpose of reducing income inequality. A similar diminution of economic incentives can just as easily result from traditional welfare-state spending programs and from the tax rates that are required to finance them. For in this context what is critical is the amount of resources transferred and not the moral or political justification for transferring them.

If today, in the conservative climate of the early 1980's, the proponents of redistribution are clearly on the defensive, the reasons are primarily economic rather than moral. The severe problems that have plagued the economy in recent years, widely attributed to the excessive growth of the welfare state, have created a climate of opinion unfavorable to any new government spending on social programs, let alone to direct income redistribution. Inevitably, the focus of public concern has shifted from questions of distribution to questions of productivity. One interesting response by a redistributionist to this shift could be observed in Lester Thurow's *The Zero-Sum Society,* published in 1980. In the early 1970's Thurow had argued in favor of redistribution on grounds of justice; in his 1980 volume, by contrast, he advocated redistribution primarily on the ground that it would provide the key for unlocking the political stalemate that allegedly was preventing the United States from restoring the health of its economy. During the past year, the press, of course, has been filled with articles attacking President Reagan's tax and budget cuts as "redistribution in reverse." But on the whole, the more serious left-wing authors have recently tended to downplay dis-

Why Equality?

Delba Winthrop

> There is indeed a manly and legitimate passion for equality
> which rouses in all men a desire to be strong and respected.
> This passion tends to elevate the little man to the rank of
> the great. But the human heart also nourishes a debased
> taste for equality, which leads the weak to want to drag the
> strong down to their level and which induces men to prefer
> equality and servitude to inequality and freedom. It is not
> that people with a democratic social state naturally scorn
> freedom; on the contrary they have an instinctive taste for
> it. But freedom is not the chief and continual object of their
> desire; it is equality for which they feel an eternal love. . . ."
> Tocqueville, *Democracy in America*, I. i., 3[1]

FROM THE FIRST, America was committed to the idea of equality; and no one in America today speaks out against equality. A proposed public policy could hardly have a better recommendation than a demonstration that it furthers the cause of equality, and nothing is more damning than an accusation that it is inegalitarian. If there is popular opposition to employing this criterion, it has surely never been mobilized under the banner of inegalitarianism. In recent years, intellectuals have joined and even surpassed politicians in espousing egalitarianism. Unfortunately, these intellectuals have done little to clarify our thinking about equality. What is the nature of America's commitment to equality? Why do we desire it? How do we expect to benefit from it? What must be done to protect and promote the equality we desire, and what must be rejected for its sake?

Today what most often tends to be rejected or suspected in the

name of equality is American capitalism. Other essays in this
volume provide evidence and argument for appraising the sound-
ness of its rejection. Here, however, it is important to insist upon
some clarity about what it is we are rejecting or suspecting. We
often use capitalism to refer to the American regime as a whole.
The confusion we create in doing so may well exacerbate, not
alleviate, our malaise. "Capitalism" does not refer merely to a
social and economic order characterized by commerce, modern
industry, and free enterprise, or even merely by private property
and its unregulated use. Rather, capitalism, from Marx's "capitalist," is the social and economic order whose end is the production of "surplus value," or profit as such, and whose essence is the
mode of production that generates and augments surplus value.
The capitalist is driven to seek profit for its own sake, without
regard for the benefits his activities may bring to him and others,
and without regard for its harms. Were the label capitalist appropriate, it would hardly enhance the attractiveness of the package.
More to the point, capitalism is, strictly speaking, an economic
order, and only in Marxist analysis and vulgar Marxist parlance
can one presume to convey the essence of a nation in a description
of its characteristic mode of production.

America's economic order is important because in the American self-understanding economics is important. But America is
also a political order, a culture, a way of life. America is a democratic republic with noble aspirations and materialistic proclivities.
Those who raise doubts about the egalitarianism of American
capitalism, be they naive malcontents or sophisticated analysts,
surely care at least as much about these aspects as about the mode
of production. Only if Marx should be correct that all this is mere
superstructure, unalterably determined by an economic substruc-
ture, would it make sense to proceed as if the proper object of
concern of friends or foes of equality in America were capitalism.
All reservations about American life are not economic in nature,
and all inequalities are arguably not economic in origin. While we
do well to begin with a proper respect for the universal interest in
capitalism and its relation to equality, we may do better to reshape
and enlarge the scope of our examination and object of our
concern.

Arguments against American capitalism or, more broadly,
against the American regime are made in the name of equality or
of "rights;" they are *prime facie* arguments in the name of justice.
Justice has traditionally been understood as giving to each his due,
or equal shares to equal persons and unequal shares to unequals.[2]
Today we take pains to guarantee the rights of criminals, or
suspected criminals, as well as to see that their victims are compen-

sated. In so doing, we intend what has been termed "corrective," or "commutative" justice, the equalization of gain and loss in criminal matters. "Commutative" justice was once also thought to apply to private economic exchanges. We assert rights to public assistance on behalf of the poor, elderly, and otherwise disadvantaged; we press for extension of the Voting Rights Act; we listen with increasing sympathy to supporters of the E.R.A. and gay rights, proponents of the rights of non-smokers and interest groups and minorities of all sorts. In doing this, we intend "distributive justice," the distribution of good things (wealth and honors) and of bad things (onerous duties) that political authorities can and invariably do distribute.

It should be clear from the outset that a commitment to equality (or inequality) may encompass a regard for justice, but need not be exhausted by it. We do not speak of unequal rights, nor, as we shall see, could we coherently do so. We speak much of equal rights, and in doing so we mean that what is due each person is the same thing, or the "equal." We can reasonably mean this if we deem human beings equal, fundamentally equal in whatever entitles them to the benefits and burdens political communities distribute. We thus imply that we know what, for political purposes, a human being is, that we know what political purposes are, and what, within the purview of politics, is good and bad for each and every one. Whether helpfully or not, we tend to refer to our desiderata as "equality." In doing so, either we employ a constricted notion of the competence of politics—which hardly seems to be the case—or our conviction that justice is some sort of equality reflects our appreciation of the human good, or happiness. Thus it is not surprising that democratic peoples feel an "eternal love" for what we call equality. Only with an awareness that what we might really have in mind is happiness can we adequately reflect on the American commitment to equality.

Equality in the abstract, however, is the philosopher's plaything or the activist's slogan, not a tool for political analysis or an end for public policy. So to take the concern for equality seriously one must begin by examining the specific kinds of equality most spoken about in America today. These are equality under the law, political equality, economic and social equality, and equal rights.

I

That equality under the law is desirable hardly seems controversial. Controversy arises when it is confused with the more problematic equal protection of the law, from which equality under the law should be distinguished. Equal protection of the law means, as the term "protection" suggests, that the law shall not arbitrarily withhold what it can provide or secure, namely, some right. In seeking equal protection we seek at least a legal guarantee and, often, political promotion of some substantive good for all who fall under the jurisdiction of the law, or we seek unrestricted access to that good for all. Consequently, this is a matter of distributive justice, not mere legality; and claims of distributive justice assume other forms we shall consider later. Equality under the law means simply that the law—whatever benefits it does or does not secure—be applied to all equally.

Equality under the law requires that no one be exempt from the law or subject to either privileged or disadvantaged treatment in its enforcement. American law is, on the whole, proscriptive, not prescriptive, so one is most often treated by it for defying a proscription. Thus, for us, equality under the law means above all equal punishment for transgressors of the law. No one shall escape punishment, much less the possibility of punishment (as did the preemptively pardoned Richard Nixon); nor shall anyone endure extraordinary punishment for reasons extraneous to the nature of the transgression (as have blacks in our country for much of its history). Equality under the law means, in effect, equal punishment by the law, or corrective justice.

Complaints of inequality or injustice under the law arise either when someone appears to have escaped the rigor of the law or to have suffered it unduly. To what extent might such injustices be a consequence of capitalism? Undeniably, unequal distribution of wealth is characteristic of, though not peculiar to, capitalist societies. People who have more, or at least enough wealth tend to hire clever, pricey lawyers who might enable them to escape some or all of their allegedly deserved punishment. The very wealthy might even try to influence judges and jurors by promising them whatever money can buy for favorable treatment or by threatening whatever sanctions wealth can command for just treatment. Indeed, it is not altogether unreasonable to suppose that under capitalism we accept preferential treatment for the wealthy because we become accustomed to the notion that the wealthy are entitled to privileges of all sorts. Or we cynically assume that the wealthy can always get off anyway. It could also be argued that capitalism creates an atmosphere in which lawyers are encouraged to think more about large fees than about justice, and judges and jurors are more likely to succumb to temptations of gain than to cries of injustice.

Such reasoning would lead to the conclusion that capitalism promotes not equality, but inequality, under the law. Even granting the conclusion, we would still want to ask whether inequality under the law is greater in capitalist societies than in others and whether it is caused by capitalism. Unequal distribution and use of wealth are no more peculiar to capitalist societies than is the materialism of those who prefer gain to justice. Nor is wealth the only currency with which one might purchase injustice. Under pre-capitalist aristocratic regimes birth alone justified not merely individual instances of inequality, but codified inequalities for whole classes of people. In communist countries thus far the issue of inequality under the law is more often than not moot because under "revolutionary legality" crime is not consistently defined and punishment is regularly inflicted altogether outside the law.

Furthermore, it is unclear that many or even most of the acknowledged inequalities under capitalism have much to do with capitalism itself. The most dramatic progress toward equality under the law in America has occurred in the last few decades, and it has been achieved by protection of the procedural rights of the indigent. As is generally known, but less openly acknowledged, the indigent criminals or suspects in question are predominantly black and Hispanic, and much of their harsh treatment is due not to their poverty or social class, but to racial prejudice. To show that racial prejudice in the United States is a consequence of capitalism would be difficult indeed. Even in the more nebulous case of leniency for white-collar crime, the softer treatment accorded these criminals is arguably not a consequence of the advantage they might have by virtue of their wealth, but rather of regard for their status, and of a sense that for some people disgrace is punishment enough. Given the incomes of clergymen as compared to businessmen, it is clear that capitalism is not responsible for our deference to particular occupations. Discrimination, be it against a race or for a profession, is distinct from and perhaps more deeply rooted than attachment to an economic order.

If it is fair to conclude that capitalism has little, if any, direct relation to equality or inequality under the law, we must still reflect further on the significance of our often expressed desire for perfect equality under the law. If our desire amounts to the wish that everyone receive the same legal punishment for the same crime, this goal might be accomplished in either of two ways. All should be made to feel the full rigor of the law, with no one's getting off easy, as was implied in the general outrage at the Nixon pardon. Or all should be given an opportunity to escape the full rigor of the law, with everyone's having the chance to get off, as is implied in the crusade to provide indigents with free legal counsel and even to have the police give them much of the advice a smart lawyer would.

If we desire that no criminal ever go unpunished and that all receive the same punishment under similar circumstances, then we are at once very demanding of people and respectful of them. We can insist on the application of a precise legal punishment only if we assume that human beings are equally and therefore fully responsible for their actions. We must suppose them to have acted with perfect knowledge of their action and its consequences and in the absence of any external constraint. For we surely think it wrong to inflict punishment for crimes that were committed either in ignorance or under some compulsion.

That human beings do act knowingly and freely is the premise not only of retributive and rehabilitative justice, but of morality itself. In punishing people because we hold them responsible for their actions we show our respect for them as moral beings. Immanuel Kant went so far as to contend that if we knew that the world would come to an end tomorrow, then the last murderer would have the moral right to be executed tonight. But that we really wish to be so hard on ourselves and our fellow moral beings is doubtful. Liberals continue to cherish and conservatives have not yet thought to mount a sustained challenge to "Miranda" rights, evidence of their abuse notwithstanding. More significantly, we would all grant that there are extenuating circumstances in the commission of crime. The decisive extenuation, admitted even by the law, is the defective nature of the lawbreaker, who is not infrequently mentally incompetent or deranged or at least swayed by great passion. It is because we could not abide perfect equality under the law if it meant equal and therefore rigid application that we tend to rest content with laws that are often little more than guidelines, flexibly applied by individuals to specific human beings in particular circumstances. We accept them despite the arbitrariness and discrimination, hence inequality, thereby made possible.

If we carried our inclination to excuse transgressions to its extreme, we would arrive at the position that equality under the law is realized when all are hardly under it at all. However commendable it is to attempt to eradicate discriminatory law enforcement, the implication of the Warren Court's criminal rights decisions must be that everyone should have the greatest opportunity to outsmart the law that any government could countenance. Nonetheless, this kind of equality is neither more possible nor more desirable than that of keeping everyone fully under the thumb of the law. Even if all lawyers were equally clever and unscrupulous, not all criminals or would-be criminals are. Would we not still envy the cleverest and most imaginative criminals who got away with the biggest and best crimes? A more serious objection is that the inclination to excuse tends not only effectively to do away with punishment, but to vitiate the very notion of crime. Alcoholism, for example, has all but become a disease, not a crime or even a vice.

We do not punish people for illness since they do not cause it. But if there is no crime or vice because there is no legal or moral responsibility, then neither can we hold ourselves responsible for and take pride in obeying the law or doing the right thing. In denying that human beings are to blame for their actions we deny them all moral responsibility and degrade them to the rank of beasts, who act by natural inclination or urge or at best by habituation. Fortunately, just as our natural sense of equity causes us to balk at equality under an inflexible law, our righteous indignation causes us to reject the thought of equality outside the law. We can conceive how we might best satisfy our desire for strict equality. But the desire itself seems incoherent when we see how it conflicts with the compassion and anger that also seem to be essential elements of justice.

A choice between strict abstract legal equality and a legal flexibility admitting of unequal and even arbitrary application is unsatisfactory under any law and in conjunction with any economic order, not only under capitalism. Of course it should go without saying, though not without considering, that we do not want to live either equally without law or equally under any old law. If white and non-white in South Africa were subject to equal punishment for violating the laws authorizing apartheid, they would be equal under the law. Closer to home, many Americans are now of the opinion that capital punishment, however uniformly inflicted, would still be cruel and unusual punishment. So even if a demand for equality under the law could be met, the desire for justice which is presumably its root would not be satisfied. Nor is justice itself always identical with the common good that should be its end—or so President Ford argued with some force on the occasion of the Nixon pardon. What is desired above all is not equality under the law, but prudent application of good laws. As the unpalatable logical extremes of equality under the law reveal, love of equality is not properly understood as a desire for strict equality or even for strict justice. It can be understood to point to the need for a proper appreciation of both the human strength exhibited in morally and legally responsible actions and the weakness exhibited in involuntary or necessary lapses from morality and obedience to law.

II

Although "participatory democracy" has not always been vociferously demanded, there can be no responsible government without political participation, and no democracy without equal participation. In recent years the demand for political equality has been vociferous. Or at least intellectuals and activists have acted as if they had heard the voices vociferating, even when they seem to have orchestrated them. In the last twenty or so years, our Constitution has been interpreted in the name of political equality to require strict adherence to the principle of one man, one vote, and to forbid the requirement that a citizen be literate enough to read about electoral issues and candidates in a newspaper or even that he understand the language in which politics is conducted in the United States. Congress has sought to secure not just equally weighted votes, but equally effective votes through the Voting Rights Act; and it has tried to equalize influence on candidates and elected officials through legislation on campaign contributions and federal financing of presidential campaigns and through regulation of lobbying practices and oversight of officials' incomes. The Executive has sought to increase, if not equalize, informal political participation by mandating public hearings and community "input" in many of its programs. Political parties have set for themselves goals, if not quotas, for proportionate representation of women and minorities on their official bodies.

It is reasonable to doubt that we have political equality in the United States today, even if it is unreasonable to assume that our regime was ever intended to be perfectly egalitarian or that it should be. It is commonly believed, also with some justification, that the lack of political equality in America, whether intended or not, is a function of capitalism. No doubt the poor rarely run for office or take an active part in partisan politics, and many do not even vote. The Senate is inhabited by millionaires, and suburban housewives and school teachers with leisure now select presidential candidates in primaries and party caucuses. The influence of the wealthy contributor to a campaign is likely to be greater than that of the anonymous citizen who allocates a dollar a year of his federal income tax to the campaigns of all major presidential contenders. Yet it is far from obvious that these political inequalities are due to capitalism and only capitalism, or that they could be eliminated simply by reforming the economic order.

It did not take contemporary students of American capitalism to show that one must have money to afford to seek and hold political office, and that the laboring poor have little time and perhaps less interest in regular political activity. These phenomena are no more characteristic of modern industrialized capitalist societies than of ancient Athens. And if wealth is not the key to political power in communist countries, neither are personal merit or public service frequently decisive. What does remain for contemporary students of American capitalism to demonstrate is that some economic, social, or political reform can remedy these defects, so as to ensure first, that men and women of ability, integrity, and loyalty, however poor or wealthy, come to hold political office and, second, that all, however poor or wealthy, take an active interest in politics. For it seems that not so much capitalism or even economic inequality, but lack of assured wealth and leisure are the economic obstacles to political participation. There may also be cultural barriers to full and equal participation that will not be overcome by any institutional reform alone. And some people may just have a natural disinclination to political activity that will never be overcome under any free regime. Capitalism may well be accompanied by unequal political participation, but it does not follow either that capitalism causes that inequality or that abolishing capitalism will bring more equal participation.

Once again, we can ask why political equality is desired anyway. Several reasons have traditionally been offered. All are problematic, but revealing. Equality is thought to be a hedge against tyranny. Society cannot exist without rules that invariably limit the freedom of individuals, but each might attempt to secure as much freedom as possible by helping to formulate the rules by which all must live in accordance with his own wishes. All rule so that no one is ruled tyrannically. Or, rather, in this way all but majority tyranny might be averted. The equal rule of each cannot be assured if the rule of all is taken to mean, as it usually must, majority rule, because there can easily be a permanent minority, effectively though not legally disenfranchised.

Even without supposing tyrannical intent, a government sometimes acts contrary to the people's good as they perceive it. Therefore the wearer of the shoe that pinches should be able to consent, or more to the point, to withhold consent. This kind of argument, however, cannot lead to the conclusion that all must share equally in rule, because not everyone has equally sensitive feet or complains as loudly as others do. Nor is knowing that a shoe does not feel right the same as knowing how to make one that does. Sometimes it is contended that the collective wisdom of the inexpert customers will exceed that of the expert, or will at least be sufficient. But this contention could make sense only if the collection of wisdom took place not at the ballot box, where each unreflective choice is finalized, but in a deliberative body where constructive debate might synthesize the bits of wisdom found in various unsound opinions. And even here there is no guarantee that the synthesis will not contain bits or even large chunks of unwisdom.

A third, somewhat more compelling argument for participation is that in being forced or at least encouraged to make political choices frequently, the citizen's capacity to make reasoned choices concerning both public and private matters is enhanced. Regular political activity is to be preferred to mere voting once every few years and to never having to formulate any opinion at all. The justification for universal participation is that the capacity of everyone to be intelligently and actively interested in his condition is promoted. But then we can only hope that we have time to wait for the capacity to be adequately developed.

The final and perhaps most fashionable reason given today is that the equal dignity of human beings mandates political equality. In fact dignity is assured with recognition of that mandate as a mandate. The difficulty in this argument is that it is not at all clear why anyone's dignity depends on an acknowledgement of universal political equality or that it does depend on it at all.

All of these arguments for political equality begin with the premise that equality and its benefits are rights. A share in authority is not to be a reward for services rendered or a recognition of demonstrated ability; justice, in the sense of giving to each his desert is not a serious consideration. Moreover, a harmony of the self-interests for whose protection political power is sought and the good of all as a whole is simply assumed or contemptuously disregarded. So is potential competence. In the context of modern capitalist societies this attitude can at least be understood, if not condoned. Today in America no serious arguments are made against *de jure* political equality. At most there is opposition to some of the means said to be necessary to secure *de facto* equality. To liberal and radical proponents of *de facto* equality it appears that the chief beneficiaries of the inegalitarian status quo are the wealthy. It is hardly argued today that the wealthy deserve a greater share in political authority than the poor because they make a notable contribution to the economy while the poor make virtually none. Even if such an argument were made, it would be untenable if one could not show that political authority is the appropriate reward for economic success. This demonstration would require proof that economic success and a willingness to own up to it every April 15th are manifestations of a kind of political competence, or that there is no real difference between political competence and the ability to make money. If every capitalist or rich man and only capitalists and rich men were capable of governing well for the public good it might seem just that the poor be effectively disenfranchised. But if the defenders of the status quo cannot make this or any better argument against measures thought necessary to achieve effective equality, then the poor need not do more than assert, as is the American way, a right to equality.

Whether argued for or simply demanded, political equality does not seem to be desired for its own sake. Rather, equality turns out to be desired because it is thought to ensure that politics will serve one's interests, whatever they might be, or at least that it will not systematically thwart them. The desire to have one's interests served points to the desire to have them served well. This could conceivably be done by a government of the few competent, who need not be elected by all, but selected according to their ability to provide for the true needs of human beings. Only if the interests or needs of various human beings differ fundamentally, or if the interests or needs of one cannot be known by another does it follow that each person who presumably knows his own needs better than anyone else, must have a say in government. Yet if it is supposed that the interests or needs of individuals which government ought to serve are not the same and cannot even be compared, then that individuals must have an equal say cannot be established. For if needs and interests differ and cannot be appreciated by others, then someone who determines that he has greater needs or higher interests cannot be denied the right to attempt to assure that government secure them. If we desire to have our unspecified or unspecifiable interests served, then we cannot show that equality is more in accord with our deepest desires than would be a tyranny of the wise or willful. With good reason the founders of liberal capitalism spoke not of self-defined interests, but of a need that could be acknowledged as universal and could never necessitate a tyranny to discover it. Their difficulty was in arguing that this most universal need—preservation— is also our greatest need or deepest desire.

Political equality is also desired as necessary to promote the

development of everyone's capacities for deliberation and judgment and as tantamount to recognition of the moral worth of
each. Or, we could say, political equality is for the sake of virtue—
intellectual and moral excellence—and for the honor which excellence should be accorded. But it remains to show both that political equality is the precondition of excellence and that the capacity
for virtue is equal in all human beings, so that a regime in which
every excellent individual governs will also be egalitarian. The
belief that all human beings conduct their own affairs equally well,
much less the affairs of the whole polity, is not supported by facts
we presently perceive. One could not seriously wish to be governed by either the Harvard faculty or by the first hundred names
in the Boston telephone directory, to be sure. But that a grant of
political equality alone could effect equal ability is dubious. And to
continue to insist on an equality of the unequal would serve only
to depreciate true ability. Recognition of excellence is needed as
much to identify it to those who aspire to it as what they should
strive for, as to reassure its possessors. Equality of the unequal
obscures excellence, making it all the more difficult to achieve the
excellence for which honor should be accorded.

From the reasons given for political equality we can infer that
we desire it in order to live as our needs or interests dictate, which
is sometimes called freedom, and to assure recognition of our
presumed intellectual excellence and moral worth, or for human
dignity. Neither is a wish for equality or justice for its own sake,
and in fact neither requires equality for its fulfillment. Does
capitalism facilitate the realization of our freedom and dignity?
The ethos of capitalism invites us to take certain needs and desires
seriously and encourages and honors the abilities employed in
efforts to satisfy them. Are these desires and abilities the ones we
really care about if our wish is for freedom or dignity?

III

When we think of economic and social equality, two quite different kinds come to mind. One is "equality of opportunity," a
situation in which each person is able to advance in wealth and
social status according to his or her merits; the other is "equality of
result," a situation in which each person winds up equal in wealth
and status to every other, no matter how.

Equality of opportunity amounts to an assurance that there will be no arbitrary obstacles to advancement by ability. The fact that someone is born to particular parents should have no bearing on whether he himself ends up with wealth and status; privilege is not to be inherited, and nepotism is to be discouraged. The fact that someone is born black or white, Catholic or Protestant, Spanish or English speaking, female or male should have no bearing, nor should the fact that someone is born to wealth. To this end free public education, for example, is instituted as a means. Natural ability and only ability should determine place.

Equality of result requires that natural as well as conventional and arbitrary obstacles to wealth and status be overcome. It is not to be supposed that nullifying all advantages of birth excepting the nature with which one is born will suffice. Any disadavantages race and gender may cause are to be compensated for by the use of benign quotas; genetic and accidental disadvantages are to be overcome as far as possible with the aid of special education programs. One's inherited nature is no more deserved than is inherited wealth, and it cannot in any case justify economic and social inequalities. Should results still somehow come out unequal, remaining inequalities are to be minimized by taxes, minimum wages, and welfare benefits, and by an enlightened public opinion that accords equal status to all occupations and capacities. Nothing can be left to nature or to chance.

Much study has been given the relation of capitalism to both equality of opportunity and result. Our present concern is not so much the conclusions to be drawn from such studies as the questions to be addressed by them. In evaluating the relation of capitalism to equality of opportunity, we must ask whether capitalism or, more broadly, an economic order characterized by private property and free use of wealth promotes or discourages "careers open to talents." How does it fare in comparison to its alternatives? Is this tendency of the economic order conducive to its stability? With regard to equality of result we need to know whether the economic order promotes or discourages equal results and whether it can tolerate them. Here the crucial issue would seem to be the place of incentives in the economy of the human psyche. Capitalism, which has relied heavily on incentives of greater wealth and status, might not survive a policy of giving no rewards proportionate to effort or ability. Nor have communist countries been successful in sustaining sound economies without recourse to theoretically unnecessary and impermissible economic incentives that lead to unacceptable unequal results. Communism's practical failure in this respect notwithstanding, its theory raises an important question. The same question is raised by our own Protestant Ethic in its original meaning. Must seemingly necessary incentives be economic, or can human beings not be moved to produce for other ends?

Both equality of opportunity and equality of result might be thought to be specifications of distributive justice and desirable for that reason. We are familiar with these principles of justice as, respectively, "from each according to his ability, and to each according to his ability," and "from each according to his ability, and to each according to his need." The first might become effective if human beings could simply adopt a natural order of talents. Is this possible? We would be required to treat each individual as if he were *sui generis,* to act as if inherited rights were simply invalid, and to assume that society does not need the stability brought by deference to traditional orderings. And is it desirable? Is there not a grain of truth, if not justice, in the second principle, with which the first conflicts? The second formula does look more like one for charity than for justice. According to it, the natural order to be respected is that of needs, not talents. The grains of truth in it are first, that we all do have needs of various sorts, as well as abilities, and second, that people may have qualities that merit recognition even if they could never be mistaken for economic or quasi-economic abilities. The difficulty in this second formulation, however, is that those who espouse it do still wish it to be the principle of economic distribution.

Clearly, the desires for equality of opportunity and equality of result are for something more than economic justice. The desire for an equal opportunity to acquire wealth and status reflects the wish to develop and display one's capacities and to be recognized and honored for them. If all human beings were equally and fully well-rounded, the development of their capacities, especially the development of one capacity among many, might well be understood as a mark of choice and freely chosen virtue. But since abilities are on the whole given rather than chosen and few people are equally good at enough things to have a meaningful choice to make, the opportunity equalized is the opportunity to act in accordance with natural intention or accident, not to act simply as one chooses. The rewards sought, wealth and status, are in effect, for fulfilling one's nature.

The desire for wealth and status, or rather, for an opportunity to achieve them, might still be understood as a desire for virtue and its recognition. But this could not be affirmed without qualification for another reason. In a free society, wealth and status invariably depend on "the market." The abilities recognized and rewarded in any society tend to be those having products or consequences that serve the needs and gratify the desires of whoever dominates that society, that is, of its regime. If needs and desires cannot be molded to reflect some non-arbitrary and true hierarchy of human excellences, then excellence will merely be defined as what satisfies dominant needs and desires. Since the likelihood of so shaping dominant desires is small indeed, then we cannot mean to identify wealth and status with recognition of virtue properly understood. Only erroneously do we desire wealth and status as recognition for true excellence. That we do almost consistently make this error must be due to the strength of the capitalist ethos in our regime.

The current preoccupation with equality of result is particularly interesting in this respect. Equality of result is presently the rallying cry of many intellectuals and of liberal and radical politicians influenced by them. It is not yet the demand of the people. Indeed, it is doubtful that the majority of Americans really care about being equal in wealth, even if equalization of wealth could be achieved without a lowering of their standard of living. Nor do the poor desire equal wealth; they desire more wealth. Who wants to live as well as the Joneses if the Joneses don't have a video-cassette recorder? It is similarly hard to believe that people desire equal status rather than status. Granted that no one wants to be looked down upon because of occupation—he wants to be a sanitation engineer, not a garbage collector. But doesn't he really want to be looked up to? If all occupations were equally honorable, none could be looked up to; honor presupposes inequality. The American hero has always been Horatio Alger, who got rich, not the man who has made it to middle class mediocrity.

True, the intellectuals who espouse the cause of equality of result rarely insist upon a perfectly equal distribution of wealth. Rarely do they argue that equality of result is an end in itself. The wealth for which they argue is said, plausibly, to be necessary for the development of human capacities. Equal or roughly equal wealth is also asserted to be necessary for the dignity to which all human beings are assumed to be equally entitled. It is, after all, humiliating to have had an equal opportunity to become a millionaire and to have failed; there is no one to blame but oneself, nothing to curse but chance. When equal dignity is the concern, then equal, not merely more equal, status is required. The plea for recognition of the equal dignity of all human beings strikes such a sympathetic chord today that its connection to economic and social status is infrequently examined. This connection has been made only by means of a contamination of the austere moral philosophy of Immanual Kant by a worldly sub-philosophic materialism alien to Kant. For Kant, the dignity of each human being does depend on a supposition of the equal moral worth of all. But Kant surely never taught either that material well-being, much less material equality, was a precondition of morality or that moral worth brought any title to worldly recognition. If, as is now contended, the end is the development of the capacity for choice of a way of life, which gives human beings their peculiar dignity as moral beings, no necessary connection between this development and material well-being or social equality has been established. While faulting capitalism for its failure to accomplish equal results contemporary moral philosophers exhibit the very concern for material well-being that animates capitalism itself.

Human beings are moved in the first instance to concern themselves with economic and social matters by the natural necessity of survival. An instinctive desire for self-preservation compels economic cooperation and restraint of anti-social passions by social conventions and laws. But the necessities of preservation cannot fully explain desires for extraordinary wealth and especially not for honor—desires to be above a concern for material well-being and to be restricted only by the standards of sociability one sets for oneself. These seemingly extravagant desires are intelligible as attempts to transcend natural necessity by means of, and for the sake of, human self-determination. The presupposition of liberal capitalism is that the necessities of preservation can never be escaped; to the extent that the desire for honor cannot be understood as proper pride in securing preservation it is deemed "vainglory." When in modern times this account of human aspirations was recognized as inadequate, it had become impossible to understand the striving to live as one chooses, and not as one must, as anything but a desire to overcome nature, for nature had come to be understood as the necessary motions of bodies. The striving to perfect the human faculties that bring honor must be conceived of as freedom and as occurring only within a realm of freedom, as opposed to the realm of nature. When freedom is thought—as it is by Marxists and even by many who still fancy themselves liberals, if not capitalists—to be effected only by perfection of the socio-economic order, the determination to free ourselves from nature remains subservient to an end to which nature impels us, the end of preservation. Proponents of capitalism's would-be successor foster the illusion that they substitute moral freedom for natural necessity. Only in this problematic way does a concern for the equality of result not assured by capitalism reflect a desire for human responsibility and excellence.

IV

Contemporary America has witnessed a proliferation of movements of various sorts for "equal rights" which cannot be classified
as legal, political, or social and economic simply. The Equal Rights
Amendment and the feminism that spawned it come immediately
to mind. One thinks also of the somewhat newer gay rights movement and the somewhat older, but still vigorous, pride in ethnicity, as well as of the attempt of the counter-culture emerging
from the '60's to establish its legitimacy. Such movements have
become so much a part of American life that the "moral majority"
currently appears as one interest group among many and is con-
ceded at best an equal right to its own life-style. The rhetoric of
these movements tends to be egalitarian in part because such
rhetoric finds receptive ears and in part because the first significant battles of their members to be what they are and be treated as
if they were the same as everybody else are often waged in the
courts under the banner of the Equal Protection clause of the
Constitution. Nevertheless, the demands of women, homosexuals,
proud ethnics, and the self-righteously unconventional are not
simply for equality, nor even for justice. Rather, what is desired is
freedom and respectability, or respectability in freedom, hence
respect for freedom.

One hears little objection to granting full legal and political
rights to such claimants; and their economic demands, equal
access to employment and equal pay for equal work, are generally
regarded as moderate and reasonable. To the economic demands
capitalism itself poses no serious obstacle. Undeniably, capitalism
gives unequal authority to the capitalist, who owns the means of
production, for would-be wage laborers must put themselves at
his disposal. Despite his ardent defense of the individual (perhaps
because of his attachment to private property and the principles
of private property) and despite his own not infrequent displays
of economic initiative and even daring, the businessman has long
been notorious for social conservatism. He, no less than anyone
else, has prejudices and occasions to indulge them. Discrimination
against women, minorities, and the unconventional has been legally forbidden in federal and state employment and wherever
government intervenes to regulate the economy, and it could be
argued that whatever advances in equality have been made in the
private sector would not have been made without this impetus. At
the same time, however, assuming that investment capital can be
found, the system of free enterprise provides unique oppor-

tunities for the disadvantaged to compete with the majority on its own (materialistic) terms even as the competitors do their own thing. There are now banks and advertising agencies owned by and serving women, prospering businessmen and professionals catering to minorities equitably and effectively, and health food stores and head shops run by patrons of healthful and less than healthful lives. Other economic orders may have tolerated different groups as what they were, but surely none has been more conducive to their social as well as economic equality than free enterprise. Nor do the theory and practice of Marxism give any greater promise. Marxism bids us all "to hunt in the morning, fish in the afternoon, rear cattle in the evening, and criticize after dinner," but this promise can be taken up only as we all become species-beings, who no longer think it important or even proper to have our uniqueness respected. If the treatment of women is typical of communist practice, women are, as one observer has aptly put it, "liberated, but not emancipated."[3]

Even less resistance to the economic rights of members of these movements would be encountered if people had no cause to fear that their satisfaction would bring more fundamental changes. But people do have cause to fear. Equal pay for equal work by women might be fine in principle, but the fact that women are equally busy at work in offices and factories must mean a fundamental reordering of the traditional American family. And what happens when the second-grade teacher on whom Jane develops the normal crush is an equally-entitled-to-access-to-employment lesbian? Rights activists want not merely a fair share of the pie, but a share of something other than the traditional apple pie.

Gay lib, ethnic pride, and the counter-culture of the '60's generation are manifestations of the desire to have one's own "life-style." Reigning American culture is attacked as mere convention, at best partial and at worst utterly contrary to nature. Conformism to it is utterly deplorable. Heterosexual love is no more natural than homosexual, soul food not inferior to clam chowder, and four-letter words no less "expressive" than rational discourse. The rejection of conventional American mores and norms in the name of equal rights is presented as an attempt to reform convention to bring it into closer accord with nature, but at the same time, the existence of a common human nature with which it might accord is denied. Therefore convention as such must be rejected. Yet it is clear that these claimants to equal rights desire respect for the way in which they exercise their rights as well as their exercise. Since respectability invariably depends on a more or less fixed standard for ranking, conventions cannot be done away with altogether; they must be remade. Leaving aside the issue of whether all life-styles are equally worthy of respect, it is hard to see how one might formulate a convention that gives equal respectability to all. One cannot be proud of one's life-style without in effect choosing it, however strong one's natural inclination to it may be. The choice of a life-style implies a preference for it above others and therefore a certain contempt for the others, however much is said about the equality of values. Just as there is no way to protect the rights of non-smokers without curtailing those of smokers, so one cannot chose a life-style contrary to that established by existing convention without undermining its respectability and offending its adherents. A battle of cultures is being waged.

There is a certain irony in the ready acceptance of the economic demands of women's liberation and other movements. Women's liberation, as the name suggests, is meant to be more about liberty than equality. And since when is working eight hours a day at a blue-, white- or pink-collar job liberation? It is liberty, or the absence of constraint, only if it is human nature to be, as Marx assured us, a conscious social producer. Perhaps the less moderate feminists are correct in taking the argument for women's liberation much further. According to them, the truly liberated woman is liberated not only from her economic bondage to men and to conventions that stereotype her, thereby defining her nature and place in society, but from dependence on any other human being for her wholeness and happiness. (Hence the significance attached to the discovery of the clitoral orgasm.) Typically, such arguments are made with reference to woman's body and the mental and psychological characteristics asserted to be fundamentally affected by the body.

In feminism as in the other movements for equal rights the desire for equality reflects an unwitting acceptance of natural necessity coupled with a desire for human dignity, but without the traditional mediation of virtue. If anything, freedom—doing one's own thing—is taken to be the meaning of virtue. Yet freedom turns out to be not only identical with one's necessity, be it sex, sexuality, or ethnicity, but an affirmation of that necessity. The life-style for which an equal right is demanded may be very different from that of the complacent capitalist, though these movements do seem to flourish under liberal capitalism. In the end they, as did Jerry Rubin, often succumb to the charms of capitalism. They can do so because they are in essential agreement with capitalism in their curious celebration of necessity, however understood. As in the theory of liberal capitalism, if human excellence can be generated and sustained by any conventional order, it is by one that affirms necessity.

V

When we express a wish for equality and a doubt that capitalism facilitates its fulfillment we do not in fact mean to worry about either equality or capitalism as much as we might have thought. Rather, our wish for equality reflects somewhat incoherent desires for living, on the one hand, as our natures—our needs and desires—dictate and, on the other hand, with dignity, according to the perfection of our capacities as we have chosen and for which we have taken responsibility. The connection between the wish for equality and the economic order capitalism as well as the disjunction between capitalism and satisfacton of our desires now seem both more complex and less crucial.

To raise the issue of the relation of economics to the ends we seek as human beings in terms of the relation of capitalism to equality, we have contended, is neither intellectually nor politically constructive. How, we might ask, has the issue come to be stated in these unhelpful terms, and why has it not been thought advisable to abandon or improve upon them? What precisely is at the root of the phenomena that have come to bear the names of capitalism and equality and of our assumption that their incompatibility is the cause of much of our dissatisfaction with American life? Are there any more constructive ways of thinking about what we want from any regime that might guide our actions today?

A brief excursion into the political theory that can be said to account for and perhaps even to have given birth to capitalism in particular and to the modern world in general is useful. For in the writings of the early liberals, notably Thomas Hobbes, John Locke, and Adam Smith, one can see why both equality and economics have come to hold such a privileged place in the thought of proponents and opponents of capitalism alike. The philosophy that first articulated the fundamental principles of modern liberalism, from which capitalism is a natural development and communism a malignant growth asserts simultaneously and inseparably the natural freedom and equality of each and every human being.[4] Natural freedom is in turn the basis of both political rights and political duties, or justice. Human beings can be naturally free only if they can be presumed naturally equal. They are free in the obvious sense of having no need to submit to the dominion of one another because they are presumed equal in two essential respects. Being roughly equal in bodily strength, thus in the ability to kill one another, each is capable of resisting any other's imposition of a government by force. Being equal in prudence, or at least in unwillingness to confess imprudence, and having a greater than equal interest in his own affairs, each is most capable of looking after himself. Therefore no one has either the natural power to impose his will on another or justification for doing so. Politics, or rule, which is nonetheless necessary to effect common enterprises, must therefore be freely consented to by all.

Human beings can be presumed naturally equal only if they are naturally free not merely from other men, but from nature itself, or at least from the intelligible, teleological nature of Classical and Christian thought. For if nature determines ends for human beings, then inequalities in prudence, which finds means to given ends, would readily be exposed. It would seem fitting that human beings be guided to their natural end, ruled by whoever might claim special knowledge of the end or demonstrate exceptional prudence. An hierarchical ranking of individuals in a community in the light of the end to be fulfilled and on the basis of prudence might seem just. In liberal thought, nature can give man only a beginning, not an end, or at best it can give a truncated end. Moreover, the beginning or truncated end cannot need to be intuited or effected by any rational faculty admitting of unequal distribution. It is the nature of a being to be, and every animate being actively desires to avoid its destruction, even if it has no notion of its perfection. In constituting beings, nature gives all beings equally the desire to preserve themselves and the right to the means thereunto, but she leaves them otherwise free from her tutelage. Hence the natural freedom and equality of all.

The natural right of every being to preserve itself entails a right to the means of preservation. If what is to be preserved is, as both modern science and political philosophy bid us to believe, a body, albeit a human body, then the means of preserving it are twofold: laws effectively enforced to deter threats to it by other human bodies and, more obviously, food, medicine, and other products of economic activity and scientific invention to remedy nature's defective production and distribution. Thus the right of nature points to its actualization with the most efficacious means of securing political order and of generating economic and technological advances.

From the novel theoretical pronouncement that all human

beings possess equally a fundamental natural right follows a novel practical political recommendation. The right of nature is a right to place one's own good above that of others, or above the common good. Previously, political philosophers had urged subordination of selfishness to public spiritedness or its sublimation by way of honor in political virtue. The theorists of liberalism sought instead to redefine the public good to make it accord with the self-interest of a body desiring above all to preserve itself in comfort. Obedience to law was to be induced by threat of punishment, including bodily destruction. At the same time law was to be limited in its scope to only what was necessary for the comfortable preservation of the political community and its members. A realm of indulgence of private, not to say selfish, desires was to be permitted and even publicly sanctioned.

As novel as the political recommendation—and tied to it—were recommendations of economic and technological development and of moral and intellectual transformations needed to stimulate this development. That human beings care a lot about the preservation and comfort of their bodies was not a new discovery; the judgment that in doing so they might best benefit themselves and others was new. No longer would political philosophers seek to moderate the desire for comfortable self-preservation with sobering reminders of human mortality and consoling myths of the immortality of the soul. Instead, the proponents of liberalism fostered and adopted modern science's redefinition of its end to make the ends of political philosophy and science as well as politics consistent with the self-interest of a body desiring commodious living. Nature's harshness was not to be acquiesced in, but overcome by a science become technological. Selfish passions, in particular the seemingly limitless desires for limited quantities of material goods could be indulged and even encouraged because their satisfaction could now be anticipated. Indeed, this very anticipation, an immoderate and anxious desire for wealth, was to be the motor of the mechanisms designed to assure satisfaction. The same political philosophy that posits the theoretical equality of human beings requires and justifies much of what we now associate with capitalism.

A newly unfettered and dignified desire for material well-being was meant to become the guarantor of not only private happiness, but of justice, or public morality. But neither justice nor happiness could be understood precisely as they had hitherto been understood. Justice might still mean giving to each his due. But corrective or commutative justice as applied to economic relations would lose all sense and eventually be replaced by "the market." Commutative justice presupposes some fixed value in the things human beings contract to exchange, a value presumably grounded in their utility to human beings utilizing them toward a given end. But as Hobbes would have it, in the condition of "meer nature" no good of human beings beyond that of the preservation of each is agreed upon, nor can the value of any particular thing for the preservation of any particular individual be anticipated. Circumstances and needs change, and "the value of all things contracted for, is measured by the Appetite of the Contractors: and therefore the just value is that which they be contented to give."[5] It is not unjust to profit from your neighbor's misfortune, nor for him to contract to work at a bare subsistence wage.

Distributive justice, too, could be divested of traditional moral strictures against greed. What is due human beings who must be assumed equal is impartiality, not more. Then, as John Locke, the father of capitalism, was to contend, the value of things provided by nature for the use of human beings without the addition of the labor that belongs to each individual is insignificant; initially, or naturally, there is virtually nothing to be distributed.[6] Whatever might be worth distributing is the product of the labor of individuals and is therefore already in a sense owned by the industrious and rational who feel the necessity of laborious acquisition. What is due the industrious and rational is not determined or limited with a view to any finite total of goods to be apportioned to each in relation to all others. Indeed, the total quantity of goods available for distribution is increased for the benefit of all mankind. Capitalist accumulation is not unjust and the "evil concupiscence" that inspires it is in fact not a vice.

The principles of modern liberalism were systematically elaborated for the first time in Thomas Hobbes's *Leviathan*. Leviathan, like the Biblical monster who swallowed up the proud, could be a kingdom of the proud if human beings could be humbled enough to concede their fundamental equality in the fear of violent death. The human beings we have learned to regard as equal are equal above all in the possibility of suffering violent death at the hands of their fellows. How could anyone fearing equally the cessation of motion toward objects of desire that bring felicity deem himself worthy of special honors, or reasonably be proud rather than simply "vainglorious?" How, recognizing that in the necessity of his motion he could not be distinguished from the rest of animate nature, could he rationally hold the specialness of man among created beings? The teaching about the natural equality of men in their anxiety for preservation is above all a polemic against the aristocratic grounding of both morality and happiness in pride.

The honor pride demands is necessarily scarce (there is nothing honorable in being average), and therefore a cause of invidious competition; peace and prosperity admit of universal, if not always perfectly equal distribution. The new justice seems to obviate the need for both the justice characteristic of pre-capitalist regimes and the pride and honor previously thought to be as necessary as justice for public morality and private happiness.

Remarkably, in the most ambitious study of American equality ever written, Alexis de Tocqueville has almost nothing to say of the connection between love of equality and love of justice. Instead, he speaks first of "a manly and legitimate passion for equality which rouses in all men a desire to be strong and respected" and "tends to elevate the little man to the rank of the great" and then of "a debased taste for equality, which leads the weak to want to drag the strong down to their level and which induces men to prefer equality in servitude to inequality in freedom."[7] The first passion, he foresaw, becomes increasingly difficult to sustain in the world constituted by liberal capitalism; the second gains ever greater strength.

At the base of our expressed demand of equality, we have argued, lie unarticulated desires not only to serve our natural necessities, but also to make manifest peculiar human excellences and see them accorded fitting recognition. A political philosophy that regularly refers us to our necessities makes it difficult for us to distinguish between the efforts we undertake by choice, and what we thereby achieve, from the things we do in servitude, or because we must. We tend to neglect yearnings beyond our most urgent and obvious needs, and eventually we come to be pained by reminders of the very possibility of striving to satisfy these yearnings. We come to envy rather than emulate the proud who would distance themselves from their necessities either by virtue of the goals they set for themselves or by the ways in which they go about fulfilling needs of all sorts. We end by stifling our own seemingly superfluous yearnings, and swallow a pride that would in any case no longer be justified. In so truncating our aspirations we effectively denature ourselves, for the fact that such aspirations still emerge in our arguments for equality suggest that they too are necessities of human nature.

Modern doctrine has so formed the human psyche that no radical reformation should be anticipated. At most one might undertake minor alterations with the hope that they will nonetheless be more than merely cosmetic. In particular, the tendency to make a virtue of necessity that has always been implicit in liberal capitalism is now explicit in contemporary egalitarian demands.

The tendency might be opposed in each instance: is homosexuality really simply in the genes, and ought this specific genetic configuration be celebrated rather than tolerated? But surely this problematic obfuscation must be addressed on the ground in which it germinated, that of capitalism. Can capitalism be a cause for pride as well as a reminder of human necessitousness? Can human beings who live in a society devoted to the pursuit of material well-being understand themselves as equal in merit and dignity as well as in need?

Indeed, it was the intention of advocates of liberal capitalism like Thomas Hobbes, John Locke, and Adam Smith to provide the striving to excel and to be recognized as excellent a newly respectable outlet in commerce, or economic enterprise. However discomforting the thought may be, there is comfort in the fact that the avarice of Americans in pursuit of material well-being engenders or supports much of what we recognize as ordinary decency or morality. Commerce seems to flourish with hard work, regular habits, and stability. So it discourages immoderate indulgence of private vices and violent political passions. (There is barely time to undertake a luncheon tryst, much less to man the barricades.) American capitalism also has a characteristic form of heroism, the working of economic miracles. Karl Marx could not help but admire the accomplishments of capitalism, even as he urged its destruction. Carnegie, Ford, and Rockefeller are legendary not for their ruthlessness, but for their successful daring and determination—not to mention their philanthropy. Capitalism's successes are a cause for pride, and the capitalist has some claim to the honor accorded virtue.

Pride in capitalism is vitiated, however, as much by an internal incoherence as by hostile doctrines. The ultimate purpose of the habits and actions inspired by capitalism remains provision for the needs and comfort of human bodies. How, on reflection, is it reasonable to risk your life or even the least of your material resources, to postpone present physical gratifications for the sake of future profits and pleasures which can never be assured? Why not leave the sweat and risk to others and then resent the pride they take in their successes? Capitalism's end undermines its efficacy as a spur to individual endeavor, making of rugged individuals impotent, yet envious and demanding citizens of the welfare state. If one tries to make a virtue of necessity, it becomes increasingly difficult to defend the necessity of virtue.

Similarly, contemporary doctrines hostile to capitalism stress the necessary end of capitalism, provision of material well-being. In this necessity all human beings are equal, and in not providing for this necessity with perfect equality capitalism discredits itself. The inequality—and necessity—of individual virtue reestablishes its credit when capitalism is appreciated as a means which is not a mere means to its most obvious end. While we can take pride in the fact that capitalism does secure the general prosperity of mankind, capitalism may ultimately command greater respect as a means to an end incidental to its own.

In justifying service of the needs of human bodies, the theory that generates liberal capitalism can hardly fail to recognize that human bodies are invariably discrete, or individual. It is as individuals that we have an opportunity for pride as well as pusillanimity. In teaching us our equal necessitousness, Hobbes and his liberal followers hoped to undermine Christian complacency and the potential for invidious pride in aristocratic morality, not to demoralize us all. Our belief in natural equality was meant to bolster the ambition and self-respect of each. Naturally free and equal human beings cannot be supposed to have arrived at a condition of sociability unless they are supposed to have done so of their own accord, with the realization that cooperation and therefore the social, economic, and political structures cooperation entails are beneficial. They must have consented, or in effect contracted, to take their places in these institutions. Having contracted, they have bound themselves to adhere to what amounts to a long-range determination of what is in the interest of each and every human being, and not to act on perceptions of present necessity. This notion of contract is crucial to liberal politics and modern morality. Man is the animal that makes promises, and his capacity to choose his necessities and act on his choices distinguishes him from other animals. Modern morality amounts to the determination to be bound by the conventions and laws we presume to have created by our contracts, explicit or tacit. Making and keeping contracts is the source of modern man's dignity, for in contracts necessity and choice are both distinguished in theory and combined in practice.

Capitalism, as distinguished from competitors from welfare statism to various forms of socialism and communism, makes the notion of contract important in economics as well as politics. A labor contract enables a worker to understand himself freely to have entered into a temporary relationship of subordination to someone who, according to democratic theory, is no better. Worker and employer have consented to meet their respective needs on this particular occasion in this particular mutually beneficial arrangement. The illusion of voluntariness created by labor contracts becomes a reality to the extent that wages rise, for people and therefore expectations become more equal and egalitarian.

Nonetheless, capitalism or any economic order organized on the principle of maximizing the production of material wealth does tend more toward equality of opportunity than of result. Efficient production of wealth dictates division of labor and concentration of capital. It did not take Marx to see that the factory worker who spends his life putting heads on pins is likely to suffer an atrophy of mental faculties at least as damaging as economic deprivation or even alienation, while the enterpreneur who constantly faces new challenges thrives mentally and psychologically as well as monetarily. Inequalities in natural ability and luck are intensified and made more obvious. Differences between employer and employee may narrow in many respects and even in many occupations, but in industry, which should be the principal occupation under capitalism, wages do not tend to rise naturally, and authority does not become less concentrated. The resulting poverty and dependence of the industrial worker endangers democracy, though not because the potential for revolution is created. It is unlikely that there will ever be such perfect equality or such complete freedom from necessity that some people will not have to work for others whether they like it or not. Constant confrontation of an inevitably necessitous condition (unaccompanied by an unfounded expectation of overcoming it) can only be demoralizing and dehumanizing.

Therefore in industry the illusion of natural equality and dignity must be preserved with the aid of organizations that give real bargaining power to otherwise impotent workers and with watchful regulation by government of industrial relations. From this it does not follow, of course, that wages can be raised to arbitrarily high levels that vitiate individual incentives or that price goods out of the market. For unearned wages "earned" cannot give individuals much cause for pride, and a capitalism that does not provide a basis for general prosperity is no source of pride for America as a whole.

America cannot abandon its commitment to equality without ceasing to be what it has always been and is. But we can think a bit more about the kind of equality to which we are committed and why we are committed to it. The natural equality of human beings, on which equality of rights is predicated, has come ever more to mean either an equality of need, and therefore a right to the satisfaction of need, or a presumed equality of moral worth that need never be tested by fact. These understandings have initiated or supported current demands for equality of result as an economic right as well as for equal political participation and for equality of life-styles. But was not the original understanding of natural equality that human beings are roughly equal in the ability to manage their own affairs and therefore that each has a right to voice an opinion or at least to withhold consent when public management of common affairs seemed called for? America is fundamentally committed to a belief in a specific equal ability that issues in a requirement of popular and limited government.

Given our express belief in the ability of all human beings to manage their own affairs well enough, we must accept the consequences of the fact that most are naturally inclined to assume that their own affairs are primarily provision for the material well-being of themselves and their families. We cannot dismiss this assumption without calling into doubt our belief in their natural or untutored ability to manage without the unsolicited direction of government or some other authority. The assumption that individual affairs are primarily economic, coupled with the requirement of individual consent, has engendered the habit of appraising regimes with an almost exclusive view to how effectively the material needs of each and every citizen can be served by its economic order. But was not the original understanding of the importance of material well-being that the enjoyment of material goods is for the sake of happiness? How many material goods we need to be happy is open to dispute; there is probably no such thing as too much.

There is, however, such a thing as too much concern for material well-being and too much endeavor to assure it. Unless, as is sometimes argued, freedom and virtue are tantamount to the activity of acquisition, then the ends for which material well-being was thought necessary or desirable are lost sight of. This much must be appreciated if demands for equality and concern over the nature of the economic order with which we must live for the indefinite future are not to become obstacles to the satisfaction of the very desires that give rise to these demands and concerns. However heated the dispute over the merits and defects of capitalism may become, it can be pointed out that the dispute is over a mere means, and that means must be evaluated in the light of the ends they serve.

This is not the occasion to examine alternatives to the American regime and its self-understanding. It is the occasion to stress that we cannot begin to clarify our own ends or to identify the cause of our dissatisfactions with American capitalism until we have understood what we mean in demanding equality. This much has become clear: What merits our greatest attention is the "legitimate passion for equality which rouses in all men a desire to be strong and respected."

NOTES

1. Alexis de Tocqueville, *Democracy in America*, trans. by George Lawrence (New York: 1969), p. 57.

2. Aristotle, *Nicomachean Ethics*, v. 1130b30–1134a16.

3. Hedrick Smith, *The Russians*, (New York: 1976), p. 124.

4. The following is based primarily on Thomas Hobbes, *Leviathan*, ch. 13–15.

5. *Leviathan*, ch. 15.

6. The following is an interpretation of the argument of John Locke, *Two Treatises of Government*, II.,5.

7. What follows relies on *Democracy in America*, I. i. 3; I. ii. 10 (pp. 400–407); II. ii. 10–20; II. iii. 5–7, 18.

Notes on Contributors

Peter Berger is University Professor at Boston University and author of *The Capitalist Revolution* (Basic Books, 1986).

Samuel McCracken is Assistant to the President of Boston University.

Jeffrey G. Williamson is the Laird Bell Professor of Economics at Harvard University.

Edgar K. Browning is Professor of Economics at Texas A & M University.

Walter D. Connor is Professor of Political Science at Boston University and a Fellow of the Russian Research Center of Harvard University.

Alan M. Kantrow is Senior Editor of the *Harvard Business Review* and a Director of the Winthrop Group, business history consultants.

Laura L. Nash is a project director on public/private partnerships at Harvard University's Center for Business and Government.

Richard John Neuhaus is Director of the Rockford Institute's Center on Religion and Society in New York City.

Stephen Miller is the author of *Special Interest Groups in American Politics* and *Excellence and Equality: The National Endowment for the Humanities*.

Marc F. Plattner is the author of *Rousseau's State of Nature* (1979) and the editor of *Human Rights in Our Time* (1984).

Delba Winthrop is Lecturer in Extension at Harvard University.